DREW
BARRYMORE

DREW BARRYMORE

THE BIOGRAPHY

LUCY ELLIS & BRYONY SUTHERLAND

AURUM PRESS

First published in Great Britain 2003 by Aurum Press Ltd
25 Bedford Avenue, London WC1B 3AT

A catalogue record for this book is available from the
British Library.

ISBN 1 85410 922 7

1 3 5 7 9 10 8 6 4 2
2003 2005 2007 2006 2004

Designed and typeset by M Rules
Printed and bound in Great Britain
by MPG Books Ltd, Bodmin

For Finlay

CONTENTS

ACKNOWLEDGEMENTS

Atomic would like to thank: Richard Adler, Gabrielle Allen, Kyoko Barrio, Chris Charlesworth, Maggie Dowling, Gary Gilbert, Steven Gordon, Elizabeth Haylett, Karen Ings, Me Julie, Orna Keisel, Nikki Lloyd, Rita Kew-Moss, Natalia Marshall, Michele Martin, Bill McCreadie, Derek Moore, Debbie Murray, Tim Murray, Nestlé, Stephanie Neuman, Barbara Newson, Marie Outhwaite, John Prater, Richard Rees, Johnny Rogan, Gwen Rudman, Laura Sadler, Frankie Sutherland, Sylvia Sutherland, Tara Terminello, Elton Thrussell, Video Blitz and Peter Webb. And commiserations to the three turtles that jumped out of the frying pan and into the fire.

Lucy Ellis & Bryony Sutherland, July 2003

PICTURE CREDITS

PROLOGUE

FULL THROTTLE

'I believe we all have two personalities running around inside us, except I have at least ten people running around in me. Acting is the way I get to use my pseudo schizophrenia.'

DREW BARRYMORE

Drew Barrymore is a paradox. She is a recovering addict who drinks alcohol; despite her traumatic childhood, she retains an impossibly sunny disposition; she divorced her parents when she was fifteen, yet still tries to help them both; she is a hopeless romantic who lurches from one failed relationship to another; she is bisexual yet has recently discovered the beauty of her own company; she's a talented actress who is content with lightweight roles; and she's an intellectual, but believes washcloths have feelings.

Above all, and despite everything, she is remarkably well-adjusted. Drew is not a Hollywood recluse, diva or prima donna; instead, she appreciates her fame, fortune, friends and family.

'Everything in life is an education,' she says. 'Good or bad, it's interesting to see what everything is all about – you don't want to get lost in it.'

Drew didn't always feel this way. 'When I was younger I used to feel I wasn't going to be around that long,' she says. 'I always had that feeling I was going to die at twenty-five. I think maybe that's why I went crazy in my teens.'*

However, after her very public disgrace (being led handcuffed into rehab as a cocaine-ravaged thirteen-year-old), Drew reinvented herself

---

*For a personal account of Drew's first fourteen years, fans should turn to her autobiography, *Little Girl Lost* (Simon & Schuster, 1990).

as an actress and producer, climbing to the giddy heights of the Hollywood A-list.

In fact, her name and face are so influential in the industry that she often appears in a small cameo just so that directors can use her as a selling point for the film (*Motorama, Sketch Artist, Scream* and *The Wonder Of Sex* immediately spring to mind).

The Barrymore surname conjures up generations of actors, while Drew's face is a peculiar combination of features. Her beauty is unconventional: her strong, prominent jaw line, generous cupid-bow lips and wide-set, down-turned eyes only really gel when she smiles.

But something about Drew Barrymore is captivating. Ever since her childhood appearances, she has displayed the powerful ability to command attention simply with her presence.

'There's something liberating about not pretending,' says Drew. 'Dare to embarrass yourself. Risk.'

1

A STAR IS BORN

It might be clichéd to say 'it was in her genes', but it's a truth that applies not only to Drew Barrymore's innate acting ability and charismatic onscreen presence, but also to her addictive personality and destructive nature regarding familial relationships.

The Barrymore and Drew families are forever intertwined in a history as complex as it is repetitive. Great actors of successive generations married two or three times and produced various offspring, leaving an extensive trail of step-siblings, cousins, aunts, uncles, nieces and nephews. To add to the confusion, many of the progeny are given ancestral names, arising in endless permutations of the surnames.

And a self-destructive streak pervades the labyrinthine dynasty: commonly known as the Barrymore Family Curse, it is an overwhelming susceptibility to alcohol and drug addiction. That said, there are yet other recurring features present in the fifth generation of the 150-year-old acting dynasty.

The story is complex, but to persevere and follow the cyclical behaviour through the years is not only fascinating, but also imperative to understanding Drew's psychological make-up and inherent characteristics. How she dealt with these ingrained compulsions is her own story, but let us start with her ancestors.

The undisputed matriarch of the family is Louisa Lane, born in London, England, in 1820. By her first birthday, she had made her stage debut in the role of 'Crying baby'. Instinctively drawn to showbusiness, Louisa travelled to America aged seven and trod the boards in New York the following year. Before her ninth birthday she had undertaken five roles in a play called *Twelve, Precisely* in Philadelphia, where she stayed on.

Many years later, Louisa assumed management of Philadelphia's notable Arch Street Theater, a tremendous coup for a woman at the time. She attracted some of the greatest actors *and* headed the bill in the repertory company she personally trained and directed. For seventy years she juggled a frenetic career, became a pillar of the Episcopalian community and raised not one but two families.

Louisa's first marriage lasted for eleven years before it ended in divorce, and her second husband drank himself to death after a year. It was her third husband, John Drew, with whom she would have children. John was an Irish comedian, a gregarious soul seven years her junior, more renowned for his drinking than his work. The couple are known to have had three offspring; Louisa Jr, John Jr and Georgiana. However, it is understood that Louisa also cared for her younger half-sister's child, Adine, who is rumoured to have been fathered by John.

The years of alcohol abuse quickly caught up with John Drew Sr, and he died of congestion of the brain in May 1862. 'Too early success was his ruin; it left him with nothing to do,' complained his widow, who mysteriously acquired a fourth child, Sidney, over a year later.

Of the five children, Adine died in 1888, followed by Louisa Jr the following year, both tragically young; Sidney turned out to be a disgrace, interested only in playing pool, fooling around with chorus girls and touring the vaudeville circuit; John Jr became a talented actor whose gala opening nights in New York invariably drew crowds from across the nation; and Georgiana emerged as a captivating comedienne.

Georgie, as she was known, was swept off her feet by a charming rapscallion named Herbert Blyth. Originally an amateur middleweight boxing champion, Herbert sought fame and turned his attentions to the theatre.

He chose his stage name, Maurice Barrymore, at random from an old playbill hanging in Haymarket Theatre – thereby changing the future identity of the family in a flash.

After appearing on stage in London, in 1875 the dapper actor travelled to America, where he fell in love with Georgie. The handsome, successful couple were married on New Year's Eve the following year.

Georgie Drew and Maurice Barrymore had three children – Lionel (1878), Ethel (1879) and Jack (1882) – but it was not long before Maurice's roving eye saw him playing opposite his leading ladies in the bedroom as well as on stage. Furthermore, he believed that a 'real man' drank, smoked, swore and gambled, and as a result his professional life rapidly began to deteriorate. Long-suffering Georgie was concerned about how her children might be affected by Maurice's eccentricities: the eldest, Lionel, admired his father but was wise enough to be fairly impervious to his ways; Ethel was permanently mortified by her embarrassing parent; but Jack was not only highly impressionable, he also shared his father's disposition.

Fortunately, as Maurice became less involved in the children's lives, their grandmother Louisa, whom they called Mummum, increased her influence. Georgie was struck down with tuberculosis, and in a family beset by early fatalities, it seemed sadly inevitable that she would not survive her thirty-eighth year, leaving her adolescent children in the care of their drunkard father and strict grandmother.

A year after losing his wife, in 1894, Maurice married a young lady almost twenty years his junior, Mamie Floyd. While Ethel was bitter towards both her father and her stepmother, Jack was to have an entirely different experience. When Mamie became weary of Maurice, she turned her attentions to his youngest son, now fifteen. Mamie's insatiable sexual appetite led to a rather abrupt initiation into the world of sex for Jack, and he was left feeling resentful towards his tutor and with a lasting suspicion of all beautiful women. It was notably at this time that he turned to drink.

In 1901, Maurice's corrupt lifestyle came to a rude end when the alcoholic was pronounced incurably insane as a result of syphilis. He was committed to a nursing home, where four years later he died, almost unrecognizable from the ravages of the disease.

*

It was left to the trio of Lionel, Ethel and Jack Barrymore to revive the family tradition of entering into showbusiness. The eldest, Lionel, initially dreamed of being an artist or composer, but, unable to make a living from either occupation, he conceded and took to the stage. The least attractive of the three siblings, he was branded a 'character actor' and achieved notoriety as such in the role of Milt Shanks in *The Copperhead*. He later secured an Academy Award for his portrayal of a drunken defence attorney in *A Free Soul*. In 1937 Lionel was confined to a wheelchair by agonizing arthritis, but ironically achieved even greater fame as he went on to play the disabled Dr Gillespie in all the popular *Dr Kildare* films, and the abhorrent banker in *It's A Wonderful Life*. His sparkling career hid the fact that for much of his life Lionel was a heavy drinker and a cocaine and morphine addict.

The second Barrymore child, Ethel, hoped to be a concert pianist, but also gave up her dreams in favour of the family business. A strikingly beautiful young lady, she became the darling of the London stage in her teens and was courted by no less than Winston Churchill and Somerset Maugham. Briefly flirting with film work during the First World War, she returned to the boards and became the first lady of Broadway for several decades.

However, one bad review of her performance as a 'matronly, dowdy' Juliet in *Romeo And Juliet* was enough to prompt Ethel to start drinking. Soon she was rarely seen without a bottle of brandy, and it began to affect her work. Fortunately, the press were polite enough to brush over her problems, saying, 'You admire her in spite of this, of that, and of the other thing.'

After accepting a personal invitation from Cary Grant to play his mother in *None But The Lonely Heart*, Ethel garnered an Oscar in 1944. Aged sixty, she successfully quit drinking after a stay at a Long Island treatment centre and was able to use her trademark aristocratic features and crisp enunciation to prolong her acting career and transfer to radio.

Jack, who had been drinking steadily ever since his upsetting sexual initiation at fifteen, was another matter. He had inherited all of Maurice's wild ways and, being a vulnerable boy raised as a man's man, adopted an attitude of exaggerated machismo to hide his insecurities: hard-drinking, profane language, whoring and roaming. When Jack got involved in fights at a young age and was expelled from school for attending a brothel, all Maurice did was shake his hand.

An avid cartoonist, Jack also abandoned his vocation to follow the family tradition, using the name of John Barrymore. A classically handsome man with chiselled features, he charmed audiences on stage and became known as 'The Great Profile'. His drinking never diminished; as he once joked, 'There are lots of [acting] methods. Mine involves talent, a glass and some cracked ice.' John spent the first two decades of the twentieth century gaining a good reputation on stage and in 1921 proved he could create the same presence on screen when he played the lead in *Dr Jekyll And Mr Hyde*. That role was followed by captivating portrayals of Shakespeare's Richard III and Hamlet.

During this phenomenal rise to fame, John had married Katherine Harris, and in 1920 the couple had a daughter, Diana. John was instinctively uncomfortable with expressions of love and refused even to hold his child. That marriage ended in divorce, as did his second, to Blanche Oelrichs. In 1926 John appeared opposite Dolores Costello in *The Sea Beast*. The blonde beauty had started life as a model and dancer, but her acting career was slowly taking off. They were reunited for *When A Man Loves* in 1927, which was carried predominantly by their real-life love affair, and the couple were married the following year.

Dolores retired from the screen to bear two children by John; the first, a girl, was named Dolores II but was known as Dede. John was disappointed, as he had hoped for a son, and when Dolores went into labour again in 1932, he promised that if the baby was a boy he'd stop drinking. On hearing that John Blyth Barrymore II had been born, the proud father left the hospital supposedly for a few minutes and returned hours later, three sheets to the wind. That same year, John senior memorably starred opposite Greta Garbo in *Grand Hotel*.

During the mid-1930s, John's personal problems caught up with him: he left Dolores when the children were just toddlers and his drinking started to seriously affect his ability to remember lines. His fourth wife, Elaine Jacobs, persuaded him to return to the stage, but his behaviour there became increasingly erratic: he began ad-libbing and frequently berated the audience. His shows turned into freakish parodies of the once great Barrymore and his excessive drinking often left him vomiting in the wings between acts.

In 1942, John's body finally gave up and he collapsed with cirrhosis of the liver, chronic gastritis, ulcers with haemorrhages, arteriosclerosis and pneumonia. Amazingly, he recovered for a brief period, but soon fell into a coma and passed away. Once one of Hollywood's most highly paid actors, John died penniless, leaving his family to sell Barrymore memorabilia to pay his debts.

*

The third generation of Barrymores fared no better.

Diana was deprived of love and affection by her father, which affected her whole life. Furthermore, she picked up on his conviction (passed down from Maurice) that women were a necessary evil and believed it. Along with a penchant for heavy drinking, she also inherited the acting gene and appeared on stage for four years, and in half a dozen movies after her screen debut in 1942.

A depressive alcoholic, Diana's name soon became synonymous with drunken brawls, disorderly conduct and arrests for shoplifting. With three failed marriages and several suicide attempts behind her, she committed herself to a rehabilitation centre. She published her autobiography, *Too Much, Too Soon*, in 1957; it became a bestseller and was adapted into a film a year later, starring Errol Flynn as her father. Her story lays the blame on a lack of parental love: her father was an absent drunk and her mother was too preoccupied with hating her father. A theme was beginning to emerge. Diana died in 1960, aged just thirty-eight.

Dede escaped the headlines by quitting acting when a director rebuked her for nervousness. She too was unable to avoid the trauma of the Barrymores: she bore four children during two marriages, but never really found happiness.

John Barrymore II followed directly in his father's footsteps. Only ten when John I died, he was disturbed and uncontrollable from the outset. Traditionally good-looking, he initially resisted the temptation to go into acting, but finally made his stage debut aged seventeen. Unfortunately, his surname preceded him, and when his appeal did not match up to that of The Great Profile, John II was branded a failure. His Aunt Ethel told him as much, saying, 'We all started sooner than that,' and concluding that he did not belong in the Barrymore clan.

John II may not have possessed the acting ability of his father, but he managed several B-movies during the 1950s, including *Never Love A Stranger* and *High School Confidential*. He did, however, inherit his father's alcoholism and soon faced numerous arrests for drink-driving, hit-and-run accidents and drunken brawling. His marriage to his first wife, Cara Williams, was violent; he ended up in jail after the first week for domestic abuse. Somehow, the couple produced a son, John Blyth Barrymore III (known as Johnny), but fatherhood did little to curb John II's unreliable behaviour.

During the 1960s, his Equity standing ruined, John fled to Rome, where he married Gabriella Palazzoli, produced a daughter (Blythe Barrymore) and increased his tally of arrests and B-movies. Returning to California, John added an array of drugs to his alcohol intake and revelled in being spontaneous, untamed and on the edge of society. This was an era when such behaviour was deemed cool, and his drug-using social circle were enamoured of his eloquence, grace and style, revering him and referring to him as 'Saint John'. It was at this wild time that John met his third wife.

*

Ildiko Jaid Mako, known as Jaid, was born in 1947, shortly after the Second World War ended, in a camp for displaced persons outside Munich, Germany. Her Hungarian parents were not married when her mother got pregnant aged fifteen, but they made the union official in order to escape. 'Everyone in the camp was waiting for paperwork to go to other countries,' says Jaid. 'My parents went through this sham marriage to get to America.'

In 1950 the trio finally made it to the land of the free and settled in Pennsylvania. Together only out of necessity, Jaid's father soon ran off with another woman, leaving her mother to rent a small abode above a petrol station. 'My mother didn't want me at all,' recalls Jaid bitterly. 'She would leave me for hours on a second-floor balcony where there was no railing. I would be wrapped in a blanket to stop me moving – I would pee in that blanket.'

After her mother remarried, Jaid felt even more insignificant. She was angry and resentful towards her mother, yet strangely idolized her father. Jaid says she was advanced and precocious as a child, reading Shakespeare aged seven, but her real interest lay in the glamorous life of Hollywood. She was certainly striking enough to appear on screen – with a petite figure, attractive East European features and long raven hair – and so she left home aged eighteen in pursuit of her dreams.

Moving to New York, Jaid enjoyed a bohemian lifestyle. Men fawned over her beauty and, starved of love as a child, she lapped up the attention. It is during this time that Jaid claims to have had a very close relationship with Jim Morrison. The West Coast-based frontman for the Doors did indeed perform in New York between 1967 and 1970, but the significance of the story lies in what happened afterwards: when Jim left for Paris (where his life soon ended), Jaid travelled to Los Angeles.

On the other side of America, she finally pursued her dream of becoming a film star. While attending acting auditions, Jaid worked as a waitress at Sunset Strip's illustrious Troubadour Club. There, in *the* live-music venue of the era, she mixed with the elite of the music scene: the Rolling Stones, the Eagles, the Byrds, the Doors, James Taylor, John Lennon and Elton John.

'I met everyone – it was a cornucopia of stars,' she says. 'Then, one day, John Barrymore II walked in.'

*

A magnetic personality, with his claim of being a Barrymore film star, John constantly had women dripping off his arm. Jaid was still bewitched by the elusive world of the movies and was inevitably drawn to him.

'He had such icy blue eyes and beautiful thick hair, like gossamer silk, perfect bone structure and great self-assurance,' she recalls. 'He gave me a killer smile and my knees weakened – John knew just how to look at a woman.'

Jaid fell head over heels for the lapsed actor, turning a blind eye to the fact that he had just been arrested, for the fourth time, for possession of marijuana. She also chose to ignore his heavy drug use and alcoholism, which brought additional foibles. 'He drove me crazy,' she says. 'He was too much of everything. He had incredible talent as an actor . . . but he was insecure and lacked self-worth. He was a brilliant, talented man, but he didn't believe it.'

The romance blossomed and the pair moved in together on the outskirts of West Hollywood. Before long they were married, this being John's third attempt, but the honeymoon period came to an abrupt end.

Like John's previous two wives and numerous girlfriends, Jaid found herself the target of his drunken abuse. In the naïve belief that she could save her husband from the trademark Barrymore drive towards destruction, Jaid suggested therapy, encouraged a spell in a rehab centre – anything to curb his temper. The harder she tried, the more violent he became.

Finally, in a rare moment of calm, the couple decided to start a family, hoping that it would solve their problems. 'John told me he wanted me as his "brood mare" because I wasn't an alcoholic or a drug addict,' explains Jaid. 'He wanted someone, he said, who could infuse the line with a great deal of strength.' However, when Jaid became pregnant, John was unable to handle the pressure and his irrational outbursts grew worse.

Jaid remembers one night in particular when he beat her and kicked her in the stomach. She curled up into a ball and did all she could to protect her baby: thankfully, a neighbour heard her cries and called the police. Incredibly, Jaid did not miscarry, but she realized that it was her responsibility to look after her unborn child and that she could no longer continue to withstand the physical attacks.

'I was going to be a mother and I knew we couldn't be together any-more,' she says.

Jaid steeled herself and told John that she was leaving him. Expecting the worst, she was surprised at his remorse. 'John kept crying for me to come back, but I knew I had to leave him . . . he was so heartbroken that he burned our house down.'

Now homeless, Jaid stayed in a friend's leaky garage until she found another apartment, a small one-bedroom place in a West Hollywood duplex. Doggedly, she continued working until finally, in February 1975, her colleagues sent her home to prepare for her baby's imminent arrival.

*

Jaid Barrymore gave birth to a little girl shortly before noon on 22 February 1975, just one week after leaving work. Despite John's violent attacks, the baby was healthy and emerged weighing 6 pounds 5 ounces after an uncomplicated labour. Jaid had picked out the name months earlier: Drew Blythe Barrymore – a good, strong, androgynous name, steeped in her husband's family history. When Jaid left the Brotman Memorial Hospital in Culver City, California, with her precious bundle in her arms, she promised faithfully to provide for and look after Drew.

A failed actress and single mother pushing thirty, Jaid could only afford to take three weeks off before she had to return to work. Not having made many friends during the five years she was with John, Jaid, desperately in need of babysitters, had few people to whom she could turn. There was a family of girls living nearby who were willing to look after the cute baby in return for a small sum. Hardly the most reliable childcare, but this was all Jaid could afford.

Working all night long at the Troubadour, Jaid attended auditions during the day. It wasn't easy, but she was determined to succeed as a single parent. 'She was my miracle child and I struggled to bring her up,' admits Jaid. 'I worked six nights a week to make sure she had everything she could possibly want.'

The one-bedroom apartment soon grew too small and when one day Jaid found Drew precariously poking through the balcony railings – a danger all too familiar to the resilient Hungarian – she decided they had to move. She was fortunate to find a two-bedroom apartment on the ground floor just over the road, although the extra expense meant that Jaid would have to take on additional shifts. 'I was too young to realize it,' says Drew, 'but my mother worked extremely hard so that I could have nice things.'

For all Jaid's good intentions, the ultimate drawback of her endless quest to provide for her child was that she was not present to fulfil her emotional needs. Drew was looked after by a string of strangers and although she says, 'I've been told that I was a very good baby, really easy and good-spirited,' all she really wanted was her mother's love.

Drew was an undeniably appealing child: she was chubby, with adorable dimples and angelic golden curls. Her good looks combined with her cheerful nature prompted one of Jaid's friends to suggest that Drew should be in commercials. Having suffered at the hands of the callous acting profession herself, at first Jaid wasn't interested in such work for her daughter. The friend persisted and, eventually, as she was taking her own baby to a local audition, Jaid and eleven-month-old Drew joined them. When the quartet arrived at the cavernous

Hollywood soundstage, they were dismayed to find they were not alone.

'It was a madhouse,' exclaims Jaid. 'There were three hundred babies at the audition; every baby on the West Coast!'

The commercial was for Gainsburger's puppy food and all the baby in question had to do was interact with a playful white puppy. However, with each infant being screen-tested individually, the wait was lengthy. When it was finally Drew's turn, the little dog came bounding in and made her giggle. She stretched out her hand and was rewarded with a sloppy lick, so she leaned in and nuzzled the pup back. For no apparent reason, the excitable canine suddenly turned round and nipped her on the nose.

Everything went deathly quiet – all eyes were on Drew.

Startled, she looked up at Jaid, then threw her head back and shrieked with infectious laughter. As the producer, who was presumably fearing a lawsuit, breathed a sigh of relief, a star was born. Everyone was immediately charmed by the affable little girl.

When they left, Jaid was secretly smarting, as Drew was not only offered a job at her first-ever audition, but she was also to be paid a sizeable fee of $2,500 for the brief appearance. It was hard to admit, but Jaid was jealous of her daughter.

2

A BARRYMORE? THEY'RE TROUBLE

After Drew's first adventure in front of the camera, life returned to normal for mother and daughter. Jaid continued to juggle work and auditions, and Drew was a contented toddler – although she missed her mother desperately. On the rare occasions when Jaid landed a part in a play or television series, her routine became harder; she was doing two jobs *and* trying to care for her daughter. All the time she justified her absence by providing Drew with all the things she never had as a child.

Stuart Margolin, an acquaintance of Jaid's, was a respected actor and playwright of many years standing, not least due to his award-winning appearance in James Garner's television series *The Rockford Files*. Margolin turned his hand to directing in the late 1970s, and in 1977 he was casting a made-for-TV film called *Suddenly Love*. He hired Cindy Williams, a notable film actress who had just signed to the smash sitcom *Laverne And Shirley*, as the young mother who begins a new life after her husband dies of a heart attack.

Most showbusiness professionals swear by the mantra: 'Never work with children or animals', but in *Suddenly Love* Margolin's hand was forced. In order to minimize the potentially painful process, he asked Jaid if there was any chance he could use Drew in the role of the child, as he was friendly with her and knew her to be a happy little girl.

Jaid agreed to help out, and Drew, who was to play a boy, was given a severe hair cut. At just two-and-a-half years old, she displayed good concentration and understanding of the situation, hitting every cue perfectly. She didn't even twitch when filming a bedtime scene: 'I remember lying on a bed, pretending to be asleep. A man came over to me, picked me up, and then someone yelled, "Cut!" '

Even her biggest scene, when the child runs to comfort the mother as she is told of her husband's death, was perfect. Everyone could see that there was focus behind Drew's performance; Jaid recalls, 'Somehow, at that age, she understood what it was all about.'

As much as Jaid was impressed, she was inwardly seething.

'I had no intention of Drew becoming a star,' she says. 'I lost the chance to read for the part of Princess Leia in *Star Wars* because I couldn't find a babysitter for Drew.'

Jaid had said that *Suddenly Love* was a one-off for a friend and she meant it. After one missed opportunity, she was not going to forfeit any other work in favour of her toddler and so she 'retired' Drew from the acting profession.

After numerous auditions, Jaid landed a small role on the hot new sitcom *Diff'rent Strokes*, starring Gary Coleman; in the improbable scenario, two black kids from Harlem live in the lap of white luxury. Thrilled to be involved, Jaid immediately ran into problems.

'The morning of the shoot, Drew got sick,' she recalls. 'The babysitter wouldn't take a sick child and I knew I couldn't show up on the set with a sick baby, so I took her from one place to another. Finally, a friend took her, but I turned up late for work. They never hired me again.' Thwarted at every turn by parenthood, Jaid was beginning to despair.

*

While Jaid fought to provide for her daughter, the one element that was noticeably missing from Drew's life was a father. Unable to count on John for any support, Jaid didn't want to bring a new man into Drew's life for fear of upsetting her – not that she really had time for romance.

Drew, on the other hand, was becoming increasingly conscious that all the families around her consisted of two parents. That said, she was also rapidly learning that her father was not a very nice person, and he seemed perversely determined to make her miserable every time she saw him.

Drew's first memory of her father is a traumatic experience from when she was just three years old. She was playing in the kitchen while Jaid was busy doing laundry, when suddenly the door burst open. Although she didn't know what her father looked like, she instinctively yelled, 'Daddy!'

John's drunken response was more like a growl and, lurching into the room, he threw Jaid to the floor. Whirling around, he turned his attentions to his daughter. John launched the little girl across the room – fortunately the laundry basket cushioned her landing. Without a second glance, he grabbed a bottle of booze, smashing several glasses in the process, and left.

Thereafter, whenever a friend asked Drew why her father didn't live at home, she earnestly replied, 'Because when he's there, he beats the living daylights out of us.'

Moving from one bad penny to another, Johnny (John II's first child, from his marriage to Cara Williams) made several appearances throughout Drew's childhood. The little girl, desperate for a man to look up to, loved her older half-brother. The unemployed twenty-four-year-old was more than happy to spend time playing with Drew. Unfortunately, Johnny had fallen under his father's spell, becoming a drinker and drug user, hanging out with hardened addicts and stealing cars.

His visits were erratic, not least due to the times he spent detained in prison, and when he did see her, there would be the inevitable question: 'Drew, you got any money for gas?'

Eager to please, each time Drew would proudly present him with a handful of change that she had been saving especially. As she grew older, Drew tried various money-making schemes to increase this stash, including selling the avocados and oranges that grew in her backyard to neighbours. It is sad to think that most of the innocently earned money went on drugs.

Drew has never met her half-sister, Blythe, but occasionally saw her maternal grandparents from Pennsylvania. They would visit reasonably often and she predictably became fond of her step-grandfather.

*

Drew turned four in February 1979 and, being an advanced little girl, reached a vital decision.

Picking the worst time to tell her mother – just as Jaid was getting ready to go out to perform in a play and then on to her waitressing – Drew blurted it out:

'Mummy, I have to tell you something very important. I know what I want to do.'

Hassled and needing to leave, Jaid chided her daughter, 'You want to behave yourself so that Mummy can go off and do her play.'

But Drew wasn't to be fobbed off.

'I've decided I want to be an actress,' she said, her eyes wide.

Despite her haste, something about the way Drew spoke made Jaid take her seriously. Postponing her departure, she sat down and explained that the auditions and rejections were soul-destroying and even when work did come, it was tough.

Drew listened intently and then simply said, 'I know it's hard; that's why I have to do it.'

Amazingly, the four-year-old's blunt clarity shocked Jaid into reconsidering her previous thoughts – and her own career. 'She knew who she was and what she wanted in life to a spooky level,' Jaid admits.

Still feeling a little sore that her career might have to go on the back burner for a while, Jaid said, 'Fine. If this is really what you want, we'll start something up and see how it goes.'

Jaid arranged a meeting for her daughter with a small-time agent, J. J. Harris. It went well, and soon after, Drew was sent on her first audition. It was for another commercial, this time for Pillsbury chocolate-chip cookies, and again Drew's confidence and cheeriness immediately won her the role. From then on the phone began ringing with alarming regularity and Harris became more like a family member than an agent as her contact with Jaid and Drew increased.

Drew was then put up for her first feature film.

Ken Russell had been a cult director since the 1960s, producing a number of bizarre, visually demanding films in which the story is often bastardized (particularly in his biopics). In 1979 he adapted Paddy Chayefsky's novel *Altered States* for film, starring William Hurt in his movie debut.*

Hurt's character had two daughters and Drew auditioned for the role of Margaret. Approximately thirty-five girls were vying for the same part. As the hopefuls gathered around Russell, he began chatting informally with the group. Drew made the girls giggle with a smart answer to one of Russell's open-ended questions, and thus enchanted the director. It was not long before Russell and Drew were conducting a one-to-one conversation while the others dragged their feet home.

The film itself was no light-hearted affair: Hurt played Eddie Jessup, an American researcher experimenting with mind-altering drugs to achieve different states of consciousness. Combined with an incident in an isolation chamber, the results of Jessup's experiments are disturbing physical changes leading to evolutionary regression.

However commanding Hurt's performance, everything took a back seat to Russell's hallucinogenic visuals and Dick Smith's remarkable make-up effects. Admittedly the movie borders on plain silliness at

*Hurt later became one of *the* leading men of the 1980s, notable for his intense and powerful portrayals of complex characters.

times, and Chayefsky so vehemently hated the results that he changed his screenplay credit to 'Sidney Aaron'. Russell's popularity had been waning since his obscure vision of *Valentino* in 1975, and this was another work designed to show off his trademark visual flair and shock tactics. As outrageousness became the industry norm during the 1980s, so Russell's flame began to fade.

Still, Drew was tickled pink to be working on a feature film with a big-name director and always bounded eagerly on to the set. 'I wasn't in that much of the movie, but when it was time for me to work, I was so incredibly happy,' she remembers.

*

As an actor bearing the Barrymore name, Drew naturally attracted much attention, but not all of it was positive. 'People would be like, "Oh, a Barrymore. They're trouble." It definitely didn't give me any advantages, but at the same time, I would never look at my family as a disadvantage,' she says.

It was at this vulnerable time that Drew had a dream about going on a fishing expedition with an old man who kept making her laugh. Drew thought little of it, until she told her mother, who just stared at her, shocked. The little girl's description of the man in her dream had matched exactly the looks and expressions of her paternal grandfather, John Barrymore I, who loved to go fishing and bought a new yacht, *Infanta*, when he was with her grandmother, Dolores. 'When I look at the stars and the moon, I always think about my grandfather,' says Drew today. 'I talk to him all the time. I feel such a deep connection to him, I really do. I feel him in my soul.'

Clearly searching for some sense of belonging, Drew experienced another vivid dream; this time, when she described it to Jaid, it appeared to draw on repressed memories of her birth. The little girl was beginning to develop a certain sense of spirituality, something she would cling to in later years.

Drew was soon back on set for another made-for-TV film – this time a biopic of Humphrey Bogart called *Bogie*, based on Joe Hyams's affectionate biography of the star. The film sketches Bogart's life up until the breakdown of his marriage to actress Mayo Methot, after which it focuses heavily on his romance with Lauren Bacall. The last film to be directed by the distinguished Vincent Sherman, who worked with Bogart in the 1940s, sadly the finished cut is poor, let down by the script and leading actors.

Again, Drew's part was just a small role, as Bogart's daughter, Leslie, but she was never happier. It so happened that Sherman had also directed her great-uncle, Lionel, and knew her grandfather, John Barrymore I. The amiable director took the time and trouble to entertain the young girl with tales of her ancestors. Drew finally felt as though she 'belonged'.

'What I didn't know was that my work was hard on my mother,' Drew later acknowledged. 'She was schlepping me all over town, taking me to shoots and auditions and fittings. It was a full-time job.' Spending a lot of time together would normally have been Drew's dream, but she was somehow aware that it was business as opposed to pleasure. While she was completely at home on set, this was in stark contrast to the loneliness she felt at their apartment.

In September 1980 Drew started pre-school at Fountain Day and proved that she was intelligent and insightful. In the classroom she mixed with other children her own age and for a while became a normal five-year-old. With the boundless energy of a child, she loved dancing, turning cartwheels and somersaults, and roller-skating.

Predictably for a girl with a passion for the stage, Drew's favourite games were dressing up and 'let's pretend'. She regularly persuaded her babysitter to pretend they were movie stars returning home from a glamorous party, rock stars on tour, fighting dragons, or just sisters staying at home while mum and dad were out.

*

The more Drew socialized with other children from 'normal' families, the more she yearned for her father. Although she was painfully aware that he was unpredictable and violent, John's absence made him more mysterious and Drew quickly forgot the bad times, instead inventing new, happier memories.

'The truth is, I always wanted a boring, functional family with proper parents,' she confesses. 'I was looking for security.' To this end, Drew talked incessantly about her father; trying to find out what he was like and asking if she could see him. Horrified by their last run-in, Jaid would not entertain a repeat performance.

Every time Jaid refused to let her see her father, Drew would lay the blame with her mother. Eventually – to get her daughter off her back, to prove a point and to give John the benefit of the doubt – Jaid gave in and arranged for Drew to visit her father. The little girl was excited to the point of bursting and arrived wearing her best dress. Conversely, John was the drink- and drug-addled, unkempt slob he had been for ages, living in a pigsty.

Undeterred, Drew set about brightening his poky apartment with some paper curtains and a cup of flowers. Just before she left, John pulled out a white teddy bear from behind a pile of junk; Drew was immediately besotted with both the gift and what she perceived as her reformed father. Apparently John was also touched by the experience and kept asking Jaid if he could look after his daughter again. The stoic single parent refused until a few months later, when she was stuck for a babysitter.

'She didn't trust him alone with me,' explains Drew, 'so she arranged for her friend, Carol, to stay over too.' Jaid's instincts were proved right: John was drunk by the time they picked him up and the couple were fighting before they even got home. Jaid kicked him out of the car, but he persisted and walked to their apartment. Carol, who was looking after Drew when John turned up, excused herself to the bedroom so that father and daughter could talk.

After watching television for a while, John began to act strangely: he turned off the lights and lit some candles. He then started to show Drew some karate moves he had learned from David Carradine, who worked on the television series *Kung Fu*. Most of the time he would just miss Drew, but every so often his leg would connect with her arm, stomach or even her head.

Drew became angry and shouted at him: 'Why do you always have to cause me so much pain?'

'What do you know about pain?' he challenged.

Then he grabbed Drew's chubby hand and held it in the candle flame. When Drew began to cry, John became more incensed; he let go of her hand and thrust his own into the flame.

The unpleasant evening only served to complicate issues further for Drew. She couldn't understand why her father had acted like that towards her, but that was the last time she would see him for many years, as Jaid's response to the blisters on her daughter's fingers was a restraining order.

Drew now acknowledges that her father's departure greatly affected her already difficult relationship with her mother.

'I realize that my father wasn't around to make mistakes bringing me up, that's why I had this idealized version of him. So my mother took all the blame,' she says frankly.

Unfortunately, during this period, Drew lost her replacement male idol: the equally irrepressible Johnny. In 1980 father and son, once estranged, embarked on a madcap caper of exhuming the body of John Barrymore I in order to cremate him as per his wishes.

It was too much for Jaid, who told Johnny in no uncertain terms to stop coming round until he had pulled himself together. Each time Drew asked her mother why she never saw him anymore, Jaid would give the excuse that he was sick, or something similar. 'I didn't really understand,' recalls Drew. 'All I knew was that someone else whom I was close to and loved abandoned me.'

*

The six-year-old Drew was next seen in another advert: this time as a flower girl munching her way through a bowl of Rice Krispies and chatting with Snap, Crackle and Pop.

Next, Drew made her stage debut at school. She was thrilled to secure the lead role in the end-of-year production of *Sleeping Beauty*. Although it was only a small affair, Drew was more nervous than she had been in either of her films because she would have to kiss Alex, the school cutie, who was playing the role of Prince Charming.

'He had brown hair, chestnut eyes and dimples,' says Drew, who remembers 'melting' inside when the time came to rehearse the kiss, despite the hoots and whistles emanating from the rest of the cast. 'With the entire class watching, Alex bent over and gave me a quick peck on the lips. It was so fast, but it was wonderful!'

Having achieved a certain degree of street credibility with her peers, Drew looked forward to returning to school in the autumn of 1981. She amused herself over the summer holidays while her mother worked all hours, occasionally returning home in time to read Drew a bedtime story; her favourites were *James And The Giant Peach*, *A Wrinkle In Time*, *Eloise* and *Charlie And The Chocolate Factory*.

Drew continued to audition for various roles, but actually suffered her first setback – she lost the lead role in *Annie* to Aileen Quinn, who was immortalized as the plucky red-haired orphan. Drew's next try-out, also unsuccessful, was for Steven Spielberg's *Poltergeist* – the role of five-year-old Carol Ann was instead won by Heather O'Rourke.* Still, Drew was undaunted, as her meeting with Spielberg turned out to be propitious, with far-reaching consequences.

*After reprising the role for two *Poltergeist* sequels, Heather tragically died of heart failure at the age of twelve.

3

WHAT'S HAPP-ENING?

By 1981, Steven Spielberg had secured his rightful throne as one of the world's premier directors with phenomenal hits such as *Jaws* and *Close Encounters Of The Third Kind,* topped by that year's summer smash, *Raiders Of The Lost Ark.*

While basking in the success of *Raiders*, Spielberg was casting two films simultaneously. The first, *Poltergeist*, was a horror movie about the paranormal invading the lives of an innocent family. Although technically directed by Tobe Hooper, of *The Texas Chainsaw Massacre* fame, Spielberg was closely involved throughout and the final cut bears more of his influence than Hooper's.

The second undertaking was a small, personal project that he had been working on and toying with for years: *E.T. The Extra-Terrestrial.* The story of a young boy who befriends a stranded alien had been with Spielberg since he was a child and was subsequently steeped in the pain of his own parents' divorce. It wasn't until he was camped out in the Tunisian desert filming *Raiders* with Harrison Ford in 1980 that the tale began to take shape.

He turned to Ford's screenwriter wife, Melissa Mathison, and outlined the themes of friendship and tolerance. He asked her to write an original screenplay, but Mathison's two children's films (*The Black Stallion* and *The Escape Artist*) had been poorly recived and she was on the verge of giving up writing. After repeated urgings from both Ford and Spielberg, she relented.

Aided by weekly meetings with Spielberg, Mathison produced a first draft in an unbelievable two months – even more amazingly, this version was hardly altered until the director and writer were actually on set with the cast. Spielberg received funds from Universal Studios and, as the project was so special to him, he even agreed to foot the bill for any budget overruns himself.

'When I started *E.T.* I was fat and happy and satisfied with having the films I had on my list,' says Spielberg. 'I just didn't feel I had anything to lose. I had nothing to prove to anybody except me.'

Spielberg gave the central character, Elliott, an older brother, Michael, and a younger sister, Gertie: he knew that the dynamics between the three siblings would be crucial to the film's success and therefore chose each child actor carefully. Having instinctively known that Drew Barrymore was not right for the little girl held captive in another spectral plane in *Poltergeist*, he requested that she audition for this other role.

By the time Drew was called up, Spielberg had seen approximately a hundred Gertie wannabes and was looking for something a bit different. The six-year-old had been on numerous auditions, but only recently had she experienced rejection. Although she tried not to let it bother her, she was understandably worried. 'Instead of taking the nervous approach, I decided to pull it together and be the exact opposite,' she recalls.

'You like acting?' offered the director, to get her started.

'I love it,' replied Drew, 'but you know, honestly, I'm a musician at heart.'

Spielberg was a little confused. 'You are?'

Without any further prodding, Drew launched into a long fictional spiel about being in a punk-rock band called the Purple People Eaters. 'We play the clubs on weekends – you know, Madam Wong's, the Troubadour, the Roxy. Stuff like that.'

Enchanted, Spielberg played along. 'And your mother doesn't mind?'

'Oh, no, she's a total rocker,' retorted Drew. 'She used to work at the Troubadour.'

Drew's years of playing let's pretend with her babysitters paid dividends as Spielberg instantly recognized her potential: 'She just blew me away . . . I thought, I can use that imagination in this picture, she can help me make my movie better. She was one of the most remarkable children I had ever met.'

Although the director was clearly enamoured with the precocious little girl, the self-confessed perfectionist called her back for another audition. The second test was to gauge Drew's emotional acting ability, her capacity to convey fear and awe – this was something which was usually overlooked in children's films, but helped make *E.T.* superior in its genre.

'I knew about fear and hurt, but I didn't have a clue what the word *awe* meant,' remembers Drew. Helpfully, Jaid provided a little drama coaching by telling her daughter to pretend she was looking at the most amazing thing she could ever imagine.

Drew took it all in her stride, and Spielberg said there was just one last requirement. Placing her in front of a microphone in a sound room, he asked her to scream as loud as she could. 'I was a little better than expected,' laughs Drew. 'They told me that I almost broke the instruments!'

Drew was the first person Spielberg hired for *E.T.*, moving on to the search for her two brothers and mother. The director found his Elliott playing a fatherless kid who wanders around the yard with a torch in the film *The Raggedy Man* – ten-year-old Henry Thomas was an obvious choice. The part of the eldest child, Michael, turned out to be the first film role for sixteen-year-old Robert MacNaughton, although he had received rave reviews of his performance in off-Broadway play *The Diviners*.

Shelley Long (pre-*Cheers*, but seen in brief appearances in sitcoms and in the spoof flick *Caveman*) was Spielberg's first choice for the role of the newly separated mother, but she was already committed to the Ron Howard film *Night Shift*. Then Spielberg spotted Dee Wallace in the little-known TV show *Skag* and immediately signed her.

The remaining adult character was Keys, the faceless authoritarian who turns into a father figure. Peter Coyote had previously auditioned for Spielberg for *Raiders*, and although he wasn't right then, the director remembered and recalled him for this role.

*

With the cast in place, filming for *E.T.* began on location in September 1981 at Culver City High School and in the districts of Tujunga and Northridge, winding up at the Laird International Studios in Culver City. Drew, who was supposed to be returning to Fountain Day school for the first grade, received at least three hours of tutoring every morning on set along with Henry and Robert. The professional teacher, licensed by the State of California, was also a registered welfare worker and made sure that the children were given rest periods and plenty of time for meals. Shooting then took place after lunch and continued until 6 p.m., although there were strict laws governing how long the children could be in front of the camera.

Drew, who was only six years old, couldn't just sit down, read the script and learn her lines by herself like an adult. Instead, her actress mother helped with some of the more difficult sections. 'We studied it at night. Then when I went to sleep, I thought about what I had to say the next day. I thought of my words and of what the scene would be,' said Drew afterwards.

The magical story starts when a group of alien botanists is disturbed by a human government task force. During the rushed retreat, one of the creatures is left behind and, narrowly missing capture, he hides in the coal shed in the backyard of the Taylor household – a single-parent family with three children.

Elliott is the first to discover the intruder and, after luring the unknown animal to his room, he wags school to look after the extra-terrestrial, 'E.T.' for short. He then entrusts his brother with the discovery, but their cover is nearly blown when Gertie bursts in on the three of them. Here Spielberg employs *that* ear-piercing scream and Drew's performance is a delightful combination of cuteness and wisecracks. Amusingly, when E.T. demonstrates his superpowers, she says 'What's happ-ening?' in the same eerie sing-song as Heather O'Rourke's 'They're he-ere', perfectly parodying *Poltergeist*.

The middle section is the comical portion of the film: as the boy and alien form a symbiotic bond, so Elliott starts mimicking E.T.'s actions. E.T. hides in the toy cupboard, making mother Mary think he is a stuffed animal, and when Gertie looks after him she dresses him up in women's clothing, replete with a wig and hat. The fun ends after Gertie teaches E.T. to speak and Elliott discovers that the alien wants to 'phone home'.

Meanwhile, the alien hunters are closing in on their target and track down the Taylors. Spielberg utilizes a classic cartoon technique of keeping the adults out of the children's world by showing them only from the waist down (except for their mother). It is only when the government officials seal off the house that their faces are revealed, namely that of Keys, who has always been a believer.

As E.T. begins to suffer from the effects of the earth's atmosphere, the rush is on to communicate with his home planet and return him to it, culminating in a fun BMX chase sequence. Backed by a rousing score by John Williams, *E.T.* is an endearing tale that remains remarkably watchable today without feeling too dated.

*

While Spielberg had been casting *E.T.*, he had employed a design team to create the extra-terrestrial itself. Carlo Rambaldi, maker of the mechanical King Kong and the aliens in *Close Encounters*, was brought in to actually construct the 3-foot-tall machine capable of walking and talking. Its eighty-five separate movements were operated by a dozen men using a complex series of hydraulic, mechanical and electrical cables.

Three versions of E.T. were built with four interchangeable heads, a separate pair of hands was used for close-up shots, and three actors wore elaborate E.T. costumes (one was a boy born without legs; the other two were a man and a woman under 3 feet tall). While Debra Winger provided E.T.'s voice for pivotal lines such as 'E.T. phone home', the bulk of the creature's vocal work was undertaken by Pat Welsh, a retired elocution teacher. The sound designer had overheard her distinctive speech in a camera store and cheekily asked her to remove her dentures and continue talking.

Despite the extensive behind-the-scenes work required to bring E.T. to life, everyone on set fell in love with him. Drew was certainly no exception and perhaps connected with the lost soul the most deeply.

'From the moment I saw him, E.T. instantly became my best friend,' she recalls. 'He was absolutely real to me – I understood that it took mechanics and some people being in his suit and a woman doing his hands to make him come alive, but I just thought that he was a guardian angel. Because he was *there*, not computer generated, he was a very real, tangible being.'

During her lunch breaks, Drew would often be found in the room where he was kept, eating and chatting away.

'I talked to him about my mother and where we lived. If it was cold outside, I wrapped a scarf around his neck,' she explains.

For a child starved of love and attention, with no real best friend, it was hardly surprising that she felt such a strong bond to the trusting alien. '[He was] a good friend – someone who was teaching me a lot about love and how to take care of someone, and how to treat people. He was one of the first most important friends of my life.'

Drew built another important and lasting relationship on the set of *E.T.*, this time of the human variety: with the director himself. They bonded straightaway when Spielberg coaxed out her elaborate fantasy about being in a band. 'He was the first person who made me feel good about being myself or living out my imagination,' she says. 'I think everyone in this world needs someone to help them find their dreams and realize their destiny, and to believe in them and make them feel like they could reach their potential.' Spielberg was touched by her refreshing attitude. 'She's wonderfully funny and spontaneous – she just melted me,' he says.

Moreover, the director recognized her latent value to his film. '[Drew] has an instinct far beyond her years,' he said at the time, 'and in this business it can pay to listen to the young.'

Indeed, for the first time in his movie career, Spielberg did not storyboard *E.T.* 'I had the feeling the boards might force the child actors into stiff, unnatural attitudes and I didn't want that. I wanted them to be so spontaneous that if something natural did come up – something that was a gift from the gods – then we'd be able to use it without the boards saying we couldn't.'

His foresight proved intrinsic to the film, with ad-libbing and accidents providing some of the most memorable scenes. 'All of us were free to offer input, but he especially seemed to like the silly things the kids came up with,' says Drew. When the children are hiding the alien in the closet, one of Gertie's brothers tries to tell her that adults can't see E.T. There was no scripted response, so Spielberg told her to improvise. 'When we did the scene again, I shrugged and said, "Gimme a break!"' concludes Drew, highlighting one of the most endearing qualities she instilled in Gertie – a smart-aleck maturity juxtaposed with her childish features.

Spielberg often took Drew aside, asking her if she liked a scene or had any thoughts, and frequently incorporated her ideas. She relished the attention, for once feeling important and useful instead of lonely and longing for approval.

*

When not required during the filming of *E.T.*, the boys amused themselves by wreaking havoc, skateboarding around the set. Drew was regularly drawn into their tomfoolery, often seen on Robert's shoulders play-fighting with Henry, who was balanced on one of the other children's shoulders. Their general aim was to 'just raise as much hell on the set as we could'.

But the shoot was not always easy. As their opposite number was usually an inanimate object, Spielberg facilitated the children's reactions by reciting E.T.'s lines, describing his actions, and one time, even dressing up as the old lady designed by Gertie.

One of Drew's first scenes includes that mirror-shattering scream when she comes face to face with E.T. 'It was really hard because they wanted me to work when I had a sore throat,' complained Drew at the time, 'but I still did it. I had to do it lots of times – the next day, I felt terrible!'

Spielberg purposefully shot the movie in chronological order, so that the children genuinely made friends with the stowaway alien, becoming closer over time. When it came to saying goodbye, the reactions were movingly authentic.

One of the biggest scenes features both Elliott and E.T. being monitored by medical staff. Rather than asking actors to learn the technical jargon by rote, Spielberg actually hired real doctors. 'That part was really scary,' he concedes. 'It was scary for me to hear the overlapping dialogue, which you don't often hear in movies, and to see the equipment.'

But if the adults found it daunting, the children, who had grown to love the alien, were horrified when electric paddles were used to try to revive their best friend. 'Drew leapt off the ground, and when she heard that explosion of electricity going into E.T., she just lost it,' says Spielberg.

'I had never seen a machine like that, I didn't even know they existed,' she says. 'I just kept thinking about something hurting the big red beating heart and it just felt like the greatest violation. All your dreams crashing away, your safety and security.' The sight of her cherubic face crumpling is one of the most touching moments in the film.

'Steven is responsible for the best advice I've ever been given on acting. He told me that when I was doing the film I should never *act* my character, that I should *be* my character,' Drew reveals in her autobiography, *Little Girl Lost*. 'What he said was so simple that it nearly skirted by me. But it's amazing how one brief sentence like that can be so profound and make such a big difference in your life.'

Jaid adds, 'He said, "Never give your daughter any acting lessons. She is the most naturally gifted actress I have ever seen. She has the stardust magic. I have never seen anyone on film who comes across the way she does." '

Partway through filming, Drew came down with a high fever, but as a dedicated actress unwilling to let anyone down, she refused to say anything. Even when Spielberg reprimanded her, saying that she didn't seem to be putting her all into her work, still the girl kept quiet. She eventually collapsed with a temperature of 105 degrees Fahrenheit and was taken to hospital, where they fed her ice chips. The director naturally felt terrible about his reproach and ordered her to stay in bed until she was better.

Spielberg treated her like a daughter and regularly invited her to his Malibu house at the weekends, where they'd play on the beach, collecting seashells and building sandcastles. 'It was so much fun to hang out with him,' says Drew. The presumptuous girl even thought of Spielberg's cocker spaniel, Willie, as their shared pet, whom the director merely housed. Jaid joked, 'When she's miffed with me, she says she's going to move in with Steven!'

And so Spielberg became Drew's godfather and mentor. His office wall still boasts a framed picture painted for him by Drew aged six which says: 'I love you, Steven,' and he gave her an arcade-size Ms Pac-Man game that Christmas.

When Drew became withdrawn and depressed towards the end of the shoot, Spielberg grew concerned and asked her what was wrong. Drew confessed that she dreaded having to say goodbye to E.T., and Spielberg sensitively promised that she could visit him whenever she wanted.

Having asked everyone to sign a confidentiality agreement to preserve the surprise of E.T., Spielberg was relieved when the sixty-five-day schedule wrapped four days ahead of time, his secret intact. The director, who had been known to mutter gleefully, 'This is going to be my little movie, my little classic,' could not have predicted the picture's impending impact.

*

In January 1982 Drew was forced to return to the boring reality of her first-grade classroom at Fountain Day. Just five months earlier, her biggest claim to fame had been kissing Alex the cutie in the school play. 'But from the moment I checked back into school, I was treated differently,' says Drew. 'The kids made fun of me. I think a lot of it was jealousy.'

For comfort, Drew turned to the kitten Steven Spielberg had given her (which, although male, she'd named Gertie). 'I told him how alone I was feeling,' says Drew, who was clearly replacing E.T. with Gertie.

Jaid had not worked for most of the time that Drew had been filming E.T., instead driving her daughter to and from the set, helping her learn lines and generally spending time with her. However, as Drew's pay (approximately $75,000) bought the pair some security, Jaid felt she didn't need to return to her waitressing jobs and turned her attentions back to her own career.

Now, just as Drew needed her to help with the awkward phase of readjustment, Jaid found herself working all hours in a demanding play at the Strasberg Institute.

An internationally renowned director, actor and master teacher, Lee Strasberg's name is synonymous with Method acting. He was famous for tutoring the likes of Marilyn Monroe, James Dean, Dustin Hoffman, Robert De Niro and Jack Nicholson. In the late 1960s a branch of his Actor's Studio was established in Los Angeles, followed by The Lee Strasberg Theater Institute, created to make his work available to a wider public.

Jaid was appearing in *Playing For Time*, a piece about Jews imprisoned by the Nazis. On Friday and Saturday evenings Drew even joined her on stage, playing a young girl about to be sentenced to death, who instead becomes the darling of a female German officer.

Both Strasberg and his South American wife, Anna, were impressed with Jaid's work and they became close friends. Anna was particularly fond of Drew and was soon made her godmother. Sadly, Strasberg died of a heart attack shortly afterwards, in February 1982.

Straight after *Playing For Time*, Jaid began work on a feature film. Coincidentally, the movie was *Night Shift*, the same Ron Howard picture that had prevented Shelley Long from starring in *E.T.* The comedy follows two morgue attendants (Michael Keaton and Henry Winkler) who turn their place of work into a nocturnal brothel for the benefit of an anything-goes hooker (Long) – and their own wallets.

For Long and Keaton, *Night Shift* proved pivotal in propelling them to fame, and for Winkler and Howard, the film marked a break away from their long-running success in *Happy Days*. It was Jaid's best shot at stardom to date.

Although she only had a minor part as a prostitute in *Night Shift*, Jaid worked or was on call for eighteen hours a day, for the best part of three months. From having her mother permanently on hand, Drew was thrown back onto a succession of babysitters, or she was dragged on to the set and told to sit quietly.

'I remember they'd always be worried that I would start screaming or hollering and ruin the scene,' recalls Drew. 'I felt the pressure of everyone watching, of being an intruder, which wasn't comfortable.'

The time apart put an enormous strain on the mother–daughter relationship, particularly when Drew caught a bad bout of pneumonia and still Jaid continued to work. Drew realized that when she was working she saw her mother all the time, but when it was her mother's turn to work she barely saw her at all. Finally, she snapped.

'Just quit this job and spend more time with me!' she yelled.

Jaid was torn.

'I wasn't pushing Drew [into acting],' she explains. 'I was the exact opposite – I didn't want her to act. *I* was going to be the star – not her!'

Eventually, Jaid came to realize that after a decade her career was still floundering, while her daughter was being courted by Steven Spielberg. Drew's cries of 'I have no mom! We never see each other! I feel totally abandoned!' hit home. 'I thought, "Why am I running after this elusive career? I am just another actress, but I am the only mother Drew has,"' says Jaid candidly.

Before the final decision could be made for Jaid to quit working altogether, she explained to Drew that, while this meant that the youngster could further her career, it also put pressure on her to bring in a substantial income. Drew later recalled in *Little Girl Lost* that she had no qualms about this, making up her mind before her mother had even finished her explanation of how life would change from now on. 'I knew that acting was in my blood, that I felt best about myself when I was working in front of the camera,' she said. 'The attention I received was great, but I also loved becoming a different person with a different name, bringing this person on a piece of paper to life.'

*

As Drew turned seven in February 1982, so began a new lifestyle in the Barrymore household. Mother and daughter settled into a schedule whereby Jaid drove her to and from school, ferried her to her various after-school classes, prepared the evening meal and put Drew to bed. This regime certainly suited Drew, but it stunted Jaid's acting ambitions, and resentment would later rear its ugly head.

Content with the living and caring arrangements, Drew was able to fully enjoy her extra-curricular activities. Every Saturday morning she attended a jazz, rock and tap class with Anthony Newley's eleven-year-old daughter, Shelby, where they performed complicated routines to 'Footloose' in black leotards and red miniskirts.

She also squeezed in two ballet classes, a karate session, and voice and guitar lessons, as well as regular shopping trips and jaunts to Spielberg's beach house. If she had any spare time, she listened to records, roller-skated, cartwheeled around the house and garden, and played with her favourite Hello Kitty accessories. Most importantly, her reading was improving (useful for assessing potential scripts), as she often demonstrated to her teddy bear.

At school, Drew regaled her peers with impressions of Charlie Chaplin, Judy Garland, Faye Dunaway as Joan Crawford in *Mommie Dearest*, Cyndi Lauper singing 'Girls Just Want To Have Fun', or any other famous person with whom she was fascinated.

Typically for her age, Drew developed crushes on a couple of television personalities. Her first was the news anchorman Ted Koppel, but she was fickle with her affections.

'I was so in love with him, I couldn't stand it. I couldn't wait till 11.30 every night, I was just smitten with him. And then one night the channel was turned, and at 12.30, Dave Letterman came into my world. And all of a sudden I had a new man.'

Sadly, Drew's new-found fun and freedom was all about to come screeching to a halt.

4

ALIEN NATION

The critics did not know what to expect from Steven Spielberg's little personal project *E.T.*; all they did know was that the Spielberg summer blockbuster was going to be *Poltergeist*.

E.T. received its first screening as an unofficial entry in the 1982 Cannes Film Festival. It was hailed with a standing ovation from the industry. Suddenly, the lightweight marketing campaign initially planned was replaced with a massive promotional drive incorporating every merchandising deal available.

Just before the end of the school summer term, Drew and Jaid flew to New York for previews; by the time of the star-studded premiere at the Cinerama Dome in Los Angeles, the buzz around town was that *E.T.* was something special.

Life at school changed for Drew irrevocably.

'Everyone wanted to know about E.T., and if I didn't want to talk about it, I was branded a snob,' she says. 'It was as if someone had stuck a sign on my back that said, "Outcast".'

Before the days of *E.T.*, Drew's occasional appearances in movies and commercials weren't considered a big deal, especially as several of her fellow pupils had done the same. But *E.T.* brought with it a different kind of fame, setting her apart from her classmates. During her ongoing struggle to be accepted, ostracism was the last thing she wanted.

On 11 June 1982 *E.T. The Extra-Terrestrial* opened, grossing a staggering $11.8 million in its first weekend. The following three weeks went against all previous trends as the weekly totals actually increased. Amazingly, the film remains Spielberg's biggest hit in America to date, yielding just shy of $400 million. Earning a further $300 million on its global release nearer Christmas, E.T. brought in a staggering $701 million worldwide – a record which stood until Spielberg's *Jurassic Park* in 1993. A further $200 million was made from the spin-off E.T. dolls, games, posters and duvet covers.

The reviews were unremittingly praising.

'The most moving science-fiction movie ever made on earth,' wrote Pauline Kael for the *New Yorker*. 'A classic movie for kids and a remarkable portrait of childhood,' said Mark Deming of *All Movie Guide*. 'Spielberg sensitively yet humorously delves into childhood innocence and experience, revealing the threat posed by adult ignorance and misplaced authority,' added Lucia Bozzola. 'With his affirmation of love and the importance of home, E.T. is something of an old-fashioned antidote to the chaos of the prior two decades.'

The industry unanimously agreed and E.T. was nominated for nine Academy Awards the following year, winning Oscars in the categories of Best Music, Best Visual Effects, and Best Sound and Sound Effects Editing; sadly the rest were lost to Richard Attenborough's *Gandhi*. The endless BAFTA nominations included Best Film, Director and Outstanding Newcomer (for Henry Thomas and Drew Barrymore), but the only win was again for John Williams's superb soundtrack, while the film secured two awards at the Golden Globes: one for Best Motion Picture – Drama, and again Williams's score, for which he also garnered a Grammy.

Drew did not leave all the ceremonies empty-handed, however: she picked up the 1982 Youth In Film Award and 1983 Young Artist Award – Best Young Supporting Actress In A Motion Picture.

As the world fell in love with E.T. and the Taylor family, rumours abounded about a sequel. Spielberg apparently reunited with Melissa Mathison to work through a storyline in which the tables are turned and Elliott and friends are kidnapped by aliens and have to contact E.T. to rescue them. 'We talked about it for a long time, and there was actually a time when it almost happened,' says Drew tantalisingly, 'but it's past now. Some sequels are great and can be pulled off, but I think usually they devalue the original.'

*

With the unexpected success of E.T., so came the equally phenomenal rise of its three child stars. One day they were all staying at the Universal Sheraton Hotel, doing normal childish things like playing Dungeons and Dragons, telling ghost stories and having food fights, when suddenly their concentration was interrupted by a news report on the television. Pictured was an incredibly long, snaking queue of people waiting to get into the Cinerama Dome. Drew, Henry and Robert sat gawping at the screen, but nothing could prepare them for the following morning.

Overnight the trio became the most famous kids in America. At first people just whispered and stood and stared. Then they clamoured for autographs, shoved their way through crowds to touch the children and fought to ask questions about E.T. For somebody who just wanted to be loved, Drew was somewhat overwhelmed by the sudden influx of attention.

'I thought it was insane. I didn't know how to deal with it and that frightened me,' Drew wrote in *Little Girl Lost*. 'I came to the obvious conclusion that very suddenly my life was going to change . . . I didn't try to figure out if it was good or bad. I was someone people knew by name. It made me feel that I must be different.'

There was no turning back – from that day on, Drew's life changed. She wasn't just adored by the public; she was also hot property as far as the press were concerned, not least due to her impressive lineage. The Barrymores' West Hollywood home was swamped by reporters, all wanting to know what Drew thought of her grandfather John, great-uncle Lionel and great-aunt Ethel. Considering that she had never met them and had only heard a handful of stories from the director Vincent Sherman on the set of *Bogie*, she merely smiled politely, saying she hoped one day to be considered as accomplished as them. Drew was also able to brush off awkward questions about her father with a brief response about only seeing him occasionally, but she didn't really understand the pressure that was being heaped on her as a fifth-generation Barrymore.

Then Drew was invited to the Shubert Theater in New York for a ceremony in honour of the acting dynasty. Mother and daughter ensconced themselves in a suite at the Mayflower Hotel overlooking Central Park, their favourite residence whenever they came to the Big Apple. Attending the event wearing a frilly white dress, white tights and shoes, with her hair tied up in long bows, an awe-inspired Drew looked startling as a child in an adult world.

After the speeches she was introduced as the youngest member of the clan and asked to stand up. She was lifted onto a chair so that she could be seen, and received a warm ovation.

'I felt strangely connected to that heritage – strangely because it was only through the complete accident of birth and nothing I did,' she says. 'Yet I subconsciously began to assume the role of the "latest Barrymore actor".'

The expectations were a lot to live up to and Steven Spielberg himself unwittingly added to the burden she bore. Famously he remarked that she was a 'perfect seven-year-old going on a mature twenty-nine', and so that was the way Drew felt she had to behave.

As the furore of the summer began to settle, Drew came down to earth with a bump as she had to return to school for the second grade. Fountain Day only went up to the first grade, so she was forced to move: Drew joined Westland School, a small, progressive private facility.

By now, however, she was considered a major movie star, and rather than this being a cool status symbol, Drew found it went against her.

'There's a difference between people you know making fun of you, and people you've never seen before just staring at you, waiting for you to make a mistake,' she says. 'One is understandable, the other is downright mean.' They say children can be cruel, and Drew experienced the whole gamut of spiteful reactions.

*

When Drew's career hit the fast lane in the second half of 1982, Jaid became increasingly involved – after all, it was their agreement that she should drop her own pursuits to look after her daughter and her professional interests.

Scripts were flooding in for the hottest new actress and Jaid spent hours poring over them with Drew's agent, J. J. Harris. Jaid was determined that her daughter's future lay on the big screen and automatically turned down any television work. She also censored projects entailing inappropriate material – with Drew having just finished work on a Steven Spielberg movie devoid of all swear words, violence, sex or drugs, Jaid was not about to expose her seven-year-old to such themes.

She vetoed one film in which Drew would portray a schizophrenic child as she thought it would upset her daughter. When unsuitable scripts crept through, Drew was sensible enough not to get involved. 'Last week we got a script with abusive language, but Drew read it,' said Jaid that autumn. 'She rejected it right off. "Mommy," she said, "I couldn't play it. I don't talk that way in real life."'

Ironically, the more Jaid became involved in Drew's life, the more alone Drew felt. Having craved her mother's full-time attention for seven years, now she had it, she believed it was under false pretences. 'Not only did I harbour a longstanding anger toward her for abandoning me, but I also imagined that my primary worth to her was the money I earned,' she recalls.

With the clarity of hindsight, Jaid can also see the problems that were emerging in their relationship as she sacrificed her dreams in favour of making her daughter a star. 'She was now the breadwinner and it was awful,' she acknowledges. 'I became less of a mother and more of a manager. I lived my life through her and was hanging out of her armpit. My mother and I hardly knew each other – I was disproportionately the opposite with Drew.'

All-consumed by acting, Drew never recognized that there was more to her chosen vocation than the natural drive of enthusiasm and ambition. It was only years later that she was able to admit to herself that her desperate need to perform was fed by her low self-esteem. 'I hungered for the love and affirmation I felt was absent from my life,' she now concedes. 'I was riddled with insecurity, always fearing that people wouldn't like me. It felt as if: "How could they? My father hates me. My mother [only] likes me for the money I earn." '

During interviews held in hotels, Jaid would sometimes lead the dialogue, allowing Drew to act like the child she was: getting in a lift and pushing as many buttons as she could; seeing how many cartwheels she could do down the long corridors; touching the ice stage at the ice show; plunging into a swimming pool headfirst; tearing through a gift department; or, when tired, sucking her thumb and twirling her hair round her finger. The mischievous girl fancied herself a modern-day Eloise, the impish character whose life at the Plaza she devoured in numerous books.

'Sometimes, I look at Drew and I can just picture her in a red suit with a little pitchfork tail,' mused Jaid to a journalist. 'She gets away with murder!' But Jaid seemed to have a firm grasp on her child's behaviour, for if Drew did something really bad she made sure that she knew what she was apologizing for. 'I don't let her simply say "I'm sorry", because she might be thinking, "I'm sorry you're such a rotten mother", or "I'm sorry you're making me say I'm sorry".

'I believe that when a child is fresh it isn't the child's fault, but rather the parent's.' Such potent words were surely to come back and haunt her . . .

*

During this whirlwind of activity, Drew was not only called upon for interviews and personal appearances, she was also invited to attend numerous award ceremonies, which inevitably had parties afterwards. Unaccustomed to and thrilled by the flurry of requests, Jaid and Drew accepted them all.

Brushing shoulders with the social elite of Tinseltown, Jaid was in her element, enjoying the glamorous lifestyle she had hoped to attain with her own career. Drew also loved the limelight but, given her youth, soon grew exhausted and found it hard to maintain the late-night pace; she would often be found curled up in a chair, fast asleep. Fortunately, the events tended to be at the weekend, so the schoolgirl could catch up on sleep the following day. Besides, it was deemed acceptable for her to be out until 2 a.m. as it was, after all, business.

During the worldwide roll-out of the film in the autumn and winter of 1982, *E.T.* reached the four corners of the earth, and so too did Drew and the publicity bandwagon. The British royal premiere was held at the Empire in Leicester Square and attended by Prince Charles and Princess Diana. Drew gave the princess one of the E.T. dolls beforehand, and they met again in a more informal setting after the screening. Apparently, the princess had to leave during the credits to fix her make-up, having cried through the ending!

Drew's next commitment was a month-long promotional tour, covering much of Europe, Scandinavia and Japan. 'I was getting to travel the world and see that there were all these different types of cultures and people,' recalls Drew, who had never before been outside of California. 'Wow – the world was so big! It made me unjudgmental towards people.'

Back in America, the spunky little girl traded quips with Johnny Carson on *The Tonight Show* like an old pro. Her bravado was for show, much like her first audition with Steven Spielberg, and due to her nerves about appearing on such an institution, Drew revealed her inner geeky self. 'I'm not cool,' she laughs, 'I'll never walk gracefully. I even tripped when I was walking out on *The Tonight Show!*'

A little more appropriately, given her age, Drew was invited to attend the opening celebrations of Walt Disney's EPCOT centre on 1 October. The second theme park at the Walt Disney World resort, the new Experimental Prototype City Of Tomorrow was connected via monorail to the familiar Magic Kingdom theme park. Designed to 'entertain, inform and inspire', the park was twice the size of the Magic Kingdom, giving rise to the nickname 'Every Person Comes Out Tired'.

The launch ceremony was hosted by veteran entertainer Danny Kaye and featured an array of famous names, including Drew, who voiced a few brief compliments about the centre.

In November Drew had a far more exciting role: she was offered the coveted position of guest host on *Saturday Night Live*.

The world-famous NBC comedy series first aired in October 1975 and by 1977 had become the highest-rated late-night show in America, surpassing *The Tonight Show*. Broadcast live from Studio 8H in

Rockefeller Center at 11.30 p.m. on Saturdays, it follows a fairly set format: a celebrity host, a musical guest, an ensemble of cast members, sketches, parodies of commercials, and a fake news segment.

The seasons from 1981 to 1984 became known as 'Eddie's Era', as Eddie Murphy was the returning cast member who dominated the show. Murphy started out in stand-up comedy at fifteen and was hired by *Saturday Night Live* by the time he was nineteen. His upbeat blend of streetwise humour, youthful arrogance and underlying rage quickly made him the talk of the show, and Murphy mania swept the nation.

Drew was especially smitten with the funny man. 'Eddie Murphy always called me Precious,' she says. 'However, he didn't exactly say it that way. He'd exaggerate it, draw it out, saying, "Praaaaaaaay-cious!" I'd break up in giggles.'

Although it was a live show, the cast rehearsed daily for a week-and-a-half to iron out any kinks and then performed a dry run for a pre-recorded show called *Saturday Night Dead*. Drew had been involved for this ten-day period, but was still understandably apprehensive as Saturday rolled around. Given her youth and anxiety about such a prestigious live show, she was excused from the traditional opening monologue. Instead, the audience were given cards and asked to write down any questions they had for Drew. The actress then made her grand entrance, accompanied by cast member Tim Kazurinsky, who prompted her with the notes. After that, it was child's play.

On 20 November 1982 Drew Barrymore walked on set as the youngest-ever host of *Saturday Night Live*. Acting like a showbusiness veteran, her nerves weren't visible and she displayed a professional maturity beyond her years. Her favourite part of the show was an *E.T.* spoof – quite a feat to pull off, considering Steven Spielberg and Robin Williams were sitting right in the front row of the audience.

Drew was a smash hit, proving that she could amply hold her own in any environment. At the close of the show, the cast swarmed around her and lifted her up on their shoulders. 'I never wanted to leave,' she remembers. 'It was the best feeling.'

*

Away from the set, Drew was as lonely as ever, still failing to fit in at school and feeling neglected by her parents.

Adding to her insecurity at home, Drew's mother was currently fighting her father for an official divorce. As Jaid was trying to rid herself of John Barrymore II for good, so too was Drew. Having spent the last few years trying to reconcile the fact that her own flesh and blood clearly didn't want her, her new-found fame (and, more importantly, salary) brought him crawling out of the woodwork.

Out of the blue one day, John called Drew, asking for money. Drew agreed and in return asked if he might wish her a happy birthday when the time came in a few months. Drew was crushed by her father's rude response of a straight 'no', not to mention his insulting reference to her being a 'so-called movie star' (of a film that he hadn't even bothered to see).

All the same, she couldn't seem to stop herself hankering after his love, and when she didn't receive it, her childish logic dictated that it was somehow her fault. Deep down, Drew knew that things weren't normal or right, but as no one was instructing her to the contrary, she kept raising her hopes, only to have them dashed again when nothing changed.

One night, John appeared to discuss the divorce in person. By now, Drew had wised up and, sick of the sight and thought of him, unleashed her pent-up anger in a very adult tirade.

'Here's to all the horrible things you've ever said to me!' she yelled. 'To all the times you've made me feel like a useless piece of garbage!'

Her father pretended to ignore her, but that only added fuel to the already-raging inferno.

'Your goddamn drinking and drug use makes me sick. I want you out of my life!' With that, she kicked a chair at him and stormed out of the room, not to see him for another seven years – a veritable lifetime for Drew.

As the Barrymore women bid farewell to John once more, Drew realized that her father's absence shouldn't preclude another man from entering their lives. A girl at school lived with her mother and her mother's boyfriend – and this planted the seed in Drew's mind of a live-in surrogate father.

Drew has since admitted that Jaid didn't have a love life, mainly because her focus was completely on her daughter. There were no boyfriends, no dates. 'The way I saw it, she wasn't *trying* to remarry,' she says.

Drew's youth and years of feeling hard done by twisted her outlook and produced a very selfish perspective on the situation – she was convinced that if her mother *really* cared about her happiness, she would find a boyfriend to replace her father. When Jaid didn't date, Drew took it as a personal slight.

*

As 1982 drew to a close, with the hyperbole surrounding *E.T.* fading, it was clear that Drew should capitalize on her fame with another film.

The trouble was choosing something suitable. Having trawled through hundreds of potential screenplays, Drew's ears pricked up when Jaid read out the script for *Irreconcilable Differences*.

The plot centres on the effect a troubled marriage between two self-absorbed showbusiness personalities has on their offspring, culminating in the child taking her parents to court in a bid to divorce herself from them.

When probed about the finer details of the story by interviewers in December 1982, Drew refused to divulge trade secrets. 'The movie is about me divorcing my parents. That's all I can say at this time,' she declared resolutely. Jaid nudged her daughter, suggesting that a bit of gossip was good for advance publicity, but the consummate professional remained adamant: 'When it's out, we'll talk.'

It was blindingly obvious why such a feisty character, desperately trying to free herself from the encumbrance of her impossible parents, would appeal to a girl who had felt neglected all her life and had finally succeeded in ridding herself of her father. 'I wondered if *I* shouldn't try divorcing my father,' Drew says. 'I thought that if I did, it would make it easier for my mother. Maybe the pain both of us were feeling would subside.'

Drew eagerly signed up for the part of Casey Brodsky; her father, Albert, was to be played by Ryan O'Neal, a successful and award-winning actor in the 1970s whose career was now in decline, and Shelley Long finally became her screen mother, Lucy, circumstances having prevented her doing so in *E.T.* Introducing Sharon Stone as Albert Brodsky's floozy, other cast members included Sam Wanamaker and Allen Garfield – there certainly weren't going to be any other children around.*

'It felt very mature,' Drew recalled. 'I went from a set of all kids to being the only kid . . . that was when I started getting into the responsibility and maturity of work life.'

Drawing on her own experiences as a key resource for this moving drama, Drew explains, 'It wasn't hard for me to get upset with my movie parents, especially considering the scene I'd recently had with my real father.'

Unfortunately, the three-month shoot was as turbulent as the Brodskys' family life. Apparently, director Charles Shyer clashed with the producers about everything from the film's overall angle down to specific scenes. The few times they agreed on something, the actors

---

*It is interesting to note that Jaid managed to secure herself a bit part in the film as 'Whispering woman', confirming that she still harboured aspirations as an actress.

then invariably found fault. Even the simplest shots began to rack up thirty or forty takes.

'It was unbearable,' wrote Drew in *Little Girl Lost*. 'Ryan kept my sanity . . . I was so emotionally drained that I broke down and cried. I hadn't ever felt stress like that and no one even looked at me sympathetically.' She goes on to describe how she would flee to her dressing room in tears, followed a few moments later by O'Neal. 'He draped his arm around me, then gave me a hug and shrugged, "Shit happens. We're professional and sometimes we're forced to work with amateurs . . . tomorrow's going to be better."'

After production wrapped, Drew was fed up with the whole acting game and on the brink of retiring. It would take something pretty special to make her reconsider and return to a movie set.

*

Irreconcilable Differences gets off to a promising start – diving straight into a conversation between Casey and her lawyer about her case. Drew, who has clearly aged since the little girl of *E.T.*, still looks young, but conversely acts like a grown-up in this adult scenario.

The story is told in the courtroom and the background is detailed in flashbacks. Lucy and Albert Brodsky enjoy a loving marriage and have a daughter, Casey. Albert's life takes an unexpected upward turn when he becomes a celebrated filmmaker, having directed a script he co-wrote with Lucy. He fails to give her the credit she deserves and, even worse, starts an affair with his leading lady (wonderfully played by a hairy-armpitted Sharon Stone).

Lucy sinks into depression, losing interest in her life, appearance and family. In a typically Hollywood-style reversal of fortune, she then has a breakthrough and becomes a best-selling author, just as Albert goes bust when his next large-scale drama flick bombs.

Casey appears but briefly in her parents' complicated lives, although long enough to show that she receives no love or attention and is far happier with the maid's family. The film concludes in the courtroom, where the media have a field day due to the celebrity of both parents.

Unfortunately, the arresting style of storytelling soon loses its edge as the recaps are too long and the glimpses of the court case are few and far between. Additionally, there is little spark between O'Neal and Long, begging the question of how they got together in the first place rather than why they split up.

As Drew's second major film, it was a perfect showcase for her advanced acting ability, with the youngster at times outshining O'Neal and Long. Highlighting Casey's contradictory character, Drew excels in an immature sulky strop, and then displays a very adult weariness and expert comic timing. The role also requires a smattering of Spanish, which Drew handles competently. Her climactic speech in court is a pleasure to watch, particularly when she admonishes that a child should be treated like a child and not a pet.

Without getting too far ahead in Drew's own story, two scenarios cannot be overlooked with regard to their proximity to her real-life experiences: the New Year's Eve party scene where a frustrated Casey downs a glass of wine, and the fact that Casey legally emancipates herself from her parents.

When *Irreconcilable Differences* was released, Drew could take some consolation from the fact that although her co-stars, O'Neal and Long, received top billing, the posters placed Drew squarely as the star. Therein lies one of the greatest problems of the movie: the original concept and selling point was that Casey Brodsky was divorcing her parents, but, far from being Casey's story, *Irreconcilable Differences* is predominantly a lame romance.

As it happens, the theme of parents fighting over a child during divorce was a common one at the time, as seen in *Kramer vs. Kramer* (1979), *The Champ* (1979) and *Author! Author!* (1982). The twist in *Irreconcilable Differences* – that the child called her bickering parents' bluff – was not prominent enough, which was a shame, as Drew's scenes were excellent.

Although the reviews were generally poor, the film touched the children of the era, who could easily identify with Casey. Achieving a domestic gross of some $12 million, it was clear that *Irreconcilable Differences* was no *E.T.* in terms of box-office appeal, but its impact on Drew's career was of comparative importance as she was nominated for a Golden Globe for Best Supporting Actress and the 1985 Young Artist Award for Best Young Actress In A Motion Picture.

As Drew earned a reported $500,000, even after paying various fees and depositing a large portion into a trust fund she and Jaid were able to purchase a lovely two-bedroom ranch-style home with a pool and sauna in Sherman Oaks, a comfortable upper-class neighbourhood in the San Fernando Valley. This move marked a considerable step up the economic ladder, and for the time being, mother and daughter were free of financial concerns.

5

TWISTED FIRESTARTER

In the early 1980s, the novelist Stephen King was at the top of his chosen genre of supernatural horror. With his seemingly boundless imagination and accessible writing style, the prolific author had shot to fame in 1974 with the publication of *Carrie*: a cautionary tale of an adolescent misfit with special telekinetic powers who wreaks a spectacular revenge on the school bullies who have made her life a living hell.

Alongside exploiting unlikely 'what if?' scenarios and all things otherworldly, King specialized in tapping into both his teenage fans' obsession with gore and his adult readers' desire to return to their childhoods and greedily devour his page-turners under the bedclothes by torchlight. By May 1983, eleven of his novels had either made it onto the big screen (with varying degrees of success) or had been optioned for filming. To give some indication of his popularity, 1980's *Firestarter* was the fourth Stephen King novel to be adapted for film in just twelve months.

Like many girls approaching puberty all too fast, Drew was a big fan of King's work. The writer's tendency to occasionally place children and teenagers in central roles – teamed with relatively acceptable and thoroughly tantalising levels of horror, sex and violence for his more youthful readers – ensured him a fan base perhaps younger than many parents would have liked. Drew read *Firestarter* at a mere six-and-a-half years of age. On turning the final page, she confidently announced to her mother:

'I'm the Firestarter. I'm Charlie McGee!'

A year-and-a-half later, her prediction came true.

In her biggest role to date, Drew was cast by Johanna Ray in the relatively high-budget, extremely high-profile film adaptation by Universal, starring alongside a distinguished cast including George C. Scott, Martin Sheen, David Keith, Art Carney, Louise Fletcher and a young Heather Locklear in her big-screen debut (perhaps a little unlikely, at twenty-two, as the mother of a nine-year-old daughter). The movie was directed by Mark L. Lester and produced by, among others, Dino DeLaurentiis, whom Drew recalls as being 'an absolute doll, so sweet and so very Italian'. Stephen King himself assisted by overseeing some of the shooting.

Firestarter, a psychological thriller, tells the story of Charlie McGee, a young girl with the disturbing ability to ignite fires purely with the force of her mind. Her parents, Andy (Keith) and Vicky (Locklear), had previously been willing participants in LOT 6 – a covert government-sponsored experiment held at 'The Shop', Virginia, in which low-grade hallucinogens were injected into ten volunteers. This resulted in Andy and Vicky developing parapsychological powers, while the other eight guinea pigs, unable to cope with the mind-altering effects of the drug, either die or commit suicide.

Andy and Vicky marry and produce a daughter – Charlie – whose own extraordinary powers of telepathy and pyrokinesis are a constant source of worry to her parents, who try their best to tame her abilities and teach her restraint. 'It's like letting a wild animal out of a cage,' explains Charlie of her unusual talent, which she can only control to a certain extent.

Charlie is inherently good, but has a childish sense of right and wrong. Unfortunately for the McGees, a ruthless division of the government, known as the Department of Special Intelligence, realizes the potential of Charlie's ability ('She could create nuclear explosions by the power of her will, and ultimately crack the planet in two!' exclaims one agent excitably) and decides to take Charlie into custody to study her and exploit her pyrokinesis for devastating military purposes. The relentless pursuit of Charlie and her father (her mother is mercilessly murdered along the way) takes place over the first half of the film: spies are everywhere, waiting at every turn. After their inevitable capture, both Andy and Charlie are forced to unleash their astounding telepathy to defend themselves, no matter what the consequences for human life.

*

All the actors for *Firestarter* were obliged to relocate to Dino DeLaurentiis's studio in North Carolina for three-and-a-half months for the duration of the shoot. The city of Wilmington and the picturesque setting of Lake Lure, also in North Carolina, provided the location shots.

For Drew and Jaid, this meant an equally exciting and nerve-wracking trip away from home – Drew's first of such proportions. 'I had to fit my whole life, literally everything in my room – clothes for every kind of weather, hair dryers, stuffed animals, books – into several suitcases,' she recalls.

Mother and daughter set up home in an old but adequate two-bedroom house in suburban Echo Park. Soon Drew would become close to her stand-in – eight-year-old lookalike Jennifer Ward, who lived with her family a few doors away. More often than not, Drew would be found sharing meals, sleepovers and general naughtiness with her new best friend.

But for now, the actress was obliged to adapt to a gruelling filming schedule. Quite unlike her comparatively small roles in *E.T.* and *Irreconcilable Differences*, her character was in nearly every scene, and much of the action took place at night. Drew learned to go to sleep very late, waking up later in the day for three hours of school in the afternoon.

Her ongoing education was obviously an important aspect that needed to be factored into the equation, and Carolyn Lennon, the teacher, provided some essential grounding under the watchful eye of welfare worker Almarie Clifford-Robinson. 'I was so tired that much of that time is a complete blur,' says Drew.

As Charlie, Drew was surrounded by first-rate actors, such as Martin Sheen as Captain Hollister, the government administrator who orders her capture, and the true villain of the piece: the late George C. Scott, who plays John Rainbird, the 'exterminator' who develops an unhealthy obsession with Charlie.

To the young girl, Scott at first appeared a frightening figure, 'a big man who looks kind of rough and gruff'. His raspy voice and one-eyed blindness effected for the movie must have been off-putting: 'He seemed like he could be mean,' was Drew's initial diagnosis.

However, Scott soon charmed Drew with their shared love of animals. His equally large dog, Max, helped break down the communication barrier, and soon Drew was cuddling the film's principal 'baddie' and cheerfully accepting adult direction from him.

'It was never like he was talking down to me, which made me feel good, like I had the respect of someone who was at the top of his craft,' she wrote in *Little Girl Lost*. 'Early on, he told me, "Drew, just forget about the camera and do your job." And I think that, along with Steven [Spielberg]'s advice, are the two best things I've ever been told.'

The other Stephen in Drew's life was also on hand to brighten her day. At 6 feet 4 inches, the heavyset Stephen King could also have proved a daunting colleague, but again this was far from the case.

'We hit it off,' says Drew. 'He's like a kid himself. You can see it in his eyes. When he gets an idea, his eyes light up, like this devilish boy full of mischief.'

A warm and friendly man with a particular affinity for children, King would spend hours in between takes with Drew, chatting amiably about everything from music, movies and TV to takeaway food. As with Scott, Drew appreciated the fatherly bear hugs and ruffles of hair, pining for what she lacked at home.

Other than the tight schedule enforced on the cast and crew of *Firestarter*, the biggest concern was the special effects necessary for a film in which fire is the main focal point. Mike Edmonson oversaw the effects themselves, also taking the credit as 'pyrotechnician'. While later reviews of the finished film's production design would range from dazzling praise ('undeniably startling') to near-mockery ('hilariously under-budgeted'), there is no question that the many explosions, hurtling fireballs and walls of flames are visually stunning.

For an eight-year-old, the behind-the-scenes realization of these effects was eye-opening and, quite frankly, scary. Incredibly, when Drew was first filmed with fire chips dancing around her, she was completely unprotected, and it was only on viewing the results afterwards that the crew decided it would be better to cover her with clear protective Plexiglass from then on. Occasionally Drew still suffered minor burns, like the time when she was instructed to stand still while flaming metal pieces were dropped around her from a helicopter hovering overhead. She became accustomed to seeing her life flash in front of her eyes as she stayed on her mark, valiantly hoping she wouldn't get hurt.

Drew and her stand-in, Jenny, were also simultaneously amazed and alarmed when they watched the first stuntman of many seem to spontaneously combust – no one thought to tell the impressionable youngsters that what was happening wasn't real.

'We didn't realize the stuntman was protected,' she grins. 'But then the fire was extinguished and he popped out smiling. "Is it hot out, or is it me?" he asked.'

*

As her friendship with Jenny deepened, Drew felt grateful to have found a peer who wouldn't criticize her or poke fun. The girls shared much in common, including a smart intelligence beyond their years.

As Jenny fast became the sister she never had, likewise Jenny's family temporarily filled a similar void in Drew's life. With the Wards she felt secure and comfortable. She envied her friend her younger brother, John, and her easy-going parents. Being naturally – and understandably – of a clingy disposition, before long Drew had perhaps become more attached to her new friends than was advisable.

'For me, just sitting at the dinner table, where the Wards said grace before eating, was a radical departure from the world I lived in back home,' says Drew. 'I was part of a family.'

Despite Drew and Jenny's unusual backgrounds in moviemaking, they were still little girls at heart. During a typical sleepover, they would loll about in their pyjamas and fantasize about the members of Duran Duran – 'with the rude and sole exception of Roger' – before slipping into the time-honoured childhood pursuit of telling each other ghost stories in the dark (undeniably heavily under the influence of one Stephen King).

Jenny and Drew were convinced that many of the houses in the road where the Ward family resided were haunted. Taking their gruesome fascination one step further, one night while staying over at Drew's house Jenny unnerved her with tales about her friend, Erika. Erika lived in a house on the same street where many people had died – apparently their spirits refused to leave. Later on, the girls were awoken suddenly by the startling noise of the bedroom blinds rolling up all by themselves.

'What just happened?' whispered Drew, by now sitting bolt upright and wide-eyed in fear.

Bang! The bedroom door slammed and the girls jumped out of their skins.

'Turn on the light!' gasped Jenny.

Drew leapt out of her bed and ran to the light switch. The place remained in darkness. It seemed that although the streetlights were on outside the house, inside there was a power cut.

Scared silly, the girls made the split-second decision to run over the road to the safety of Jenny's house (where Jaid was at this point is anyone's guess). As they unlocked the front door, though, it initially refused to budge. To all intents and purposes it seemed like someone – or something – was trying to keep them in the house.

Now screaming in terror, the girls ran back to Drew's bedroom and climbed out of the window, finally reaching the welcoming lights of the Ward residence.

When daylight came, the events of the night before were all too easily forgotten – that is, until Erika invited them both to stay overnight at her house.

The evening passed without event, but just before saying goodnight, Erika had the grace to reassure her guests, 'Don't worry if you hear footsteps in the middle of the night . . .'

Needless to say both Jenny and Drew woke up in the small hours when footsteps were heard. At least, they *sounded* like footsteps. Whatever the source of the phantom stomping, it was enough to inspire another moonlight flit, again back to the safe haven of Jenny's family home.

*

Infamously, Drew's experiences on the set of *Firestarter* were notable for more than it being her most challenging role to date. For it was during the wrap party at the end of the shoot that the child took her first drink.

The celebratory gathering was held at DeLaurentiis's beach house. When Drew and Jaid arrived, the place was already swarming with merry revellers saying their fond farewells. By now, sociable Drew knew most of the people involved in the film, be they actors or technicians. Slipping away from her mother, she sidled up to two members of the crew who were nibbling hors d'oeuvres and swigging champagne.

'Hey, I bet I can down two of those glasses,' said the eight-year-old.

'Sure you can, Drewster,' one of them replied, to the other's laughter.

A glass was filled and passed to Drew.

She had never so much as tasted anything alcoholic before, but she had attended enough parties to know that drinking was considered normal behaviour and that the more people drank, the more fun they seemed to have.

Drew studied the glass carefully, swirled it around, noticing how the bubbles burst at the surface. How refreshing it seemed – and besides, it wasn't that much liquid after all. It couldn't do any harm. Lifting the champagne to her lips, Drew daringly gulped it down as the crew members cheered her on.

But it didn't end there. Someone had the brainless impulse to refill her glass, and although the girl was already feeling a little woozy, she polished that one off too . . . before passing out.

When she came to, Drew was confronted by her concerned mother. What on earth had happened? When Drew explained that she had been drinking champagne at the party, Jaid dismissed it as 'one of those things'. After all, wrap parties didn't happen every day, and next time she would be more vigilant. She requested that Drew 'stay away' from alcohol in the future, and thought no more of it when her daughter readily agreed.

*

After the best part of four months in Echo Park, the inevitable happened: Drew had to return home with Jaid. She was upset that she would have to leave behind the many friends she'd made and felt torn and depressed.

After the success of *E.T.*, her Golden Globe nomination for *Irreconcilable Differences* and the probability that this film would also be a hit, it was likely that there would be other films – and therefore other friends – to be made in the near future. Still, tears were shed. It was the Ward family she'd miss the most.

'Saying goodbye was one of the most difficult and emotional things I'd ever done in my life,' she recalls. 'I broke down and cried and pleaded with my mom to stay.'

While Drew's future friendship with Jenny seemed uncertain, Stephen King's fondness for his young charge was undiminished, and shortly before *Firestarter* premiered she was invited to stay at his house in Bangor, Maine, for a fortnight. Another ready-made, transient family was created, with Stephen and his wife, Tabitha, and their three children: Naomi, Joe and Owen.

Drew spent her time happily snacking on King's homemade French toast and revisiting her love of ghost stories at bedtime, sitting in the author's office – a converted attic with its own clear potential for eeriness.

'Stephen doesn't just say a monster jumped out,' says Drew affectionately in *Little Girl Lost*, 'he describes a monster in the goriest details, with eyeballs dripping blood, bashed-in noses, hatchets for fingernails and always a fondness for defenceless little girls dressed in their nightgowns . . .' When Drew's teeth began to chatter in fear, the author would pack her off to bed, where she would lie, toes curled in anticipation of a fictional fiendish ambush.

Although Drew wasn't aware of it, in actual fact King was a closet alcoholic continually battling with his own, very real demons. By the following year, he would have added drug addiction to the list, but, as he says in his autobiography, *On Writing*, he 'continued to function, as a good many substance abusers do, on a marginally competent level'.

The reviews for 1984's *Firestarter* were generally positive and Drew's performance was rightly picked out as the high point of this ominous, thought-provoking movie. These days, *Firestarter* is regarded as something of a cult piece, and, while it is inescapably dated and rather too long, there is an uneasy sense of the inevitable throughout. This is helped by Tangerine Dream's understated electronic soundtrack, which gives the film a doom-laden *Terminator* (also from 1984) feel. Opposite the genuinely menacing George C. Scott, David Keith as Charlie's father is particularly intense, with an authentic hunted look.

As with *The Terminator*, the obvious premise is 'Us versus Them'. However, the secondary theme here is a girl and her father's utter devotion to one another. Keith and Barrymore's relationship seems effortless and thoroughly believable on screen, and it begs the question, with her practically fatherless background, how did this make Drew feel? Also, in the film her mother is killed by the agents, so her father is effectively a single parent – which mirrored in reverse the real-life Barrymore family situation. Drew would have been called on to simultaneously examine and ignore her own experiences, and with this in mind it has to be said that her performance is extraordinary.

'Drew is such a natural actress,' praised director Mark L. Lester at the time. 'She has instincts that are incredible.'

'She carries the whole film on her tiny shoulders,' agreed one critic. 'What's so remarkable about the young actress is the wide range of emotions she conveys with enormous conviction, some of which pull at the heart strings.' Cute, pretty and lisping, Drew has a couple of brief hammy moments but is otherwise at her best acting out the extremes of fear, anger and joy.

Unfortunately, there are umpteen holes in *Firestarter*'s plot. Why can Rainbird get close enough to shoot both Charlie and her father before either of them senses him with their telepathy? And why is he accompanied by men wearing protective flame-retardant suits while he's clad only in a leather jacket? Why doesn't Charlie sense 'John the friendly orderly' (Rainbird) is evil? Why don't the agents film their captives in every room? The list goes on and the ending is equally all too convenient, but overall this tale of a child's trust abused is engaging, entertaining and occasionally frightening; perfect for teenagers and Stephen King fans alike. The domestic gross of over $15 million was respectable, and Drew's performance was even tagged as Oscar-worthy.

The future looked extremely bright.

6

THE PERFECT ANTIDOTE

'Steven Spielberg once told me that my daughter is an old soul, and I have to agree with him. One minute Drew's a playful nine-year-old talking to her dolls and stuffed animals, and the next she's twenty-nine or an old woman of seventy-five.'

JAID BARRYMORE

As Drew slowly adjusted to life back in Los Angeles, an inescapable buzz surrounded her which she did her utmost to ignore.

'She will be bigger than Tatum O'Neal and better than Meryl Streep!' were the bold words of a major studio boss, hoping to sign the eight-year-old into a three-picture, $5 million deal.

Drew's response was twofold. Her well-developed business acumen came first. 'Let me tell you that I will always act in movies and be the best actress that I can,' she graciously reassured her public during one of several press conferences. 'But, when I grow up I'm going to get two degrees. One each in producing and directing . . . and I also want to be known as a dancer.'

In such potentially intimidating situations, the youngster always appeared well briefed and able to filter out the more influential journalists from the hacks. Always she was professional and polite, outwardly seeming far wiser than her tender years. 'Drew and I have talked about priorities,' Jaid testified, 'and to her, being professional is the most important thing.'

It sounded as though mother and daughter had rehearsed a list of stock answers about Drew's future plans, including a desired remake of Victor Fleming's sea adventure *Captains Courageous*, with Drew in the little boy's role of Harvey Cheyne (previously played by Freddie Bartholomew). There was also talk of a part in a dramatic adaptation of one of Drew's favourite fairy tales, *Alice In Wonderland*, scheduled to take place in England later in the autumn, and a musical proposed by the award-winning Broadway dancer and choreographer Tommy Tune. While the latter failed to materialize, the former turned out to be the darkly controversial Dennis Potter story of the true nature of the relationship between Lewis Carroll and Alice Liddell, the child who inspired the author's whimsical novels. Amelia Shankley played the young Alice in flashback sequences, while the unpalatability of the story was offset by Jim *The Muppets* Henson's recreations of Carroll's characters – sadly, Drew failed to get involved in this acclaimed project.

Drew also revealed she was writing a screenplay called *Kim*. 'It's a serious comedy about a little girl and her mother,' she said, but as with *Irreconcilable Differences*, sensibly refused to elaborate further: 'I can't tell you what it's about – that's a secret – but I'm going to play the mother.'

Drew's second and more natural response to all the attention was pure bewilderment. 'Stardom has always been a role which I've never really accepted,' she said during a quieter moment. 'It's never seemed real, like anything I could identify with.'

If Drew thought stardom seemed unreal, she had only reached the tip of the iceberg.

*

Having previously been exposed to the occasional Hollywood party, the invitations now flowed in constantly, and Jaid and Drew began to attend glitzy events on a regular basis. Presently it was only a couple of times a month, as a special treat.

Jaid's justification for keeping her daughter out so late was that the summons were mainly to attend necessary business-related events, such as the Golden Globes or the People's Choice Awards. No one even raised an eyebrow when Drew was spotted at such occasions, yet when it came to a private party in a nightclub, murmurs were heard. 'I was expected to explicitly draw the line between business and social,' Jaid says.

Inevitably, though, the fine line between the two became blurred and the mother-and-daughter team enjoyed a vast array of gatherings, usually mixing with the same crowd. It seems that Jaid never stopped to consider employing the services of a babysitter for the social events.

'The party-time environment was intoxicating,' Drew later admitted. 'I loved it for the same reason I hated school. I belonged.' Because Drew was a celebrity in her own right, she was accepted and adored without question. She has since likened the exhilarating feeling of being at the centre of such attention to a 'big security blanket'.

A good example of a typical evening out for the actress and her mother would be dancing all night at a disco like Studio 54 (for which Drew was soon given her own entry card), or dining till the early hours at a cutting-edge restaurant like Ma Maison. At the former, Joan Rivers clearly remembers leaning over a balcony and seeing Drew on her mother's shoulders, frantically waving up at her – the point being it was way past midnight and Drew was only eight. At the latter, and along the same lines, the little girl was famously photographed nodding off at a table, while the mêlée whirled around her in a haze of cigarette smoke – and worse.

There were just 'so many parties', a dozy Drew groaned in one interview. 'Sometimes I'm so tired that I wish I could be alone so I could sleep. I *love* to sleep . . .'

Of course, one might question why Jaid would take a child into the grown-ups' playground of drinking, drugs and sex. Jaid's defence, warped though it is, has always been that because her own mother had abandoned her, 'I wanted Drew with me twenty-four hours a day, seven days a week. I loved her so completely that I took her with me everywhere.' And so her underage daughter became used to nights so late they were more like mornings, X-rated adult conversation, and, of course, alcohol by the champagne bucketload.

'In a way, it was all quite innocent,' says Drew. 'I was always by far the youngest person wherever I went, and I'd float around, talking to people or keeping to myself.'

However, on occasion Drew's childish naïvety afforded her fellow partygoers much amusement and her mother much mortification. In *Little Girl Lost*, Drew memorably relates a story in which she watched an unspecified horror movie on cable TV, featuring an explicit sex scene. To Drew, who knew no different, the hugging, kissing and rolling around in bed looked like a great deal of fun. The following day, her Barbie and Ken dolls were having a whale of a time, but the situation reached its climax (pardon the pun) during an unorganized get-together.

As the night was still young, the adults stood around mulling over where they should go and what they should do later on. Little Drew piped up with her suggestion for the evening's entertainment.

'Why don't we have sex?' she proposed.

As jaws hit the floor within a 10-metre radius, Drew was confused by the reaction.

'Isn't it like a joyride?' she continued, using an expression she'd heard in the movie. To Drew, sex sounded exciting, like going on a ride at a fair. But poor Jaid didn't know where to look. Perhaps it was time to start monitoring her daughter's preferred TV viewing.

Drew's innocence at this time notwithstanding, even the child herself realized her outrageously developed social life was extreme.

'By the time I was eight-and-a-half, I felt like I was some abnormal, crazy girl,' she admits. 'I could walk up to the door of any nightclub and they'd say, "Hi, you're that little girl, come in . . ."'

*

In September 1983, Drew wasn't best pleased to be enrolled for the third grade at the Country School. A private establishment situated in the Valley, Country may have been chosen because the staff were happy to 'look the other way' when it came to enforced absences for filming.

It was her third school in as many years – and of course Drew had also received individual tutoring on each film set she had attended. To Drew, the concept of education must have seemed like an endless blur of faceless teachers with whom she could not form any particular bond. But, even worse, she was now the new girl all over again. Drew faced hostile stares, whispering behind her back and petty jealousy, all from a strange group of kids who had known each other for years.

'Around this time I quit hanging out with people my own age,' she recalls. 'I didn't think I could relate to them or that they could understand the kind of life I had.' This, of course, is something of an understatement.

'Third grade was a lesson in futility,' she continues. 'Compared to what I knew existed out in the world, school was just plain boring.'

An intelligent child, Drew could have worked hard and achieved top grades. After trying – and failing – to integrate herself among her classmates, Drew just didn't see the point. Although she didn't consider herself above it all, she was restless and unable to muster enough interest to study seriously, and averaged a C grade for all her subjects. In her own words, she found herself stuck in a 'rut', and she couldn't be bothered to pull herself out of it.

As Drew admits, the teachers consequently 'came down hard' on her. 'I loved learning, but I was never very good with authority or being patronised, because I pretty much had to raise myself.' Having been forced into a reasonable facsimile of adulthood by both her mother and the grown-ups with whom she worked regularly on film sets, it is hardly surprising that she experienced clashes of personality with her would-be mentors.

Perhaps with her mother's precedent in mind of analysing the Bard at just seven years of age, the only subject Drew was prepared to turn her attention to fully was English. It could be that the plays, prose and poetry reminded her of her favourite film scripts and became an empty canvas for her fertile imagination. But Drew's tastes in literature were to get her into trouble with her teachers.

'I would turn in a book report on, say, Henry Miller, and they would give me an F because they didn't consider him a "proper" writer,' she recalls. 'But he wrote literature, and they shouldn't have been closed off to certain authors because of what they wrote.'

In truth, Drew's English teacher must have been completely fazed by the student's fascination with this now legendary beat writer, who had died just three years before, not so far away in his Pacific Palisades home. Miller's classic 'stream of consciousness' style and complex – and frequently X-rated – existentialist musings were a million miles away from the authors preferred by Drew's peers, such as Mark Twain, Robert Louis Stevenson and Joel Chandler Harris. For poetry, Drew studied the Los Angeles poet Charles Bukowski, and her favoured musician was Jim Morrison of the Doors – two personalities intrinsically linked with adult vice. All Drew's classmates were still glued to *Sesame Street*.

'I had a different childhood from anyone I knew,' underestimates Drew today. 'I thought that it was normal . . . Mom didn't have many friends and neither did I.' Drew's listing as one of twelve 'Promising New Actors Of 1984', in Volume 36 of John Willis's *Screen World*, probably did nothing to relieve her position as class outcast.

*

After Drew's ninth birthday in February 1984, she began to become a little more aware of her appearance. She had always wrestled with the concept of image versus reality and now it became a problem.

'The public saw me as "Drew Barrymore: Movie Star", while I viewed myself quite differently – as a sad, lonely and unattractive girl with not much to her advantage,' she says.

Although Drew was in fact undeniably pretty, she was also quite plump. Two years previously she had announced in an interview that she was 'practising my exercises so I won't be so chubby'. Unfortunately, in recent months she had been gaining more weight. But that wasn't the worst physical problem she had to deal with – at least, not yet. Having worn a retainer since the age of seven, now Drew's teeth were fitted with unsightly metal braces, and it would be five long years before they would be removed for good.

Not that this latest acquisition prevented Drew from launching her latest conquest. No doubt influenced by all the Hollywood parties, the little girl longed to become part of that fairy-tale world for real. Her nightlife was full of adults kissing and cuddling and the insinuation of sex – so Drew became obsessed with boys.

And it seems that boys also became obsessed with her. Rarely those in her class – oh no, they were far too mundane (and always poking fun at her anyway). No; Drew was a celebrity in her own right – and the famous notoriously attract hangers-on, no matter what their age.

At first, Drew didn't aim too high.

'Let me describe my very first kiss,' she says, quickly forgetting poor Alex. 'I was nine and this little boy took me out to a movie. When we got back to my house, he fumbled to kiss me at the door.'

In most cases, the inexpert embrace would have ended there and the young lovebirds would have said goodbye. But, most humiliatingly for the boy in question, in an attempt to garner popularity, Drew had arranged for some girls clutching handmade scorecards to hide out in the bushes nearby and judge the boy's 'performance'.

'So when he planted the big kiss, the girls held up pieces of cardboard with numbers on them. You know, 9.9, 9.5, 9.7 . . . To me, he was a total ten!'

Equally memorably, during a visit to Disneyland, she ventured into a haunted house with a boy whose name now escapes her and began to make out. Imagine her embarrassment, not to mention pain, as the boy – who was also wearing braces – clumsily lunged towards her lips and their teeth locked together as the two sets of braces became momentarily entangled!

Drew has also admitted to snogging Jordan Knight (who in 1984 had just joined the fledgling pop band New Kids On The Block) in *his* braces, to the romantic strains of a Whitney Houston song. Whether or not young Jordan was the true identity of the haunted-house kisser has never been confirmed.

Although she was still so young, Drew also claims that she 'dated' Stephen Dorff (the son of composer Steve Dorff) while she was in third grade. In a couple of years' time, teenage Stephen would become fairly well known as an actor himself, appearing in TV shows like *Roseanne* and *Married With Children* and later progressing to movies.

Sadly, despite her fame, Drew wasn't always as successful with boys.

'I practised this dance routine to Madonna's "Burning Up" to sing to this guy Peter Shane,' she remembers. 'But I was too nervous to dance so I said, "You quench my desire" [a lyric from the song]. Needless to say he didn't give me the time of day . . .'

*

Drew's pursuit of the opposite sex coincided with a reignited interest in alcohol. The fainting episode at the *Firestarter* wrap party a distant memory, in March 1984 Drew attended the actor Rob Lowe's twentieth birthday party, held in an L.A. nightclub.* She had found a soul mate in Jaid's best friend's daughter – to whom she gives the pseudonym Gigi in *Little Girl Lost*† – and that night Gigi came along for the ride.

'I knew I was going to take a drink that night,' Drew recalls. And what a setting to indulge in: many of the members of the legendary Brat Pack were there: Lowe, his younger brother Chad and stepbrother Micah, Emilio Estevez, Demi Moore and Melissa Gilbert, among others. Even though many guests were underage, almost everyone had some kind of drink.

In spite of her tender years, in these surroundings Drew was considered part of the 'in' crowd, and she loved showing off to Gigi with all the celebrities she knew, even introducing her to Lowe and giving him a little birthday kiss. After a few turns on the dance floor, Drew had the bright idea of surreptitiously lifting one of the cold bottles of beer left on the bar.

Succeeding in their mission, the two little girls then ran to the bathroom, where they proceeded to down the bottle between them. Feeling giddy with excitement and the alcohol, they returned to the bar and repeated the act, and were delighted with how suddenly everything seemed rosier and everyone seemed friendlier.

'I began to flirt, innocently, with Emilio Estevez, whom I had a crush on. It was like batting eyes at your big brother.' Lucky Drew was carried to the dance floor by Estevez, who hoisted her up to his waist and gave the nine-year-old actress her first-ever slow dance.

As she glanced around the swaying club, she mimicked the other girls with their boyfriends. 'I nuzzled in close to Emilio, wrapping my little legs around his waist.' It was the perfect antidote to being teased at school. 'My heart was thumping.'

After a few more dances (and a few more swiped beers), Drew fell in with Lowe's twelve-year-old stepbrother, Micah, and soon they started making out, again in imitation of the older partygoers. Bold Micah caused a commotion at the end of the evening when Jaid announced it was time to leave. In front of Drew's mother, he 'grabbed my arm, pulled me back, took me in his arms and we started to kiss,

---

*Drew's first run-in with Rob Lowe occurred when she was seven. 'Rob Lowe heard I had a crush on him. I got the chicken pox, and he called and invited me to his birthday party – I can't tell you how much it meant.'

†When Drew recounted her life in *Little Girl Lost*, she changed some names to protect those near and dear to her.

like passionate thirty-year-olds'. Dumbstruck, Jaid started to chastise her daughter, but having had a few drinks herself, it didn't seem that big a deal, so she let it go.

And so Drew came to believe that being intoxicated by liquor and pursued by the opposite sex was the best way she could relax and escape her life's many downsides.

*

While Drew had been in North Carolina shooting *Firestarter* back in 1983, her buddy Stephen King had been so impressed with her performance, professionalism and onscreen presence that he wrote an episode in his next film especially for her.

'One day Stephen asked me if I wanted to be in his next movie, and I said, "Sure," thinking that I'd hear about that in a few years,' she recalls in *Little Girl Lost*. 'But the next day Stephen handed me a portion of a script to read. He'd written it overnight. "It's great," I told him a few days later after reading it. "But can't I have a couple of days off now?"'

King's next big-screen venture was *Cat's Eye*, a trilogy of horror fantasies with dark twists, loosely linked by a mysterious wandering tabby cat. The first two parts, *Quitters, Inc.* and *The Ledge*, were adapted from short stories from the author's best-selling collection *Night Shift*. The third part, *The General*, was Drew's finale and her chance to shine. However, a bit like the cat, Drew had small interlinking parts dotted throughout the first two tales, which allowed her to don an array of none-too-flattering disguises.

Quitters, Inc. is a black comedy, starring James Woods as a habitual chain-smoker, which explores the unorthodox methods used by a company professing to stop their clients from smoking. It provides some wry observations on the widespread and highly fashionable American 'self-help' movement of the early 1980s. The late Kenneth McMillan then stars in *The Ledge* as a cold-blooded gambler who forces his wife's lover (Robert Hays) to take a life-or-death walk on a ledge situated fifty storeys up a high-rise building. Both stories investigate human vice (smoking and gambling) taken to extremes and beyond.

Although Drew appeared briefly as a shop-window mannequin in between tales and as the daughter of James Woods in *Quitters, Inc.* (credited only as 'Our Girl'), her main role was as ten-year-old Amanda in *The General*. Here, against her mother's wishes, she adopts the stray cat, naming him 'General', and in return receives protection from a tiny-but-deadly troll who is trying to steal her breath as she sleeps.

*

For Drew, *Cat's Eye* was a joyful reunion: with Stephen King, with producer Dino DeLaurentiis, and with much of the old crew from *Firestarter*. Although the director, Lewis Teague, was new, filming once again took place at DeLaurentiis's North Carolina Film Corporation studios and on location in Wilmington. Drew and Jaid returned for the length of the summer holidays and rented another house – this time just one door away from their beloved Ward family. For a second time, Jenny Ward was used as Drew's double during filming. 'Seeing Jenny made me so incredibly happy,' says Drew. 'I thought my life was complete.'

However, at first the new Drew took a bit of getting used to for her best friend. Although it had been less than a year since they were last together, so much had happened to the actress. She had been exposed to so many new things that initially the two girls found they no longer had much in common; Drew even spoke differently, using slang she'd picked up in Los Angeles. But before long their differences melted away and it was just like old times. As before, Drew became a permanent fixture at the Ward household, and the pyjama parties recommenced in earnest.

For six days each week both girls were obliged to be on set, whether filming or not. Typically, the day would start at the studio dressing rooms at 7.30 a.m. Drew would be accompanied by her mother and her tutor, Almarie Clifford-Robinson. Half an hour later, Drew would be on set, rehearsing her scene for the day. Eleven thirty would signify lunchtime – and some valuable playtime with Jenny away from the adults.

Back on set by 1 p.m. at the latest, the cameras would start rolling and much of the afternoon would be spent filming. James Woods was a favourite on-set companion, as was Candy Clark (Drew's mother in *The General*).

The only day Drew and Jenny would have off would be Sunday, which of course unofficially began late every Saturday afternoon. Drew would arrive with her overnight gear in tow, Gayle Ward would provide iced tea, fried chicken and mashed potatoes, and the girls would play in the garden with Jenny's cats or go bike-riding. At night Drew would teach Jenny the latest dance moves from MTV, to a soundtrack of Jenny's 45 rpm records. 'Borderline' by Madonna was a particular favourite: 'Our giggling probably kept the neighbours up all night.'

One noteable amusement for the girls, which was nearly as entertaining for their adult audience, was a much-rehearsed rendition of *Mommie Dearest*. Shortly before bedtime, all grown-ups present would be summoned upstairs for the recital, in which Jenny played Christina Crawford. Drew played one of her best-loved characters, the hateful mother, Joan, so memorably portrayed by Faye Dunaway in the film. As in the highly strung, highly camp biopic, there was much shouting of orders, slamming of doors and, of course, 'beating' of poor Jenny with wire coat hangers, which invariably ended up with the girls on the floor in a heap of flailing limbs, tangled hair and giggles.

*

One key scene in *The General* is when Amanda discovers her pet parakeet, Polly, lying dead in its cage. The mini-murder is the bloody work of the evil troll, but General receives all the blame from Amanda's raging mother. In turn, the little girl, who knows General is innocent, throws a tantrum at her mother, blaming her for the gory pile of feathers.

Filming this scene required Drew to scream, shout and, above all, cry realistically. In between takes, she would retreat to a dark corner and refuse to talk to anyone until the cameras began rolling once more: 'She feels it breaks her mood,' explained Almarie Clifford-Robinson. At the time, Drew wouldn't tell her tutor about how she summoned the tears, but eventually she confided in Candy Clark, the other key player in this part of the film.

'I'd never told anyone my method before,' says Drew. 'It seemed mysterious to others, I suppose. But there wasn't any secret.' Every time the actress needed to cry, she forced herself to think about Gertie, the little kitten given to her by Steven Spielberg after *E.T.* had wrapped, who had one day made a brave bid for freedom and sadly never returned. 'He was the only one in the world I could really talk to,' she explained to her onscreen mom. Drew was so distraught at the memory of losing the kitten that the tears never failed to materialize.

Predictably, something that also reduced Drew to tears was when *Cat's Eye* wrapped at the end of the summer. Again, she couldn't bear to leave behind all her friends, especially Jenny, and return to the horrors of school. But she had no choice: it was the actor's life she had chosen.

'I loved the life I had [in Wilmington], but I knew it wasn't mine,' she says. As Jaid and Drew sped away to the airport, Drew came to the realization that her idealized existence within the warm embrace of the Ward family was really no different to any of the film parts she took on.

'They were a fantasy brought to life. A dream . . . I knew that the next day I'd wake up and it would all be over.'

*

Unfortunately, *Cat's Eye* has not stood the test of time as well as *Firestarter*. With its *Tales Of The Unexpected* atmosphere, the lacklustre production, direction and special effects seem rather mediocre and dated, and as a whole it's all a bit lame. Hardcore fans of Stephen King would probably have been quite disappointed, and indeed King himself was said to be unhappy, deeming the linking of the three stories with the tabby cat (reportedly exacerbated during post-production) gauche and off-putting. Also, as a horror movie, *Cat's Eye* doesn't really earn its 15 rating, although it's possible the occasional use of bloodshed could give younger teenagers – who back then were probably a lot less hardened than today's teens – nightmares.

That said, there are several scenes of violence involving animals: a cat being electrocuted and later dicing with death on a busy freeway, a pigeon being kicked to death, and both the cat and the parakeet being stabbed by the troll. Worryingly, there is no notice in the credits stating 'no animals were harmed in the making of this movie'. Some of the gore is avoided by using implication alone, but watching the cat jumping up and down among sparks on a supposedly electrically charged floor and twice dodging traffic makes for uneasy viewing.

Still, *Cat's Eye* has its good points: the humour is dark, the scenarios clever and Drew's segment is silly but entertaining. Stephen King readers get to play spot the reference throughout, and there are solid, watchable performances, notably from James Woods, Kenneth McMillan and Drew herself.

The nine-year-old actress actually receives top billing (having previously received only second billing for her far greater role in *Firestarter*). This is technically quite justified as she helps link all three stories together, but it is specified that this is 'in order of appearance', perhaps to avoid offending the more experienced actors on parade throughout the trilogy. As Amanda, Drew is engaging and plucky, and convincingly cast – later in 1986 she would receive a nomination for the Young Artist Award for Best Starring Performance By A Young Actress In A Motion Picture.

Cat's Eye grossed $9 million. Commercially and artistically it wasn't a patch on *Firestarter*, and for the first time there were whispers in Hollywood that Drew Barrymore's star was waning.

7

SHOWBIZ MOTHER FROM HELL?

Although half of Drew's *per diem* for *Cat's Eye* went into her college fund, she was no more interested in going back to Country, to start fourth grade, than she had been the year before. September 1984 saw the actress begrudgingly return to a classroom not rigged up in a film-set trailer. It didn't help that she had fallen slightly behind her fellow classmates, despite having been tutored throughout the summer shoot.

Maybe Drew was resentful at having to buckle down to 'normal life' again, or maybe she was paranoid, but her overriding memory of this period is that her teachers were much less understanding about her absences than they had been the year before. Drew says she was criticized for placing her career above her education and believes they were jealous of her success.

'Grade school for me was torture,' she remembers. 'I mean, I could not win these people over to save my life.'

One example the actress gives of the teachers' unkind treatment of her is when one of them called her 'stupid' in front of the whole class. Apparently Drew had failed her in-class assignment.

'I wanted to crawl inside myself and die,' she recalls. Drawing on her acting ability, Drew managed not to show her true feelings. 'I sat there, stone-faced, crying on the inside and completely humiliated. Why that teacher seemed bent on destroying me is beyond my comprehension.'

Sadly, there was also no escaping the fact that Drew was now suffering from a weight problem. She wasn't *that* big, but then everything seems magnified at nine or ten years of age.

'I was heavy because I ate avocados all day, not realizing they were fattening,' she explains. Drew's favourite calorie-laden fruit still grew on a tree in her backyard, and she thought nothing of eating five a day. 'I sat outside with a spoon and a salt-shaker, and I was in purgatory when the avocados weren't ripe,' she continues. And the avocados were only the beginning.

'Being famous as a kid meant my eating habits were crazy. I could have anything, basically, so I ate junk and more junk, any time, any place. Nobody told me not to, so I got bad skin, bad hair and I became fat.

'It's amazing how a few extra pounds all of a sudden makes you an entirely different person. It's so wrong, because it's not who you are.' Unfortunately for Drew, an ailing self-image wasn't the only thing she had to deal with as the taunting began.

'There was this nasty group of guys who were constantly on my case,' she revealed in *Little Girl Lost*. 'They delighted in belittling me. Their torment was endless.' Drew would be called unkind names such as 'Fat Ass', 'Fatso', 'Porky Pig', 'Cosmic Cow' and 'Drew the Poo'. The gang would throw books at her and make her cry on a daily basis, but naïve Drew was determined that she had suffered enough rejection in her life and, despite herself, did her best to make them like her. It didn't work.

She tried to wear the same kinds of clothes as they did, in a fruitless effort to fit in. This simultaneously opened the door to a love of bizarre combinations which unfortunately only made her persecutors laugh harder. 'I would wear a polka-dot shirt with striped pants, because that's how I was feeling. There are pictures of me with horribly uncoordinated, clashing clothes on – I didn't care because I was showing the world who I was.'

Most of the time Drew accepted the bullying in the same way that she had put up with her father's neglect and cruelty, but one day Jaid stepped in and became Drew's ultimate hero.

'One time, in school, this bully took a flying leap onto my back and knocked me onto my blacktop,' remembers Drew. 'My chin came off my face. I went to the emergency room, got a thousand stitches, and my mother brought me back to school with this huge bandage on my face. She found the bully and said, "I will *kill* you if you lay a hand on my daughter again." What kid doesn't want her parent to say that?'

Often when a parent – particularly a mother – intervenes between school bullies and their victims, the victim loses even more credibility, and Jaid's well-meaning interference could have unintentionally made matters much worse. Whether or not this was the case for Drew, her lasting impression of this miserable period of her life was sheer desperation.

'I was very lonely. I lived on my own and mostly stayed home. I was just a really unhappy girl.'

*

Thoroughly depressed at school, Drew sought new ways to rebel. One time, when Gigi and her mother arrived at the Barrymores' for the evening, both Drew and her friend were inexplicably bursting with excitement. They each had a secret and in a flash they ran giggling into Drew's bedroom.

Independently of each other, they had both managed to smuggle some cigarettes. Their amalgamated stash was equivalent to a whole packet's worth. The pair promptly locked themselves in the bathroom and smoked every contraband stick.

Unusually for such an avid clubber, Jaid detested the smell of cigarettes and refused to have them in the house. So when she called to say it was time for Gigi to go home, the friends, feeling somewhat sick from the excess nicotine, panicked. Diving for the sink, they repeatedly brushed their teeth and scrubbed their hands and faces until they were sore.

Then, with their most critical heads on, they smelled each other's breath.

'The breath check,' says Drew. 'It was my first and certainly not my last.'

Amazingly, neither Jaid nor Gigi's mother noticed the stale odour that must have clung to the girls' clothes; they suspected nothing.

'I realized that I'd gotten away with lying to my mom,' says Drew. 'That was an eye-opener – as well as an invitation to try the same thing again.'

After her inauguration session, the nine-year-old continued to smoke illicitly at home, but she wasn't always as lucky. The first couple of times Jaid discovered cigarette butts, Drew escaped with just a lecture. The third time, she was actually caught red-handed. As punishment, Jaid decided to ground her daughter . . . but then a party invitation arrived that appealed to both of them. So Drew was allowed to go, and the grounding was completely forgotten. 'It was becoming clear that rules didn't apply to me,' says Drew.

Drew smoked regularly from then on, thrilled to have another tool under her belt to make her appear older. As cigarettes are also a well-known appetite suppressant, it is likely that Drew found her new habit helped her to gain some control over her weight.

Although Jaid did her best to enforce house rules, like daily chores, homework, Drew keeping her bedroom tidy, and a set bedtime (9 p.m. during weekdays and non-party nights), any sense of strictness and order was now going straight over Drew's head. The only thing she took seriously was her nightlife, and it was too much for the single mother to keep an eye on her all of the time.

'I had tried to be all things to Drew – mother, manager, drill sergeant, friend,' Jaid insists. 'I was almost disproportionately there because I was there so much for her.'

The already unnatural mother–daughter relationship soared to new levels, and by now there was no turning back.

*

Drew increasingly sought out the otherworldly rush she got from being allowed into Hollywood's trendiest parties and, as Jaid too revelled in the party-hearty lifestyle (for her own, different reasons), the twice-a-month outings rapidly increased to once, twice or sometimes even five nights a week.

Drew felt she fitted into this adult life far better than she did at school: at the parties she was famous and cool, and everybody wanted to be her friend. There was no chance of fading into the background as Hollywood's youngest nightclub attendee.

It wasn't just the attention she craved; it was the whole event, from start to finish. Just like her mother, the girl would spend hours getting ready and choosing her outfit. Drew's preferred party dresses were often of the fairy-tale-princess-meets-adult-sex-siren variety: either pink and fluffy with sequins, fur or frills; or as grown-up as she could find with swathes of glistening satin sitting somewhat uncomfortably on her young shoulders. Her hair was styled immaculately and she would sneak as much of her mother's make-up as possible. It was like getting into costume for a role or going to a movie premiere every time. Of course, when she arrived there would be the shouts of the journalists, the blinding flashbulbs of the waiting photographers and the exciting boom of loud music as the Barrymores made their way into the club.

The best bit for Drew was the recognition. It was so unusual to find a child at such events that she was spoiled rotten. 'People treated me like a little toy, always telling me how cute I was, patting me on the head or giving me a playful squeeze,' she says.

Gradually Drew's need for attention grew so great that she would nag Jaid to take her out even when her mother felt like a rare night in. With her childish reasoning, she didn't understand why she was being treated like an adult on film sets and in nightclubs, yet wasn't allowed to just go out when she pleased. She had already come up against authority with her schoolteachers and didn't like it one bit. Regular bickering sessions developed.

'I'd want to go out and party; my mom would want to stay home,' she recalls in her autobiography. 'I'd storm out anyway. It was a tug of war that marked the start of what became my constant struggle for more freedom.' Drew became desperate to grow up and not have to report to anyone else – she says that her role models were the exciting people she saw living it up at the clubs in their finery: drinking, smoking, dancing and staying up way past a nine-year-old's bedtime.

Alongside Studio 54 and the Hard Rock Café in West Hollywood, one of Jaid's favourite haunts for herself and her daughter was Helena's, the fashionable and exclusive club in Silverlake. Packed with celebrities ranging from Warren Beatty, Jack Nicholson and Anjelica Huston to Madonna and Sean Penn, it was owned by a former actress who was a very close friend of Jaid's, and who was evidently happy to turn a blind eye to the presence of a minor.

'Everyone at the club knew me,' says Drew. 'I knew them. It was kosher. To me, that club was like a second home.' Jaid's reasoning also followed the lines that her friend's club was 'safe', and so long as they were both there she could keep an eye on her daughter.

Gradually, though, a routine developed whereby Jaid and Drew would arrive at the party together, and then they would separate and socialize with their respective friends. If it seems unthinkable that a pre-teen would be present in this environment to begin with, her mother's laissez-faire attitude meant that she was literally free to come and go as she pleased, and expose herself to things she shouldn't.

The Hollywood director Joel Schumacher recalls seeing Drew at Helena's. Unlike most of the other partygoers, he was shocked and ill at ease with the child's presence. 'Her mother, Jaid, was there all the time and she brought Drew, who was the only child there,' he says. 'I was concerned about her being in a place like that at two or three in the morning . . . she saw some incidents.' Around this time, Drew was given the nickname of 'The Badger' by actor Gary Busey, because she was 'shorter, faster, closer to the ground and always darting around' the club.

*

Even though they were regulars at Helena's, Jaid was uneasy about her daughter mingling alone with strangers and wanted to provide her with a companion closer to her own age. Of course, underage clubbers were not exactly two a penny, but, as with Gigi and her mother, Jaid and Drew befriended a couple of single parents with teenage daughters in similar circumstances to their own.

A couple of the girls were aspiring actresses – although not in Drew's league – and all shared in common a hatred of school and authority, and a love of parties and naughtiness. When writing her autobiography, Drew disguised her friends' names to protect their identities, and the monikers she chose besides Gigi were 'Chelsea' and 'Amy'.

Still very much the baby of the group, Drew looked up to her new friends and began to copy their look. Her attire became distinctly less cutesy and increasingly sluttish. 'We dressed to kill – miniskirts, black lace, high heels, heavy make-up, perfume. The works.' When Jaid went to check on the girls' progress, she would coo over how adorable they looked; but on the contrary, the prepubescents virtually resembled hookers.

The trio, regulars at Helena's, egged each other on to sample the adult delights that were all too readily available. Always a great lover of dancing, Drew's actions headed in a different direction as she emulated the adults' provocative movements. 'We'd try especially hard to look sexy on the dance floor, mimicking whatever moves we saw the older women make.' Despite her age, and due to her ridiculous outfits, Drew often attracted the attention of older boys and she rapidly learned the art of flirting.

But that was relatively harmless compared to her next step.

'I was smoking constantly and doing everything I could to be bad,' admits Drew. 'It wasn't long before I began thinking, "Well, if I smoke cigarettes, I can drink."' So, in the same way that she had started smoking, Drew began drinking furtively with her friends when they stayed over at each other's houses.

At first, they just snuck the odd one or two glasses. Then, realizing that all her problems seemed to drift away after a few drinks, along with her inhibitions, Drew began to physically crave the forgiving haze of alcohol. She began hankering for the same relaxed state of mind while she was dancing at the clubs, and devised a plan to acquire beers based on her experiences at Rob Lowe's party.

Chelsea and Drew were regular smoking companions at Helena's, climbing upstairs to a loft that was sectioned off from the public. They thought of it as their private balcony and delighted in leaning over and spying on the revellers below. There, the girls would pull out their secret stash of cigarettes (begged, borrowed or stolen) and light up. As the balcony overlooked the bar, Drew realized they could keep a lookout for unattended or unwanted drinks.

'When we spied one or two, we'd make a beeline down the stairs, swipe the glasses and quickly bring them back up,' she says. Drew began to view alcohol as the ultimate accessory – after all, it helped make her appear older than her nine years.

Before long, the terrible twosome were regularly passing out in their clandestine balcony hideaway. Having drunk themselves into a stupor, the girls would actually black out for a couple of hours, waking up with monumental headaches – a cruel combination of the alcohol and lying next to the speakers.

But that didn't stop them. In fact, getting away with such excesses only encouraged the pair; a night without ending up inebriated seemed like a night wasted.

'As soon as people forgot I was the girl in *E.T.*, they got to know me as Hollywood's youngest alcoholic,' says Drew. 'I didn't drink to have fun. I drank to get drunk.'

*

Drew's schooldays were brightened up considerably when she realized she 'had feelings' for her classmate Brecken Meyer. At one year her senior, he was just the type she was beginning to identify as hers: older, floppy brown hair and cute.

They had known each other since the third grade and were already quite good friends, but then Gigi noticed Drew's lingering glances in his direction – and that Brecken was repaying the compliment.

One night, Brecken phoned on the pretext that there was a girl called Tracy who was pestering him to 'go steady'. He didn't like her and wondered if Drew could think of any way to divert her unwanted attentions? Quick as a flash, Drew offered to step in and pretend to be his girlfriend.

At first the arrangement was only supposed to be a make-believe relationship, but then Gigi and her scheming came along. One day after school at Gigi's house, Drew's nosy friend demanded to know if the 'steady' couple had consummated their relationship with a kiss. When the pair tentatively shook their heads, Gigi decided that they should start, there and then, and try six rounds of making-out under her watchful instruction.

'I have no idea where she picked up her expertise,' laughs Drew. By round six, the kids were smooching passionately. 'Thanks to Gigi's coaching, we spent nearly an hour instructing each other exactly how we preferred to be kissed!'

From then on, Drew and Brecken regularly indulged in French-kissing sessions, and Drew later concluded that this temporarily satiated her need for physical affection. In the absence of a father figure who could hug her and kiss her goodnight, this childish version of adult intimacy made her feel more of a person, validated her. By her own admission, Drew was utterly 'boy crazy'.

*

On 22 February 1985, Drew reached double figures. As a treat, Jaid organized a surprise party in New York for her starlet at the ultra-trendy disco Limelight. Having built up a circle of friends in the Big Apple whenever they stayed at the Mayflower Hotel, Drew was not averse to the trip, but instead fancied a quiet dinner with family and friends to celebrate, just for a change.

Alarmed that all the preparations would be wasted, Jaid enlisted the help of one of Drew's friends, a teenage model named Stacy who was also from a broken home, to persuade the birthday girl to attend. Stacy lured Drew there with the promise that Matt Dillon, over whom she regularly drooled, would be there. Drew agreed, with butterflies in her tummy about meeting the hunky film star, and looked forward to following Stacy round the New York clubs during their stay.

Dressed up to the nines, the pair arrived at Limelight, where Stacy led Drew up to the private gallery.

'Surprise!' the ensemble yelled.

Drew certainly was surprised. Jaid had executed the perfect secret soirée, brimming with balloons, streamers and the obligatory cake. There was only a slight tinge of disappointment when Drew discovered that her knight in shinning armour wouldn't be there after all; instead, she danced the night away with eclectic composer Frank Zappa's dazzlingly named children, Moon Unit and Dweezil, and Stephen Pearcy, the lead singer of the rock group RATT.

Shockingly for someone turning ten, Drew was unable to enjoy herself properly as, being the centre of attention, there was no way she could pilfer a beer.

'All I thought about was drinking and smoking – instead of what a nice surprise the party was,' she admits, revealing her alcohol-driven, brattish side.

At ten, Drew took her clubbing seriously, now with or without parental supervision. 'I would sleep over at a friend's house and we would sneak out,' she recalls. 'I didn't care what anyone thought. I was accepted in the club world, I felt I belonged.'

While Drew may have felt she belonged in the adult environment, the press were less inclined to agree. A newspaper photo of the prepubescent partying at 2 a.m. prompted an uproar. Jaid was tried by media and found guilty, as a foregone conclusion, of not exerting enough control over her daughter. She was branded the Showbiz Mother From Hell.

Jaid's perverse line of defence starts with the fact that plenty of other children smoked and drank at that age; Drew was just singled out as being the most famous. 'All the kids at the private schools did it,' she retorted. 'If Sally Schmutlich took drugs, what kind of a headline would that make? Drew Barrymore, America's sweetheart, was doing it, and that's why her problems made the headlines.'

Then Jaid changed tack, insisting that the fault lay with Drew for being too independent and rebellious. When that fell on deaf ears, she admitted that she took Drew to Hollywood nightclubs – but 'it was never as often as people said', which obviously made it all right. Finally, her lame excuses boiled down to: 'I was trying to be a "cool" mother. I wanted her to experience everything life had to offer.'

Eventually Jaid had to accept *some* blame, and the truth began to seep out.

'Sometimes I wonder if our problems started because she had the fame and success as an actress I always wanted,' she conceded. 'Maybe I was jealous that she was getting to do everything I'd dreamed of. There were times I bitterly resented her.'

So, if by turning a blind eye to her daughter's activities Jaid was able to indulge in the life she believed she deserved, then that was how it would be.

That is not to say that Drew was innocent. Although still a child, she was resorting to downright devious methods to attend clubs, smoke and drink. By her own admission, she was 'just a belligerent, horrible little nightmare – totally out of control'.

As her smoking, drinking and partying had increased, so Drew relied on her acting ability to pull the wool over her mother's eyes and cover her tracks. She chewed gum and regularly brushed her teeth to mask the smell of smoke and drink, she turned on her sweetest cheesy grin when detailing her previous night's fun at a friend's house, and she gradually learned to act sober when she could barely stand.

The mother–daughter relationship became ever more complex as new dimensions were added, particularly when one party was unaware of these changes.

*

Throughout 1985, Jaid mistakenly continued to trust her daughter's stories of her whereabouts and activities. She made another error in trusting those around her.

Alex Kelly, the name given in *Little Girl Lost* to a male model in his mid-twenties, had somehow ingratiated himself into Drew's circle and, more importantly, the Barrymore household. He was considered a good friend of Jaid's and Drew loved hanging out with him – presumably looking to replace both her father and brother in one go.

Drew particularly loved Alex's cherry-red Corvette and frequently begged him to take her for a spin. One time she persuaded him to take her and Chelsea to Magic Mountain, a white-knuckle amusement park, for the evening. On the way home, just before midnight, the young girls used their feminine wiles to convince Alex to stop off for some beers. Obliging their wishes, he even had the foresight to pick up some cups so no one would become suspicious.

The Barrymores were also friendly with Carlo Ponti and Sophia Loren, and Jaid and Drew regularly visited the Italian movie producer and the actress at their picturesque ranch in Thousand Oaks over the summer. The two Ponti boys, Carlo Jr and Edoardo, were a few years older than Drew, but they all swam, played tennis and raced go karts in the driveway together. Drew loved these getaways, as the Ponti household reminded her of happier times with the Ward family. However, it would not be long before Carlo Jr would fuel her bad habits.

While Chelsea encouraged Drew's wild behaviour in the clubs, the actress was introduced to a new substance through Amy.

Or, more specifically, Amy's mother.

Another close and supposedly trustworthy friend of Jaid's, Amy's mother was a divorcée and musician who often acted as 'chaperone' to her daughter and Drew. However, Amy's mother was a little more lax about smoking, and while driving the girls home one night she lit up. But this was no ordinary cigarette. Although only ten-and-a-half, Drew recognized the heady, sickly-sweet smell filling the car.

Drew had been given the usual lectures at school about the dangers of marijuana, she had heard the horror stories about child users being caught by the cops, and she had even been told of parents stealing their children's stash. She had never tried it . . . till now. Ever curious, she was dying to ask for a puff, but kept quiet for fear of admonition.

Imagine her surprise when Amy's mother casually offered the marijuana to her passengers. Drew was wary, but seized the opportunity. The gold pipe and a Bic lighter were passed back to Drew and, with a bit of coaching, the seasoned smoker soon got the hang of puffing the weed. Greedily inhaling the illegal substance, Drew and Amy finished most of the pipe and, high as kites, decided they liked this new sensation. Back at Amy's house, her mother and the three girls continued to smoke, but by now Drew was getting disappointed.

'I'm not stoned,' she complained – and then burst into uncontrollable fits of laughter.

When Drew realized she had found the ultimate drug for relaxation, she readily added it to her repertoire of escapist vices. Amy's mother happily shared her supplies and the bizarre group of musicians and waifs that gathered at her house were always up for an impromptu party.

Although marijuana is not supposed to be addictive, Drew later acknowledged that its calming qualities are powerfully seductive. She soon became hooked on the drug as another method of forgetting her angst. Unlike cigarettes, pot is famous for giving the user 'the munchies' and beer is extremely high in calories, so Drew's weight ballooned once again.

But it wasn't just her physical appearance that was affected. With another criminal activity to hide, Drew's lies to her mother became more frequent, adamant and blatant. Along with her increased desire for privacy, she became more irritable and difficult. Such behaviour only exaggerated the awkward barriers already present between the pair.

'I couldn't see that she was reacting to the way I treated her,' says Drew in hindsight. 'We fed off each other, egging each other into more extreme behaviour and reactions.'

Before long, Drew had withdrawn completely, having as little as possible to do with her mother and viewing every moment of contact as an unwanted intrusion. The fighting really began as their relationship turned into a constant battle for independence. No matter how hard Jaid tried to make the rules, Drew would break every one.

Remarkably, considering Jaid had witnessed the same erratic behaviour in her ex-husband, she somehow remained blinkered to Drew's increasing dependence on alcohol, and now drugs.

8

I'M A NORMAL LITTLE GIRL.
I AM NOT GROWING UP TOO FAST

As Drew piled on the pounds, not only was she getting grief from the school bullies, but, far more critically, she was being overlooked on the work front. Was she really a has-been at ten?

Her biggest problem was that while she had long since ceased to be a cute little 'un, she had yet to develop into an attractive teenager (no matter what the regulars at Helena's thought). She was at that awful in-between stage: heavy, and moody with it.

Although keen to stick to film, lean times dictated that Drew had to accept television work, and in 1985 she starred in a new gender-bending ABC adaptation of the Mark Twain novels, retitled *The Adventures Of Con Sawyer And Hucklemary Finn*. Drew was the lead, Con Sawyer; her little sister was endearingly played by another budding child star, Melissa Joan Hart (who went on to find magical fame as the star of *Sabrina, The Teenage Witch*), while her sidekick, Hucklemary Finn, was portrayed by Brandy Ward.

Other than this piece, Drew was unemployed for most of the year, save one token project with her godfather. Over the summer of 1985, Drew had visited Steven Spielberg on the set of his latest movie, *The Color Purple*, for want of something better to do. There she met Whoopi Goldberg, the star of the feature in her Hollywood debut, with whom she built a lasting rapport.

Spielberg was creating, producing and part-directing a television series called *Amazing Stories*. Drew was more than happy to be one of a host of guest stars in Spielberg's latest project.

The *Stories* series, running from 1985 to 1987, was clearly inspired by such great shows as *The Twilight Zone*, *Alfred Hitchcock Presents* and *Night Gallery*, and initially served as a nursery for Spielberg's infant ideas. But something in the series failed to spark and there were few memorable episodes in the collection of uneven adventures. Those that stood out tended to be the comedies, while those concentrating on serious issues were dull and tedious pieces.

Drew appeared in a cameo as a train passenger in the opening episode, *Ghost Train*, aired on 29 September. The poignant little tale of a phantom locomotive was possibly one of the better of the bunch, but was too low-key to launch the series successfully.

Pushing into 1986, Drew fared a little better. Turning eleven, she was still struggling for work and so took on a cartoon voiceover in *Star Fairies*. This charming story centres on a princess star fairy named Sparkle, who lives in Castle WishStar. She is responsible for grant-ing the wishes made by children when they wish upon a star. Overwhelmed by her tasks, Sparkle hires five helpers. Then along comes a little girl, Hilary (voiced by Drew), who is very upset but cannot think of a wish that would cheer her up.

It is hard to imagine that either Jaid or Drew saw much potential in a voiceover, but alongside the much-needed financial gain, Drew was nominated in the 1987 Young Artist Awards for Exceptional Young Actresses in Animation.

Drew's other small project of the year was another series, this time based on the novels and short stories by the famed science-fiction author Ray Bradbury. Also akin to *The Twilight Zone*, *Strange Tales: The Ray Bradbury Theater* features Drew in an episode titled *The Screaming Woman*. She appears as Heather Leary, a young girl whose penchant for lies backfires when she hears the sound of a woman's screams coming from beneath her feet.

Fortunately, as far as Drew was concerned, filming for the above pieces took a minimal amount of time, leaving her free to pursue her frenzied social life and substance abuse. Conversely, in promotion for these projects Drew reassured interviewers time and again how wholesome she was. She professed an interest in swimming, Monopoly and playing with her friends, then gallingly comforted the public that she was not caught up in Hollywood folly by stating: 'There are many things in life, apart from being a movie star, you know. I just don't want to disappoint anyone. I want to make all the right decisions.' Furthermore, in response to Spielberg's comment that she was mature beyond her years, she cheerily replied, 'I'm OK. I'm a normal little girl and I am not growing up too fast.'

*

Drew returned to school for the fifth grade at Country in September 1985; her flirtation with Brecken a thing of the past, she was once again wretched. She still took time out for filming, which no doubt disrupted her failing studies, and her all-night partying and drug use made it that much harder to get up in the morning. Soon she was moping around school like a zombie: furthermore, she was still being bullied.

The school gang continued to make her life miserable, and eventually, in the spring term of 1986, the principal called Jaid and the other mothers to put an end to the problem. As only Jaid and one other parent bothered to turn up, little was resolved: Jaid felt frustrated that she couldn't help and Drew sunk lower into her funk. Consequently, she leaned more heavily on the uplifting high she got from drugs.

'[It's] called self-medication,' she explained in *Little Girl Lost*. 'Instead of dealing with whatever pain or troubles you have, you medicate them. The problems are still there, you just don't feel them until the drug or alcohol wears off. Then you medicate again.'

Relief finally came in the form of work. Having been out of the circuit for a while, Drew was grateful to be offered a lead role in a movie, no matter that it was made for television. The project was called *Babes In Toyland* and the best part was that it was to be filmed in Munich: Drew and Jaid were able to escape their problems in Los Angeles for four glorious months over the summer. Perhaps with a change of scenery, mother and daughter might even get along?

Arriving in Germany, the Barrymores had just a couple of days to kill before production started. As luck would have it, Rod Stewart arrived in town for a concert. The once-respected singer's career had hit a slump in the mid-1980s as he favoured stardom over musical integrity; nevertheless, his loyal following included Drew Barrymore. Her (albeit waning) child-star status still held some clout and she was invited to join him on the tour bus for the trip to the stadium, then hang out backstage. A rocker at heart, Drew was in heaven; Jaid, with her colourful Troubadour past, must have been spitting with jealousy.

After a fantastic concert, Drew accompanied the motley crew back to the hotel. Rod and his then girlfriend, Kelly Emberg, disappeared to their room, but Drew stayed up with the band, drinking all night. As if in a scene from *This Is Spinal Tap*, the group filed outside at four in the morning and started playing their instruments as loudly, and no doubt badly, as they could. After a stern word from the manager, the ridiculously drunk band piled back into their rooms and passed out. Jaid was none the wiser.

When they finally surfaced the next afternoon, Rod asked Drew if she wanted to go to Vienna with him for the weekend. Jaid actually contemplated the crazy plan for a while, but eventually put her foot down as Drew had to start work on Monday.

That was it. Drew was not used to hearing the word 'no' and erupted in a spectacular temper tantrum, as only eleven-year-old addicts can. So much for the idea of cosy mother–daughter bonding sessions.

Fortunately, as soon as Drew arrived on set and began mingling with the cast and crew, she felt the familiar sense of security and calmed down. Unlike much of her work, *Babes In Toyland* was a children's film and many of the actors were nearer her age. In fact, Drew soon acquired a boyfriend, fifteen-year-old Michael, and the two were regularly locked at the lips in between takes.

Not having witnessed many of her daughter's snogging sessions, Jaid was a little alarmed and took it upon herself to finally give her daughter a very basic 'birds and the bees' talk. Drew was still a 'good girl' in that department, but Jaid's lecture only prompted her to fight even harder for independence.

Clashes with Jaid aside, the summer of 1986 actually proved most enjoyable for the actress, who felt confident and empowered by her surroundings. She had regular sneaky cigarettes and occasionally swiped a quick drink, but by leaving her nagging insecurities back in Los Angeles, Drew was temporarily less dependent on diversionary substances.

*

While *Babes In Toyland* may have been enjoyable for Drew to film, watching it is another matter. Victor Herbert's story was first adapted in 1934 by Laurel and Hardy, and remade to a lesser standard in 1961 by Walt Disney; it seems a real shame to have bothered with this inadequate re-remake. The version available on film today is an hour-and-a-half long, but the original cut aired at Christmas 1986 at an inconceivable three hours.

The first most striking thing is Drew's appearance. She had changed considerably in the year she spent largely off screen: now her face was longer, her features more adult-like, her hair mousy-brown and frizzy, and she'd gained some height. With a bit of imagination, it is possible to see how she could have passed as a teenager when all dolled up.

Drew plays Lisa Piper, a mature eleven-year-old who no longer plays with or believes in toys. Causing trouble at the shop where her elder sister works, Drew is delightful as the mischievous sibling. Her sister's boyfriend drives the girls home during a terrible blizzard (it is wise to mute the sound during the atrocious 'Cincinnati' song), and in a freak accident Lisa falls out of the car on a sled and careers headfirst into a tree. Knocked unconscious, she is transported to Toyland, where her friends and family from the real world are reincarnated as fairy-tale characters.

Mary Contrary (Jill Schoelen) is about to marry Barnaby Barnacle (Richard Mulligan), although she really loves Jack-Be-Nimble (Keanu Reeves). In stopping the wedding, Lisa and her new-found friends discover that dastardly Barnaby is plotting to take over Toyland and it is their job to stop him. Asking the Toymaster for advice, it turns out that he cannot help them as Lisa doesn't believe in the magic of toys. There ensues a farce, consisting of stolen cookies and flower-power go karts that make bubble noises. Needless to say, Lisa rediscovers her faith in toys, saves the mythical town and returns home in time for Christmas.

The ending has two scenes notable only for their relevance to Drew's life: the first acknowledges E.T. as a reindeer flies across the moon; the second is her character's epiphany: 'Life just made me grow up too fast. I always wanted to be a kid, I always wanted to play with toys. I really am still a kid.'

For all the film's downfalls, Drew is undeniably enchanting as the reborn child Lisa Piper, proving that she can act syrupy-sweet when necessary – it also makes it easier to understand how Jaid was sucked into believing her lies. This role saw Drew nominated for the Young Artist Award For Best Young Female Superstar In Television in 1988.

*

Returning to Los Angeles in the autumn of 1986, Drew was, as always, sad to say goodbye to her on-set friends and she became withdrawn and depressed. Worse, she dreaded facing her tormentors at the Country School and all her insecurities came flooding back.

Jaid remembered how Drew had connected with Gertie, the kitten Spielberg gave her, and since it had run away, she thought it would be a nice idea to find a replacement. She took Drew down to the animal shelter and together they selected an old, fat cat. Calling him Pizza, Drew again used the moggy to confide her deepest fears.

Sensing her anxiety about the school bullies, Jaid decided to enrol her daughter in another small, exclusive and expensive private school for her sixth grade. By the time Drew attended Cal Prep, she was fed up with being the new girl for the fourth time in six years, but admitted that anything had to be an improvement over the last two years.

Instead of struggling, Drew was pleasantly surprised to find that she was finally at a school where she could mix with eleventh and twelfth graders; although several years her senior, she could relate to their maturity and after-hours activities. Even more amazingly, the teenagers didn't laugh her out of their circle as one would imagine, but instead found her to be on their level, due to her lifetime's worth of experience.

'The older kids laughed at my jokes, listened to my stories and accepted me for who I was,' says Drew. Spared the petty jealousy she had come to expect from kids her own age, she found her confidence grew.

Of course, the crowd Drew chose to hang around with weren't the nerds, and her social life was catapulted into uncharted territory. Her new gang were regular truants, preferring instead to get drunk or high. As many of her friends drove, Drew was now mobile without having to rely on Jaid. Weekdays usually consisted of killing time at the malls, smoking dope and moaning about their miserable lives; weekends involved getting up late in the afternoon, watching some television, cruising around town until midnight, smoking more dope and watching the *Rocky Horror Picture Show* or raiding someone's parents' drinks cabinet.

Drew quickly fell into step with her new crowd. 'I was confused,' she admits now. 'I was hanging out with a lot of older kids, conforming to this image I'd created for myself of a super-sophisticated kid who could drink, smoke and take drugs.'

By indulging in these antics, not only did Drew feel accepted, but she also rose above her depressions. The hangovers the next day left her feeling lower than ever, so she simply self-medicated her way out of it again. 'I decided being loaded was the new way of life. My depressions were more frequent and deeper than ever before and that was the only way I could rise above those depths.'

This way of life gathered momentum as the school year progressed and soon took on an identity of its own. Weekend partying spilled over into weeknights, and, unlike the period when they were clubbing at Helena's, Jaid had very little involvement. The more Drew desired her freedom, the more Jaid tried to step in, and the inevitable clashes became daily occurrences.

Jaid was sure she was living a nightmare. For all her faults, she was at heart a caring mother who could be counted on to throw a surprise birthday party, help choose a new pet or defy the school bullies. The more Drew pulled away, the more she tried to help. History was repeating itself as Jaid fell into the same volatile co-dependent relationship she had experienced with John.

During one nasty argument in the car, Drew finally snapped in the face of Jaid's tirade of abuse and slapped her. The loud crack as her hand hit her mother's face reverberated around the car and stunned the women into silence. Drew was grounded for two weeks, one punishment that Jaid actually enforced.

'I would never have treated a friend that way,' Drew admits now. 'But she was my mother and I knew that no matter what I did or said, she'd come back.'

What the Barrymores failed to do was sit down and talk about any of their feelings – Jaid's resentment and frustration over her daughter's career; Drew's feelings of abandonment and her vulnerabilities. It was impossible to save the relationship without them both facing up to a few home truths, but neither had the guts to tackle such issues.

In January 1987, not long before her twelfth birthday, Drew had another particularly vicious fight with her mother. Before slamming her bedroom door, Drew had swiped a bottle of extra-strength aspirin.

For an interminable length of time, she sat and stared at it, contemplating how peaceful it would be to close her eyes and end all her pain. She even envisaged herself swallowing the pills and wondered how long it would take. But for some reason she stopped.

She grabbed some alcohol instead and drank herself to sleep.

*

During this terrible time, Drew accepted another job in the hope of dragging herself out of her rut. *A Conspiracy Of Love* was another made-for-television movie, and was unfortunately just as lame as *Babes In Toyland*.

In the storyline, Joe Woldarski (Allen Fawcett) has walked out on his family a few years previously, leaving his wife, Marcia (Glynnis O'Connor), and daughter, Jody (Barrymore), living at his parents' house. Jody has a strong bond with her grandfather (Robert Young) and loves living with them, but as her mother begins to build a new life, including a romance, it is only appropriate that they move out.

As Jody continues to see her grandfather, Marcia decides to limit their contact to help her start afresh. The pair continue to meet in secret, but Jody feels let down when she discovers her grandfather's trophies are fake and most of his stories are nothing but dreams. At the same time, her father, whom she also idolizes, reappears. Overhearing her mother asking for a divorce and telling him they are moving to New York, Jody runs away – the predictable reunion is corny, with a large helping of American patriotism.

Despite the inferior script, Drew instils a healthy dose of realism, fun and infectious cheer into her character, building a good rapport with Robert Young. She looks a little chubbier than when last seen in *Babes In Toyland* and noticeably wears layered clothing to hide her fast-developing figure.

The fact that work had really dried up, and all she was being offered were a few low-grade made-for-TV films, needed to be addressed. Jaid was unable to talk to Drew, and so it was down to J. J. Harris to lay the cards on the table. 'Nobody would tell me why I couldn't get work, but finally, when I was twelve, my agent sat me down and said, "You have to lose this weight,"' Drew recalls. 'I looked like a damn butterball, couldn't even get a job because I was so fat!'

Drew admits that she tried the 'easy' option of making herself vomit, bulimic style, but fortunately she soon realized that was not the answer. Although the drink and drugs were not helping, it was her penchant for junk food that Drew tackled. She had never been properly instructed in the habit of eating healthily and so went on a fast learning curve. Along with a low-calorie diet, she endured two hours of exercise per day and finally began to see some results.

That was only half the battle, however, as she found that if she strayed from her regime, she quickly put the weight back on. Naturally this depressed Drew and so she sought solace in her preferred substances again.

When Drew and Jaid spent time at the Ponti–Loren ranch over the summer of 1987, the twelve-year-old pushed herself even further. Carlo Jr and Drew spent a lot of time together, but their activities were not as innocent as before. 'In the same way that we used to spend the day swimming or running around, we drank and got stoned at night,' she says.

One night Drew downed one too many vodka shots and was violently sick in the bathroom. Assuming that she would be caught, Drew couldn't believe her luck when she was able to pass it off as a stomach ache.

Another time, while smoking pot, she experienced a full-blown anxiety attack. Normally very animated while high, Drew became unusually calm, then introspective and depressed. Suddenly she went pale, had trouble breathing and her heart started racing. She later said, 'It totally scared the shit out of me,' and vowed to stay off the stuff for a few days. It wasn't long before she was smoking again.

Over the summer, without any acting work lined up, Drew needed cash to keep her in the lifestyle to which she was accustomed, and so she took on part-time work at a video rental store. This might suggest that Jaid had squandered the money Drew had previously earned, but in fact that was not the case at all. She had used some for the family's day-to-day living expenses, and saved the rest in Drew's trust fund. 'If anything, she has always been overly conservative about saving money,' says Drew. 'She'd give me a bit of cash, but let me earn extra spending money.'

Back at Cal Prep in September 1987 for the seventh grade, Drew's life continued its downward spiral.

9

THE ANSWER

In December 1987 Drew's bank balance, at least, got a boost when she won the role of Cathy Goodwin in the family drama *See You In The Morning.*

Drew herself wasn't so sure. She had taken on the TV movie *Conspiracy Of Love* primarily because she needed the money, but after auditioning for this latest Warner Brothers production, perhaps the repetitive theme of children caught up in divorce began to grate. Her part was a minor one – although important within the context of the movie – and it just didn't seem that appealing anymore.

When Drew heard that she and Jaid would be required to up sticks and relocate to New York for four months, she was livid. The girl who had been so excited each time a new film presented itself and had positively adored packing her belongings and preparing to meet a new set of friends, had now been replaced with a moody, surly soon-to-be teenager. She didn't want to go.

'Who cares about a stupid movie?' she retorted to her mother, who was trying to reason with her.

Jaid didn't know what to do – this was not the enthusiastic actress of old. Certainly the relationship between mother and daughter had been suffering for several years now, but this was the first time Drew Barrymore seemed positively indifferent to a dramatic opportunity. Perhaps she was just being ratty because of the current restrictions on her diet and the struggle to lose weight?

Of course, the true reason behind Drew's petulance was not so much that she was going to be separated from her Los Angeles pals – *again*, as she snapped at her mother. After all, she had already made several close friends in New York, notably Stacy, the model. It was more that, being forced to uproot to a relatively unknown city some 3000 miles away, Drew was unsure where her regular supply of booze, fags and pot would come from.

But contracts had been signed and Drew was obliged to go. Although she cried all the way to the airport and whinged throughout the flight, there was no turning back. She and Jaid were installed at New York's Mayflower Hotel the following month.

'Being forced to work over my objections clinched the impression I had of my mother as the enemy,' Drew recalls. 'All she wanted from me, I believed, was the money I earned.'

*

See You In The Morning relied primarily on the names of the prolific actor Jeff Bridges and Farrah Fawcett, best known for 1970s TV series *Charlie's Angels*, as estranged couple Larry and Jo Livingstone. Directed by Alan J. Pakula, the plot centred around the emotional progress of Larry and Jo with their next families: both parents are given a second chance at marriage, but Larry in particular has to work hard at finding his way into the affections of his stepchildren, who are mourning the death of their father, while still finding time for his own offspring.

Although the drama focused mainly on the divorcées adjusting to their new marriages, the child characters were notable if only for their casting: Drew played the troubled adolescent daughter of Larry's second wife; Lukas Haas (the child star of 1985's *Witness*) played her younger brother, Petey; and Macaulay Culkin made his second celluloid appearance as Billy Livingstone, a couple of years before shooting to major stardom in 1990's *Home Alone*.

Drew had several fleeting appearances to film and a couple of key scenes at best, but she still had to be on call for the whole four-month shoot. By law, she was also obliged to be tutored for three hours every day on the set, which she was beginning to resent in a big way.

In a bid for diversion, Drew made contact with Stacy, who was by then living with her older sister. Stacy had everything Drew felt she hadn't: looks, maturity and, above all, absolute freedom to come and go as she pleased. Stacy's SoHo apartment immediately became Drew's second home and soon the model was introducing Drew to all her pals. Ones that dabbled in everything from marijuana to cocaine.

At seventeen, Drew's latest best friend was still underage for the fashionable clubs she frequented all night long, but modelling had taught her how to apply make-up and wear clothes that made her appear far older. Drew was still one month shy of turning thirteen, but her celebrity had always been her ticket into these adult venues, and so the two became regular clubbing partners in crime. Yellow cabs were their chariots, cigarettes their accessories, and cocktails and beer their poison.

Drugs, of course, were their diet.

The members of Drew's new gang were seemingly sophisticated New Yorkers, for whom taking marijuana or cocaine was as much an everyday occurrence as grabbing a bite to eat. And apparently drugs were as easy to come by as a newspaper – marijuana could be bought at a newsstand outside Stacy's apartment. 'It was thirty-five cents for a paper and five bucks for a tiny bag of pot,' says Drew.

Failing that, there was always an abundance of drugs for sale out on the streets or in the clubs. 'All you had to do was order them, just like a drink,' says Drew of the latter. 'Then a quick exchange of money in a dark corner and the deal was done.' The idea of a twelve-year-old trading cash with drug dealers goes so far beyond sordid it's almost unimaginable, but this was what Drew's addiction had led her to.

Surprisingly, at this point the actress restrained herself from trying the designer drug of the time: coke. It frightened her, perhaps appearing *too* grown-up, if that was possible. And so she stayed permanently stoned on joints and drank herself into oblivion.

The trouble with alcohol was that it had after-effects. For a young girl who, in between diets, probably wasn't eating properly anyway, the built-up resistance of an addict wasn't always enough.

One night Drew downed seven Long Island iced teas and was horribly sick all over a table in a nightclub. Even her fame wasn't enough to persuade the club's manager (who had earlier turned a blind eye to Drew's lack of ID) to let her stay. Drew was forcibly thrown out, with the threat that she must never return.

Blindly weaving her way down the street (for once, her protector Stacy wasn't by her side), Drew drunkenly hailed taxis until one took pity on her and drove her home. But when she staggered through the front door, reeking of vomit, there was Jaid – with a face like death itself. For Drew had promised she would be home by 1 a.m. – and that was six hours ago.

Establishing eye contact as best she could, the stinking child managed a pitiful 'Hi, mom' before passing out in a heap on the floor.

The next morning, Jaid gave Drew one of the worst lectures of her life and grounded her for two weeks. Somehow, some of Jaid's ranting and raving sank in, and Drew realized that she was behaving in a thoroughly amateurish manner. As an actress being paid to complete a job, she had a responsibility to the director, producer, crew and cast members of *See You In The Morning*. She needed to be punctual and, above all, she needed to be sober.

As Drew begrudgingly agreed that her mother had a point, she vowed to restrict her wild partying to the weekends. A modicum of professionalism returned and for a while things went quiet.

*

Of course, Drew's secret nightlife was kept exactly that: a secret. Jeff Bridges, Farrah Fawcett and Alice Krige (Drew's onscreen mother) had no idea what a mess their young co-star was in. In fact, the situation was almost farcical, because they would all jolly the moody girl along with sympathy and encouragement. 'If I seemed glum and depressed, which I often did, they chalked it up to adolescence and tried cheering me up,' she says. Bridges in particular made a good impression on Drew: 'Jeff's kindness kept me grounded.'

To an extent, Drew also paid a little more attention to her tutoring, but found it impossible to keep up with the work. She simply wasn't interested and was often suffering from either a hangover or a craving for one of her many vices, which made her feel ratty and lose concentration. Unfortunately, any hours she missed she would have to make up on Saturdays – taking away from her precious party time.

Meanwhile, Jaid had decided that she liked New York enough to invest in a second home there. It would provide a good base for future films on the opposite side of America and save money on hotel fees in the long run. By the time Drew's thirteenth birthday came around, the Barrymores had checked out of the Mayflower and moved into a large two-bedroom apartment on 68th Street and Broadway.

However, Drew's birthday brought nothing but a fresh lapse in maturity. Worryingly, Drew began to exhibit violent tendencies and would vent her pubescent fury on household objects – smashed vases and crockery lying splintered on the floor were a common end to yet another fight.

After one such colourful tirade, Drew ran out of the house, having snatched her mother's purse. Jaid was too exhausted to follow and collapsed in the bathroom in tears. Drew hesitated momentarily at the sound of her mother's anguish, but then continued her flight away from the apartment. With the money in the wallet she bought a pair of roller skates, just like her friend Stacy's. Skating became her preferred means of transport over the unreliable and expensive taxis.

*

The two methods of celebrating Drew's thirteenth birthday were so completely opposite, it was preposterous. The clean-cut version was a small and sedate party held on the set of *See You In The Morning*, complete with little-girl birthday cake, ice cream and balloons. In spite of herself, the child who was desperate to grow up actually quite enjoyed herself, revelling in the attention of the friends she had made during the shoot.

However, away from her professional responsibilities, Drew decided it would be cool to go and get a tattoo done. And why stop at one?

'I got most of my tattoos when I was thirteen,' says Drew. 'I went tattoo crazy and got six of them between the ages of thirteen and sixteen.

'I wanted to show people that I'd grown up. I didn't have tattoos done to shock people who remember me as a sweet little girl, I had them done because I like them. They're such fun.'

Drew's first experience at the tattoo parlour was a test of her conviction, however.

'When I walked into the tattoo shop I really wanted daisies because that was my favourite flower,' she says, 'and the guy didn't even know how to draw a daisy.' After a moment or two studying his limited designs, the tattooist scratched his head.

'You get a rose,' was the best he could offer.

'All right,' said the thirteen-year-old.

And because she wanted the tattoo – any tattoo – done so badly, Drew passively agreed to his suggestion instead of holding out for her first choice or going elsewhere. It was only later that she had the desired daisies added in.

'That was my first tattoo and it's not really that cute, but I like it,' she says of the rose on her inner left hip. 'It reminds me of how I would have taken anything, not necessarily the thing I wanted. Now I have a great deal of patience.'

The rose/daisy fiasco was only the start of a lifelong fascination with permanent body art. Over the next three years, Drew would add to her collection a tiny blue moon and a selection of angels. The former is to be found unusually placed on her right big toe and matches one of her friend's tattoos.

As for the cupids, situated low on her back and reaching further down to her bottom, she says, 'I got the angel tattoos because I love angels.' During a rare time of peaceful relations with her mother, Drew would even ask for a cherub holding a cross which bears her mother's name, 'Jaid'.

*

Over the next two months in New York, Drew found another way to pass the time: a boyfriend. His name was Bobby, and although he was into drink and drugs just the same as all her other friends, he was otherwise a clean-cut, A-grade private-school student destined for a top university.

They met one night while Drew was out clubbing with Stacy. Drew fell in love at first sight, but it was only after a fortnight of pointedly hanging out at the same club in the hope of crossing paths again that Bobby really took notice, taking Drew upstairs and wooing her with champagne and kisses. 'I was totally infatuated with him,' Drew recalls. 'The next day he called and from then on we were inseparable.'

The relationship was passionate to say the least. On the positive side, Drew was charmed with the little things Bobby would do, like buying her roses and picking the thorns off the stems. But on a more negative note, Bobby was jealous by nature and was always accusing his best friend, Sam, of making moves on Drew. As their relationship deepened, his drunken, stoned allegations would lead to physical fights. One night Drew and Bobby practically brought a nightclub to a standstill with their inebriated screaming and punching. A couple of drinks and smokes later, it had all blown over, and they were smooching to 'their song', New Order's 'Blue Monday'.

Although they weren't sleeping together, Drew's teenage love affair gave her the temerity to spit it all back in her mother's face. While in New York, Jaid's social life had been surprisingly low-key, and it had been some time since she had enjoyed a romantic relationship of her own. Drew, in her twisted and hazy logic, held this against her mother – after all, Jaid had failed to provide that ever-hankered-after father figure as a replacement for the real thing.

'You know what?' hollered Drew during one of their many vicious catfights at the apartment. 'You need to get laid!'

It was the final straw – for that evening, at least. Jaid peeled a $100 bill from her wallet and flung it at her daughter's feet.

'Get out!' she retaliated. 'You don't like it here? Go find someplace on your own. See if you can do any better by yourself!'

It was the first time Jaid had ever blatantly refused sanctuary for Drew, be it physical or emotional. Drew's rudeness deserved punishment, but Jaid's reaction was no less shocking.

Drew ran out of the apartment and roller-skated straight round to Bobby's home on the Upper West Side, where he lived with his parents. Fuelled by alcohol and rage, Drew was surprised that neither Bobby nor his mother seemed to care very much about what had just happened – she was allowed to stay overnight, but only after Jaid was telephoned to be informed of her errant daughter's whereabouts. In the cold light of day it must have all seemed very childish.

Mother and daughter came to an uneasy truce for the few weeks left in New York. Drew skated from Stacy's to Bobby's and back again, spending most nights away from the tense atmosphere back at the apartment.

*

See You In The Morning would not be released until 1989. Grossing less than $5 million, it wasn't particularly successful, and although Jeff Bridges did his best to liven up a dull script, it was soon reduced to the ranks of video mediocrity. Although some reviewers found the tale of divorcées and their stepchildren 'touching', it is really just an unremarkable and extremely superficial melodrama, inaccurately billed as a comedy, where the families play 'musical chairs' and nothing much really happens.

Considering what was going on in the background, Drew's performance is surprisingly subdued and low-key. Still looking fairly chunky in spite of her diet, her lifeless hair and pale complexion highlight her 'awkward' stage of adolescence – and all those late nights and illegal substances. Her two key scenes show her lying in bed with her mother, discussing her large breasts, which apparently don't run in the family. Then, in a bid to resemble her attractive mother, she has a makeover, which leads to her shoplifting and subsequent arrest by the police. The only real stretch acting-wise must have been affecting a loving bond with a maternal figure.

'That was a very bizarre time in my life,' Drew would later conclude about the film. 'I was a little confused – a lot confused.'

*

In April 1988 the Barrymores left New York for Los Angeles. Despite her initial tantrums about the temporary move, Drew had predictably grown to love her new friends, and spent a whole day on the telephone in tears as she said her goodbyes.

Other than the much-detested school, there was now nothing on her horizon until *Far From Home*, a film which she was due to shoot in Nevada in mid-July. Almost immediately after returning home, Drew was stir-crazy. What could possibly liven up the barren months stretching ahead of her?

Many paths of addiction follow a fairly predisposed sequence, and Drew's was no exception. She had watched Stacy, Bobby and all her other New York friends use cocaine, but had always resisted, basically because she was afraid. 'I was around it often enough not to be naïve about its thrilling high,' she admits.

But back on L.A. turf, Drew decided it would be 'cute' to try out something heavier than pot. The setting for her next experiment was her high-school prom, where her chosen drug was in plentiful supply.

Putting on a brave face in front of her friends, when the time came for Drew to snort her first line of coke, she was so frightened she could barely see straight.

'I thought I was going to have a heart attack,' she recalls in her autobiography. 'A friend held my head straight so I could snort better. And I needed the help. I was so drunk and so stoned I could hardly walk.'

But the rush was wonderful. She had expected she would feel good – but not that good. And the excitement of being so daring – especially at school – only pushed her to try more and more. After a couple of lines, Drew's friends then handed her an innocent-sounding 'coco-puff' (cocaine in a cigarette), and she began to float above the clouds.

Over the next two months, Drew's usage of the drug underwent a slow-burning progression. Gradually she began to take more as the cravings kicked in. 'Just thinking about it caused my palms to sweat. I loved cocaine. Period.'

As Drew herself explains, part of being an addict is the never-ending quest for 'the perfect antidote to pain'. In fact, a hundred years earlier, cocaine, a powerful psychostimulant alkaloid found in the leaves of the South American shrub *Erythroxylon coca*, had been a highly effective and widely used painkiller. Found in tonics, cures for toothache and patented medicines, it was sold over the counter and available in such respected establishments as Harrods department store in London until 1916. The popular 'soft drink' Coca-Cola (containing around 60mg of cocaine per serving until 1903) was introduced in 1886 as 'a valuable brain-tonic and cure for all nervous afflictions'.

To Drew it provided the Answer. Alcohol, her first love, was great, but the hangovers were terrible and made it difficult to work. Cigarettes and pot were fun – but that wasn't the kind of entertainment Drew was looking for anymore. Cocaine, however, was right up her street.

'It was like standing on top of a mountain and yelling, "Eureka! I found it!"' she says in *Little Girl Lost*.

Taken in the way Drew did (inhalation rather than injecting), coke had no after-effects that she could detect, and thus it allowed her to overcome her ongoing depression. Even better, when taken in combination with alcohol, its buzz would enable her to avoid the dreaded hangovers the next day. Best of all, it killed all hunger pangs and was therefore fabulous for losing weight. What she couldn't see were the many downsides to the drug, with addiction being the most obvious one.

Soon Drew was well and truly hooked.

'My mind seemed to have a huge neon sign in it that blinked non-stop: Coke. Get Coke. So I did.'

On the face of it, Drew was having a wonderful time, living on a permanent high and escaping her inner demons. But one image will stick in her mind forever from this period of gratuitous binging.

Sitting alone on her bathroom floor one afternoon, Drew carefully arranged several neat lines of coke on a hand mirror. To the sound of her stereo, she methodically inhaled each one, savouring the rush. When she came to the end of her supply, she knew she needed more.

As her heart pounded and her hands shook, Drew thought she was incredibly happy. But as she searched the mirror for the very last specks of the drug, she saw that her face was awash with tears. She hadn't even realized she was crying.

'I remember telling myself, "Get a grip, girl. Get a fucking grip." But, I guess, it was too late.'

10

COKE. GET COKE

'Like most parents of kids with drug and alcohol problems, I had no idea what was going on. People want to know where I was. But the question is still somewhat of a shock.'

JAID BARRYMORE

For months, if not years, Jaid and Drew had been at each other's throats. Jaid had suppressed any suspicions that there might be more to her daughter's aggression, erratic mood swings, poor grades and general unhappiness than straightforward adolescence. Confronting the girl only exacerbated their arguments. For a long time, Jaid couldn't stomach the truth: after all, she'd been there before, with John Barrymore II.

There were still several weeks to go until the beginning of *Far From Home*. Drew was clearly going out of her mind with boredom and Jaid just couldn't face the fights until the diversion of filming began. Something had to be done, she decided.

On 28 June 1988, Drew unwittingly provided the best excuse Jaid could hope for. Out on the town on a pub crawl way past her 10 p.m. curfew, she phoned her mother in a drunken, spiteful temper.

'I want you out of the house by the time I get home,' she slurred. 'I don't think you're treating me fairly and so I want you to leave.'

On the telephone, Jaid calmly agreed she would leave and spend the night at a friend's house. But instead, she stayed put. This would be the night when things would change for the better.

When Drew finally made it through the front door, having downed thirteen beers in a race with a friend, she was livid to find her mother waiting up for her.

'What the *hell* are you doing in here?' the teenager shrieked. 'It's *my* turn to be Mom. Get out!'

But Jaid refused to move. She stood there, blank-faced. Her silence lit the fuse. Lumbering around the room and swearing her head off, Drew began to throw things. Glasses, vases, plates and ornaments all went hurtling through the air and smashed on the floor around her mother, who for some reason wasn't screaming and crying the way she normally would. Momentarily giving up, Drew decided to refuel.

'I need another drink!'

'You can't drink in the house,' came the placid response, but it was lost on Drew.

'Fuck you!'

As Drew reached the kitchen, she heard the muffled sound of her mother talking on the phone.

'She's very bad,' Jaid was saying. 'You need to come over right now and pick her up.'

Somewhere in the back of her beer-addled brain, Drew knew that what she was doing was wrong, very wrong.

'Oh my God,' she thought in her stupor, 'she's finally gone and called the police! I'm going to be walking out of here in handcuffs and everyone's going to find out . . .'

Drew panicked, thinking that if she could only down one more beer, then everything would go away. The idea of being led out of the house after a scene with her mother and taken to jail was something she'd always been scared of, but never thought would actually happen. Shaking, she reached for the fridge.

The doorbell rang. Drew could hear her mother rush to open it. She began to cry.

*

Instead of the police, there stood Chelsea and her mother. Drew was so relieved she could have burst out laughing, but she could barely stand. As she was bundled into the car she enquired, 'Where are you taking me?' When she heard it was hospital, not jail, she slumped in the back seat and thanked her lucky stars.

Jaid had been increasingly worried about her daughter's erratic behaviour for some time, but remained at a loss as to how to handle it. When they returned to Los Angeles from New York after *See You In The Morning* wrapped, they found that Chelsea had been put in a rehab centre. Drew hadn't seen her since, as their lifestyles were completely different now that Chelsea was clean, but Jaid, on the other hand, had spent hours on the telephone with Chelsea's mother and, through the sobs, began to realize that Drew was in the same position and needed the same help.

'It was the toughest thing I ever did,' says Jaid. 'I was the one who had to get her in there and I was the one she blamed. But I knew without rehab, my daughter would wind up killing herself.'

So, with assistance from Chelsea and her mother, Jaid committed Drew to the Adolescent Substance Abuse Program Center (ASAP), a private hospital specializing in the treatment of drug and alcohol users, situated in Van Nuys, California.

Founded in 1979 by psychiatrist Dr Lewis, the ASAP Family Treatment Center is specifically aimed at helping teenagers. No matter what their background, Dr Lewis discovered there was a significant pattern with adolescent users – they dabble around age eight, start using regularly at eleven and are admitted by the time they are fifteen – a timeline Drew had more or less followed to the letter.

The treatment consists of months of intensive therapy whereby the patient confronts the issues behind their addictions. Through a combination of various group sessions and the daily practice of a twelve-step belief programme, they identify and resolve their problems. As well as helping the addict break their individual cycle, the centre also focuses on rebuilding familial relationships destroyed by the patient's behaviour, and resocialization. The $500-a-day bill was picked up by Drew's health insurance.

When the actress, who couldn't even walk by this time, was unceremoniously dragged into the centre, she was simply grateful not to be in a cell. She assumed that she would just be there for the night so that she could dry out, but at some point during the lengthy admission process the reality of the situation began to dawn on her.

In a small, sterile room Drew's height, weight and medical history were noted, along with details of the substances she had consumed that night. Jaid was present during this administration exercise and was not only horrified by Drew's chain-smoking – she was dumbstruck when she heard her daughter had progressed from cigarettes to cocaine. It was almost dawn before the process was complete: Drew was led through to a box room with a bed and blankets where she could crash. After the door was locked behind her, Jaid drove home, numbed by the whole experience.

Harsh overhead lights were turned on at 7 a.m., something which Drew would have to get used to. She was taken to an examining room to give a blood sample, then allowed to sleep for a little longer and clean up before being introduced to Betty Wyman, her assigned therapist. During the rest of the first day, Drew was shown around the hospital and introduced to the room-mate she calls 'Tina' in *Little Girl Lost*.

The initiation had been gentle in comparison to the regimented routine that followed and the extensive list of rules and regulations that had to be obeyed. Along with set times for meals and bedtime, patients had a rota for schooling, therapy sessions and even showers. Smoking was allowed (which is surprising, given that Drew was underage), but it was considered a privilege and could be curbed for misbehaviour. Other punishments were also given out for any fraternization between girls and boys, skipping the timetable, refusing to co-operate with the orderlies and so on and so forth.

But the strict schedule was a breeze in comparison to the emotional work required from Drew. Her first and greatest problem was not opening up to her therapist or anyone in the group, but admitting her problems to herself and confronting the monstrous girl she had become.

Dr George Blair, the resident psychologist, and Lori Cerasoli, a counsellor and former ASAP patient, led the group sessions, which consisted of twenty children talking about their problems; the idea being that they all listen, realize they are not alone and help each other process their issues. During Drew's first two-hour session, she was announced as a new patient. Some of the other residents had recognized the actress and voiced concerns that she might receive special treatment, but they were assured this would not be the case. On the outside Drew was all sweetness and light, but inwardly she was fuming. She wished she were anywhere but there – jail probably seemed preferable.

'When I first arrived at the hospital, I was extremely standoffish, the most distant, obstinate person in the entire hospital,' she admits.

On Drew's second day at ASAP Jaid brought in a suitcase of clothes. That was when it really hit Drew that she was there for the long haul. Sitting sullenly in the corner, closed off to the world, Drew twirled sections of hair round her fingers and spoke to no one. She refused to answer questions, rebuffed anyone who tried to get close to her and remained impervious to the discussions going on around her. How could anyone even begin to understand the problems she was suffering?

She felt the whole process was lame.

'Hi, I'm Drew. I'm an addict and alcoholic. And I have two days of sobriety,' she said, through gritted teeth.

She didn't believe a word of it.

Part of the therapy was a session including the patient's parents, with the aim of reintroducing the child to a balanced home. But for the meantime, Drew was furious with her mother for locking her up in an institution. She was sure it proved that Jaid didn't love her.

Indeed, there was no love lost between Jaid and Drew as they walked into the meeting separately. Drew bristled with resentment: Jaid suffocated under guilt.

*

Drew's twice-weekly one-to-one sessions with Dr Blair started off the same way as the group meetings, as the patient refused to open up. However, as many of the other teenage girls found, Dr Blair's youthful enthusiasm and good looks eventually broke down the barriers, and she let him into her world on their second get-together.

As for the individual family sessions, despite Cerasoli's attempts at diplomacy, Drew and Jaid tended to end up in screaming rows. Finally, they got to one of the roots of the problem:

'Why don't you just be my mother instead of my manager?' demanded Drew.

Jaid thought she understood how Drew was feeling and desperately tried to reassure her that it wasn't true. When she defended her actions, Jaid was hushed by the counsellors, who explained that it was important for her to listen and not argue back.

Gradually Drew showed signs of progress. She eventually spoke up in one of her other sessions. One girl was complaining about her parents when something snapped inside the actress, who retorted, 'Why don't you just be grateful that you have a mother *and* a father?' Having remained determinedly mute until then, she surprised herself as much as everyone in the room by her outburst.

But as all good things must come to an end, so too did Drew's therapy. Upon her famous daughter's admission to ASAP, Jaid had explained that Drew would be required on set for *Far From Home* just a fortnight later. It was a contractual obligation that she could not shirk, but any help she could receive before then would obviously be beneficial. The staff at ASAP reluctantly agreed to treat and then release Drew after just twelve days, on the proviso that she was brought straight back after her shoot finished.

Jaid was mindful not to undo all the hard work of the last two weeks and asked Betty Wyman if there was any way they could provide Drew with the support she would need while she was away. Using the technique designed to help resocialize patients, a former ASAP attendee, Diane, was assigned to travel with Drew to provide valuable, unconditional twenty-four-hour support.

When it came to her departure, the biggest surprise came from Drew herself: the scared little girl who had lashed out at institution-alization actually didn't want to leave the safety net of rehab.

Drew approached her part in the murder mystery *Far From Home* with more vigour than any other film in years. She and Jaid were particularly keen on the project because at a career level it would be very much a 'coming-of-age' movie, with Drew's fourteen-year-old character, Joleen Cox, losing her innocence in many ways. It was Drew's opportunity to begin to make the transition from child actor to teen star.

The Barrymores flew into the tiny town of Gerlach, situated on the edge of the Black Rock Desert in Nevada, on 11 July 1988. They were accompanied by Diane, whom Drew grudgingly began to respect.

Gerlach had a population of just 350, three bars and absolutely nothing to do between shoots. It had once been a mining outpost, benefiting from the gold rush of the late nineteenth century, but now it resembled one of those ghost towns in cowboy movies where fragments of desert foliage blowing down a dusty street is the biggest excitement on offer. All of the cast and crew agreed that it was literally like being marooned. The location alone was to prove a severe test of Drew's mettle.

'If anyone had asked me one month earlier if I could have stayed sober, I would have laughed and said, "No way!"' says Drew. 'However, not only did I survive, I had a pretty decent time.'

In fact, the true appeal of *Far From Home* (other than Drew's performance itself) is the atmospheric beauty of the desolate surroundings.

In the film, Joleen Cox and her father (Matt Frewer) are stranded in the fictional town of Banco when they run out of gasoline on the last day of their cross-country vacation. Forced to stay in a shabby trailer park while her father works out how to get them home, Joleen attracts the attention of two very different teenage boys, Jimmy and Pinky, also living in the park. Going out of her mind with boredom, Joleen's position as she hangs around the trailer park in the searing heat, searching for distractions, wasn't so different to Drew's own real-life scenario.

Surprisingly, being so far away from civilization had its own sobering effect on the addict. It gave her time to take long walks, sunbathe, chat to the cast and crew, and, most importantly, to think. Sharing a room with Diane, Drew began to open up to her about her troubles, and was proud to say that she stayed away from the bars.

'In that small a town, it was pretty hard to get away from yourself – and the fact that I didn't blow my sobriety gave me a small measure of confidence that I was on the mend,' she recalls.

But after just a fortnight in Gerlach, the production moved on to Carson City, a smaller version of Las Vegas. It housed ten times the entertainment available in Gerlach, in the form of bars, clubs and casinos.

Drew's 'party girl' persona woke up with a bang. She had never been gambling before and fancied giving the exotic-looking tables a whirl. As she had been doing so well over the last two weeks, Jaid agreed for her to attend a casino with some friends from the crew. Dressing up 'like Scarlett O'Hara', Drew pretended to be twenty-two and strode confidently into the den of vice. Immediately the sexy-looking girl with the red lipstick and substantial cleavage was offered something to drink.

'No thanks,' she replied, not pausing to think twice.*

This looked like fun. First Drew played craps, throwing the dice for a friend, before moving on to blackjack. After winning $180 from her original $20 bet, Drew's heart began to race and she experienced a rush similar to that provided by the drugs and alcohol she had been weaned off only three-and-a-half weeks earlier. Confidently she moved over to the roulette table, but there she lost all her games – and money. Wisely, the teenager decided to retire to bed before she went too far.

Diane was waiting for her back in the hotel room.

Full of the adventures she'd had, Drew bubbled over about how she wanted to go gambling again – hey, Diane should come with her next time!

Gently, Diane explained to Drew what was happening: her addictive personality was fighting just below the surface, struggling to break through. It wasn't necessarily the gambling itself – although that could certainly prove a problem if it was allowed to really kick in – no, it was her love of partying that had been reawoken.

Diane wasn't Jaid, and although she was shocked, Drew actually listened to the older girl's explanation that Drew was going straight back to her old habit of forgetting she was only thirteen and convincing herself that she was a grown-up, able to cope with a grown-up lifestyle. There was something about the way she said it that made Drew catch her breath. After all, Diane had been through it all herself – she knew what she was talking about from bitter personal experience. It was an important moment.

Drew was never going to change her very essence – she loved socializing too much and understandably justified it as her reward for

---

*Funnily enough, this would mirror a scene from *Far From Home* itself, where the character Jimmy tempts Joleen with a drink, and she turns it down.

working long hours on the set while simultaneously studying with the set teacher, Scott LaValley. But if she could go out – admittedly not as much – and resist all the temptation put in her way, she would be a better person. So, although Drew continued to visit the bars and casinos while resident in Carson City, she exercised considerable self-control.

'It was painful,' she says of each and every time a friend would order a drink in front of her. 'I'd stare at it, feeling incredibly anxious, like I wanted to grab the glass and down it. But I didn't. I really wanted to be sober. It was a constant tug-of-war.'

And she managed it: Drew stayed sober for the entire shoot.

*

Far From Home yet again places Drew in the surely uncomfortable position of playing a child of divorced parents. In this instance, she has gone on holiday with her Los Angeles journalist father.

While stone-cold sober, Drew's acting ability improved in leaps and bounds, and although the film as a whole is an unremarkable tale of teenage lust and murder, Drew's performance is mature and thought-provoking. She copes admirably with some challenging scenes, such as an attempted rape, and the slowly dawning realization that one of her friendships is not what it seems.

However, for better or worse, the most obvious thing about Drew's performance as Joleen is her physical appearance. Whether it was down to the dieting, the weight she'd lost during her cocaine binges, the twelve-day detox in ASAP or simply growing up, Drew's days of puppy fat were long gone.

Instead, viewers saw onscreen a beautiful, curvaceous woman. Although in this movie Drew has evidently yet to grow into her facial features, she is slim and voluptuous – her ample bust making several appearances of its own in a skimpy black bikini and the occasional wet T-shirt. Looking wholesome and tanned, her huge almond eyes framed with heavy brows, Drew/Joleen barely clings on to her childhood with her multiple watches and earrings, lisp and braces.

In the trailer park, murder is an everyday occurrence. The inhabitants are stalked by an unknown serial killer and the film builds up a strong atmosphere of tension, making excellent use of the barren surroundings and sets, such as the disused, unfinished hotel building. The heat is so intense that people walk around in their underwear (Joleen is no exception), and the ominous desert storm towards the end foretells a much-anticipated explosion of teenage rebellion, frustration, desire and violence.

Essentially a quasi-erotic rites-of-passage movie, *Far From Home* is at times genuinely frightening and at others a bit childish. Joleen is writing a journal, which is translated into voiceovers – in particular, the 'life is just totally un-*fair*' overdub is particularly cringe-making and unnecessary.

Described accurately by one critic as an 'offbeat thriller with comic overtones' on its release in June 1989, one of the highlights of the movie is the hilariously over-the-top performance by Susan Tyrrell as the trailer-park landlady. The directorial debut of Meiert Avis, *Far From Home* is somewhat let down by an unclimactic ending.

11

BABY STEPS

When *Far From Home* wrapped on 5 September 1988, as per the agreement, Drew was flown to Los Angeles and immediately taken back to the ASAP centre.

Over the summer, Jaid had sold their luxurious pad in Sherman Oaks and bought a smaller place that was easier to maintain, but still had two bedrooms. Drew wouldn't see it for a while. Nor would she go back to school for eighth grade with her friends at Cal Prep.

Suddenly rehab once more seemed like an institution, rather than a safety net. The barriers had been raised once again. Having stayed sober for nearly two months, Drew was convinced she was cured.

'I didn't want to face that I was still as much an addict as when I first entered the hospital,' she admits now.

She soon learned, admittedly the hard way, that there was a stark difference between being 'clean' and being 'dry'. The former is the goal: to be a contented soul without the desire to use and abuse substances, to be able to deal with problems in a different way and not return to old habits. The latter, however, signals that although technically sober, the patient is still following old patterns associated with the time when they were addicted, hanging around with the same crowd who are still using, so the temptation is constant and it is all too easy to give in.

Ridiculously, after less than a week back in rehab, Drew had to leave again. This time she was required in New York to dub some dialogue for *See You In The Morning*. Having made no headway in six days, and sensing Drew's deluded state of mind, the staff at ASAP were adamant that she shouldn't go. But Jaid knew that Drew had to fulfil her contract and wanted her to audition for a play while in New York to give her a goal for the end of her treatment. She reasoned that Drew had seventy-six days sobriety and what harm could be done in just one week in Manhattan?

On 12 September Drew flew to New York, where she hooked up with Stacy, and at first managed to stay sober and out of the clubs. Just three days later, at 11 p.m., Stacy and Drew entered one of their favourite nightclubs.

She was dry, but not clean. An innocent trip to the toilets an hour-and-a-half later was all it would take to try her resolve.

'Do you blow?' asked one of the girls as she opened her purse and got out a packet of coke.

'No, I stopped that,' replied Drew, feeling strong.

'You don't mind if we do it in front of you, do you?' the girl continued, having already started to cut lines.

'It's OK, guys,' said Drew, desperate to be cool. 'Go ahead.'

Drew stayed and watched the girls. She could almost feel the burn of the cocaine as they inhaled. She remembered the high as she watched them turn lively and giddy. It was unbearable.

'You sure you don't want any?' the girl pursued.

Drew burst into floods of tears, checked her watch (12.37 a.m.) and gave in. She just needed a little pick-me-up. So she did one line. Then another.

Even during the illicit high, Drew was furious with herself for breaking her sobriety. Worse still, the hospital would find out as they would analyse her urine when she returned.

So she turned to Stacy and said, 'As long as they're going to know, I might as well do some more.' There was a dealer in the club, but he wouldn't sell less than a gram of coke. Drew flashed a wad of $10 bills at him.

*

High as kites, the girls staggered home at about 7.30 a.m. Slipping all too easily back into the lies, Drew told her mother she had spent the night at Stacy's. Wanting to believe the best from her daughter, Jaid bought it. Later that day, she also allowed Drew to borrow her credit card with some story about returning a clock she had bought.

Drew's intentions were far more elaborate. She brandished the plastic in front of Stacy and suggested that they live out their greatest fantasy – jetting off to Hawaii with just the clothes on their backs. Stacy was up for it.

Calling out to Jaid that they would be back in an hour, Drew and Stacy jumped in a cab and headed for LaGuardia airport. At the booking desk, Drew exercised her celebrity status and acting skills to use the credit card in the name of Ildiko Barrymore.

Soon Drew and Stacy were on a plane bound for Los Angeles with onward tickets to Hawaii for the following day in their hot little hands. At regular intervals Drew cannily phoned her mother to ask permission to stay out just a little longer. Jaid was beginning to get restless and gave her daughter a deadline of the following afternoon to return, or she would call the police.

Once in Los Angeles, the terrible twosome arrived at the new Barrymore condo, where they decided to take Jaid's BMW and go out to dinner. Drew realized that she had forgotten her set of car keys (which begs the question: what was a thirteen-year-old even doing with a set of car keys?) and so hunted for the spare set.

Drew drove – illegally – to a restaurant, where she telephoned her mother again. This time, Jaid called her bluff.

'That's it, I'm going to call the police,' she said.

'Do whatever you bloody well want,' snapped Drew, 'see if I care.'

Drew and Stacy went back to the apartment, stuffed some suitcases with clothes and raced out. They drove to a friend's house, but were soon being tailed by a police car. Although driving with a minor behind the wheel, Drew and Stacy were in fact more concerned with their stash of coke sitting on the dashboard.

Stacy turned to Drew for advice and the cocksure youngster told her to calmly put her hand on the dashboard, fold up the packet and slip it in her pocket. Somehow, they managed to extract themselves from a very awkward situation . . .

When the pair awoke after spending the night in the car, they realized they were out of coke and so went to a friend's house to get some more. Drew was so high she dented two cars trying to parallel park outside. The runaways then hit the department stores with Jaid's credit card, which was by now reported stolen. Some cashiers refused the card, while others with older systems accepted the transactions.

Back at the Barrymore apartment, Drew and Stacy gleefully tried on their purchases, snorted four lines of coke each and prepared to go to the airport.

They were completely oblivious to the man and woman who quietly entered the apartment behind them.

Caught off guard, Drew was handcuffed and led out to a waiting car. She was extremely fortunate to be spared the indignity of jail a second time.

The intruders were in fact private detectives hired by Jaid to return the wayward girl to rehab. Rubbing salt into the wound, the agents were thrilled to meet the child star and quizzed her about E.T. and making movies. When they uncuffed her, they actually asked for her autograph.

Re-entering ASAP just one week after leaving for New York, Drew was in a state. Running a high temperature of 102 degrees Fahrenheit, she was dehydrated, 5 pounds lighter, shivering from cold sweats, agitated and too weary to sit up properly.

After the readmission process, ASAP's regimented routine was again spelled out to Drew, only this time they were going to be even tougher. She felt tricked by her friends and family, and trapped. Soon the drugs in her system curdled to venom. While waiting in the dining room, Drew flipped; her outburst was only suppressed by four technicians and the use of restraints.

In therapy, Drew went straight back to square one. She resurrected her protective shield. She sat hugging her knees to her chest with her head down. She refused to talk or let anyone in. She became a virtual recluse.

Having broken not only her sobriety, but also the trust of the staff, the rules were far stricter the second time around and Drew was not allowed any work privileges. She was woken at 7.30 a.m. each day, then she made her bed, had her breakfast and headed to the classroom for a morning's worth of school. After lunch she had therapy, followed by dinner and more meetings. The schedule was unrelenting. Her rehabilitation included one-to-one sessions, therapy groups, family groups, multifamily groups, doctor groups and recovery groups, as well as specific substance abuse programmes and studying the twelve steps. Not forgetting homework, of course.

As with the other two times she entered ASAP, Drew resented her mother. Sometimes she claimed she only experimented with drugs and was not an addict; other times she pontificated poetically that a bird cannot be locked in a cage. The end result was always the same: she felt abandoned and institutionalized.

For weeks Drew maintained her harsh exterior, wallowed in depression and made little progress in any of the sessions. The friends she had made previously (one close friend in particular she called 'Edie' in *Little Girl Lost*) were now finishing their treatment and preparing to leave, while Drew was stalling at the start of the long road to recovery.

Then she met a boy. In *Little Girl Lost* she called him 'Rick', and there was no mistaking her attraction for the blond-haired, blue-eyed bad boy. Although sexual contact of any description was strictly forbidden, the pair started dating. As Drew had deep-rooted problems concerning the men in her life, the ASAP staff ruled that it was imperative for her to steer clear of such a relationship while resolving her issues. But prohibition was like a red rag to a bull.

Each and every time Drew was caught with Rick she was punished with the Intensive Treatment Programme (ITP). This usually meant that the patient was restricted to her room when not in classes, but in extreme cases, for repeat offenders, the severity of restrictions correlated to the offence.

In the first month-and-a-half Drew set a hospital record as she was put on ITP more than fifteen times. Her crimes weren't always Rick-related – sometimes they were for tardiness, sloppiness or smoking in her room – but the worst was kissing Rick in his room.

Before long, the rascal had given his bracelet to another girl, and Drew was forced to deal with her issues about men on her own.

*

Shortly after her brief affair ended, Drew was called into Cerasoli's office where she was told to call her mother. There was bad news: Jaid's father had passed away.

Bursting into tears, Drew realized that she had been so wrapped up in her own selfish little world that she hadn't even stopped to consider other people.

Her normal response to the loss of her grandfather would have been the escape route of drugs, but instead she was forced to deal with her feelings of grief and regret clear-headed. She wrote him a posthumous letter. That was the first step on the uphill climb.

Finally, in one group session, Cerasoli was determined to drag the little girl out of her shell.

'Have you hit your bottom?' asked the counsellor.

Drew had often heard therapists say that if you haven't hit your bottom, you cannot begin the process of recovery. She thought she knew what hitting bottom meant and admitted it.

Again, it was baby steps. She still didn't talk, but at least she started to listen. Slowly, very slowly, over the autumn of 1988, Drew began to confront her problems again. The therapy was progressively permeating her thick skin.

At first she despised being treated like a child, but eventually conceded it 'was the best thing that could have happened to me. Being deprived of the simplest things, like sitting under a tree, riding in a car, or taking a walk, was totally humbling.'

One thing she was forced to speak about was her celebrity: one night *E.T.* was mentioned on the news and a picture of Drew as Gertie flashed up on screen. Stuck in the rehab centre for months, Drew was beginning to enjoy the safety of anonymity and being a 'regular kid' – she had almost begun to forget that she was famous in the outside world and it scared her. Rather than bury her fears, she opened up in therapy and found the support and help she received invaluable.

By early November, Drew's improvement was still hit and miss. Some days she made enormous advances, others she regressed. When Jaid came to family sessions, Drew remained difficult and prone to flaring up. The ASAP staff felt it was high time for Drew to tackle her complex relationship with her mother.

Summoning up her courage, Drew elaborated on her previous accusation – that she felt Jaid was more of a manager than a mother. Jaid sat and listened.

'I just let down the sacred guard and allowed her back into my life, and she reacted like a mum, with total love,' remembers Drew. 'That was the best feeling in the world. When she finally said it was time for her to go home and sleep, I wouldn't stop hugging her.' When they met the following day for therapy, Jaid brought Drew a sandwich, asked how she was and didn't once talk about business. What's more, in time Drew started to reciprocate by listening to her mother's own complaints.

Their rocky relationship seemed to be on the mend.

12

GETTING STRAIGHT

Once Drew had showed consistent signs of improvement, she was allowed to join the Growth Group. This was the facility the ASAP centre used to reintegrate patients into society. Outings to movies, concerts, parks, bowling alleys, barbecues and softball games were all chaperoned by recovering addicts. There was a straightforward lesson to be learned from the fun days out: it was possible to enjoy life without getting high.

'Growth Group kept me hungry. I didn't want to give it up. It made me try hard in groups and in my family sessions, and the harder I tried, the better I felt,' says Drew. The programme was clearly working.

Drew's sponsors assigned to support her through Growth Group were David Crosby and his wife, Jan Dance. As a founding member of two pioneering American bands – the Byrds and Crosby, Stills, Nash & Young – Crosby was a heavy influence on the future of folk rock during the 1960s and 1970s. Sadly, as is often the case with celebrities, he is more often recognized for his larger-than-life offstage antics, particularly his decade-and-a-half-long battle with drug abuse.

Crosby's cocaine and heroin use started in the early 1970s and continued through to the mid-1980s, when he and recording-studio engineer Jan Dance were repeatedly charged for drugs and weapons possession. Crosby was put in a drug rehabilitation clinic in lieu of a jail sentence, but after he escaped there were no second chances: on his capture, he was sent to prison. In 1985 the couple finally kicked their habits together, a struggle which Crosby details in his staggering autobiography *Long Time Gone*, and they were keen to help other addicts come clean. When Drew met the musician, he had reunited with Stills, Nash and Young for the album *American Dream* and was also experiencing success with his second solo effort, *Oh Yes I Can*.

It was very important for Drew that she was paired up with people who not only identified with the descent into drug addiction, but could also put it in context with the pressures of fame. Drew immediately bonded with Crosby and Dance. Attending AA meetings as a trio, they also enjoyed everyday things, such as eating out, going to the cinema and spending quiet nights at home. Drew found she could talk with Jan about anything. They shared similar experiences and she was a good listener.

Coincidentally, there was another link, which proved priceless. 'I'm an old Hollywood kid and I knew her story,' says Crosby. 'I felt she had been dealt a short deck, you know, a fifth-generation alcoholic, and I didn't want to see her go down the tubes. I knew her father back when I was using.' Drew was stunned to find out that Crosby and John Barrymore II had mixed in the same circles and she interrogated him for all the information he could remember. Even more remarkably, Betty Wyman's drummer husband, Dallas Taylor, was a friend of Crosby's, an ex-addict and also knew Drew's father.

These twists of fate led to Drew's next major challenge: talking about her father, with the ultimate goal of dealing with her problematic relationships with all men as a consequence of his behaviour. Drew had not spoken to John Barrymore II in nearly seven years, and her lasting memory of him was of the time she screamed at him for being a lousy father and kicked a chair at him.

'With the encouragement of my friends at the hospital, I plucked up courage to call him,' she said. 'For the first time in my life, my father said, "I love you, daughter." I said, "I love you, father." I was laughing and crying at the same time, thinking of what it would be like to have a family. Then I reminded myself that my father is gone from my life.'

Of course, one phone call could not negate a lifetime of abuse: something more needed to be done. Wyman had sometimes found that role-playing could be a useful tool in therapy, particularly for an actress used to playing characters. Similarly to Drew's posthumous letter to her grandfather, Wyman wanted to set up a dialogue whereby Drew could air her feelings about her father. Obviously John Barrymore II would not have co-operated in such an exercise as Jaid had, so Wyman looked for a stand-in.

Crosby was the prime candidate, but he had already built a nurturing relationship with Drew which could cloud the issue. Instead, she turned to her husband. As hoped, Drew found it as natural as acting work, and Dallas Taylor knew enough about John to let her vent while also providing some answers. Gradually Drew learned that it was all right to love her father, but it was impossible to have him in her life.

*

By December 1988, Drew was a stronger, healthier person and, although obviously nervous, felt she could finally make it on her own. 'For weeks I kept on asking when I'd be able to leave,' she recalls. 'When I did get a date, I just burst into tears with this big smile on my face.' She was due to leave just before Christmas.

Believing that she had cured her addictions and their root causes, Drew thought she might tell her story. She realized that as a celebrity she could use her experiences to stop other teenagers with similar insecurities from turning to substance abuse. She just wasn't sure how or when to present herself, but that decision was rudely taken out of her hands.

Jaid was waiting in the reception at ASAP to take Drew to a regular dentist appointment one day. A man claiming to be a father looking to check his child into the clinic was also there. As he was leaving with all the information, he turned to Jaid and asked her opinion on the centre, as a mother of a sick child. Naïvely trusting, Jaid began to answer his questions until she felt they were becoming too personal and specific. At that moment Drew bounded through the doors and hugged her mother.

'Aren't you Drew Barrymore?' enquired the impostor. 'How's your treatment going?'

Drew and Jaid ran to the car, but it was too late – at the eleventh hour, their cover had been blown. The tabloids were going to have a field day. ASAP's switchboard was inundated with reporters fishing for any details. Then they heard that the *National Enquirer* was set to splash a sensationalist version of Drew's battle across their pages. Concerned at how Drew would cope with this overwhelming pressure, staff at ASAP offered to allow her to go home a week early to deal with it, or to stay on in the safety of their centre.

All the temperamental Barrymore genes exploded and Drew erupted in a raw rage. Her mother and agent had gone to great lengths to keep her treatment quiet, and she knew plenty of famous people whose drug use was excused by some mystery illness – why was she, of all people, being exposed?

When she had calmed down, she carefully mulled over her options: she could either ignore it, deny it or admit it. Drew was of the opinion that it was usually best not to respond to gossip, but having already considered telling her story, she planned a counterattack that would show the world she was a success story – not an out-of-control addict, as the *Enquirer* was bound to say.

In her last week at ASAP, Drew sat down with Todd Gold, a reporter from *People* magazine, and spent seven hours describing her ordeal.

When she left the safe confines of ASAP on 21 December 1988, Drew had been sober for ninety-six days, she was 25 pounds lighter and looked and felt beautiful.

*

Christmas had always been a difficult season for Drew, as it is traditionally a time when families gather together. This year, she concentrated on self-preservation and spent a quiet festive period at home with Jaid in the apartment she'd only seen on a few occasions, and rarely sober.

The new year, however, was another matter. On 3 January, the *National Enquirer*'s headline read: 'E.T. Star In Cocaine And Booze Clinic – At 13! The Shocking Untold Story'.

The public were staggered. *E.T.* co-star Henry Thomas summed it up, saying, 'It's kind of shocking that this little girl you knew when she was six and in pigtails was doing cocaine.' The Barrymores were besieged by phone calls and reporters staked out their house.

Always resilient, Drew seemed to be holding up. She even found work, although it was a little unorthodox. ABC were filming an after-school special entitled *Getting Straight*, a drama about teenage drug use. It was shot at the ASAP hospital in Van Nuys that Drew had only just left. The short film follows Jeff Hoyt, a sixteen-year-old who can't believe he's in the unit and won't admit that he has an addiction. He believes his fellow patients, other teens at varying stages of the programme, are losers. Drew took on the all-too-familiar part of Susan, an addict, alcoholic and bulimic.

The star of the show is Corey Feldman. Feldman, four years Drew's senior, had been acting since the age of three, had a recurring role in *Mork And Mindy* at the beginning of the 1980s and broke into movies aged fourteen with a superb performance in Rob Reiner's *Stand By Me*. *Getting Straight* also featured another former child star, Tatum O'Neal, as Susan's counsellor. The daughter of Ryan O'Neal, Drew's screen father in *Irreconcilable Differences*, Tatum's career had somewhat peaked with an early Oscar win for *Paper Moon*, and she had not worked since 1985.

Unfortunately, the message film is a little too neatly wrapped up, but there is an outstanding scene where the teenagers confront their parents, during which Drew oozes realism. Although at the time she said she was happy to do the film to help other teenagers, she ungraciously admitted years later, 'Believe me, from being the most famous child in the world to doing an after-school special is kind of a bummer.'

During the second week of filming, Drew's counter-exposé was printed in *People* magazine. She said of her decision to tell her story: 'I wanted people to know that I wasn't shooting heroin every night. I wanted people to know I had a problem and that I was just getting treatment for it.'

She was relieved to have her version of events in the public domain and, more importantly, was thrilled when *People* magazine received several sackloads of positive letters. Of course, there were a few responses expressing horror at Drew's or Jaid's behaviour, but the vast majority were from well-wishers, praising her for being so brave and saying that her article had helped them.

When Drew was interviewed while filming *Getting Straight*, she came across as an odd mix of an immature girl who liked fish because 'they don't meow and they don't smell', and a world-weary adult who had dealt with addiction and rehabilitation. She explained that she was sober, but she was taking it one day at a time. She now had a different circle of friends and, although she was sad to say goodbye to her old crowd, she knew she had to remove temptation and move forward.

For a couple of months after *Getting Straight* Drew dated Corey Feldman, who had also led quite a full life. By the time he was fifteen, the actor's parents had embezzled all the money he had earned as a child star, so he sued them and became legally emancipated. Unfortunately Feldman was not averse to indulging in cocaine or heroin himself (rather ironically, given his role in the film) and within a year-and-a-half was arrested twice for possession of both drugs. 'Any kid can screw up. But if you have money and fame and no privacy, you can really, *really* screw up,' he later lamented.

*

Struggling through the early months of 1989, Drew appeared to be dry rather than clean as the new group of friends she insisted on hanging out with turned out to be drug users. The media, having only just unearthed the scandal, seemed determined to bring her down and printed several stories about Drew being seen drinking and snorting cocaine in clubs.

Back at school after an extended hiatus, Drew kept her head down while her publicists issued statements refuting the claims: 'Drew's doing well. She's right on schedule with her rehabilitation. There have been no setbacks.'

She was also busy writing her own story in full. 'Opening up about my childhood really helped me come to terms with what had gone on in my life,' she says. 'Writing is a marvellous way to get things out of your system.' Drew wasn't the first Barrymore to pen an autobiography. Diana's book *Too Much, Too Soon* was a bestseller, and the triumvirate of Barrymore actors, Lionel, Ethel and John, had all published their own memoirs over the years.

All the major publishing houses were interested in Drew's story, but she chose Simon & Schuster, as they allowed her to dictate what was said (such as changing various names to protect her friends) and the direction of the book. 'Of course, since I am not an author, I had to have a co-writer, and they were very flexible about who I would use,' she adds. Reunited with Todd Gold, the *People* magazine reporter to whom she had bared her soul while still in ASAP, Drew began work on *Little Girl Lost*. As she wrote in the prologue, she was still undergoing intensive outpatient therapy, but was 'excited to be free in the world again and able to tell the happy story of my recovery'.

Feeling empowered by her revelations in therapy concerning her relationships with men, Drew felt comfortable enough to go the extra step, despite the fact that she was under the legal age of consent. Shortly before her fourteenth birthday, Drew lost her virginity. She has kept the identity of her one-time-only lover secret, not least because the experience was less than memorable.

Instead, come March, Drew had found a new boyfriend from Beverly High School. Naming him Sam in *Little Girl Lost*, Drew was bowled over by the dark-haired sixteen-year-old. After a relaxed dinner date, he took her to his parents' boat, where instead of a bottle of champagne, he had laid out a bottle of Evian in an ice bucket.

However, that Drew seemed to be coping was just an illusion.

On the eve of her sixth month of sobriety in mid-March, Drew went out with a friend she called 'Andie' in her autobiography. Andie was another wild child, and while she and Drew were driving around Hollywood together, she produced some marijuana. She lit a joint and absently passed it to Drew. Without any qualms, the recovering addict took the spliff and inhaled. She didn't want to break her sobriety; she just wanted to get high.

Drew managed to convince herself that her reasoning was acceptable, but as the dope wore off she lost her nerve, realizing what she had done. Just as Andie turned to Drew, a car coming the other way crossed the central reservation and collided with them. Drew was thrown headfirst into the windscreen and was knocked out.

Groggily, Drew came to and a shaken Andie took her home, where Jaid fussed over her. In the midst of all this love and attention from her mother, she couldn't possibly tell her about the joint.

The following day, Drew was awarded a chip to mark her six months of sobriety. Jaid was bursting with pride; Drew was overwhelmed by her deception.

Andie promised to keep quiet and Drew returned to normal life. She did well at school, started auditions for work and began dating an actor she calls 'Peter' in *Little Girl Lost*. She continued to attend her AA meetings and outpatient therapy, and soon managed to convince herself that she had nearly eight months of sobriety.

*

In the middle of May 1989, it happened again. For no apparent reason, Drew and Andie got stoned in the middle of the afternoon. They were so far gone that they actually missed the Bangles concert they were due to attend that night.

This time, Drew found it harder to ignore her relapse. During one poignant AA meeting, a patient expressed the remorse she felt after getting loaded and lying about it. The message hit home. Drew was consumed with guilt.

As Drew was struggling to deal with her culpability, so she found that her life began to fall apart. The old habit of fighting with her mother resurfaced; she became more reclusive and began pushing both Jaid and Peter away. With nowhere else to turn, her mother and boyfriend formed an unlikely friendship, which only fuelled Drew's feelings of rejection. After one particularly bad fight with her mother, Drew went and talked to David Crosby. Although this helped, she neglected to mention the real problem, so it was no solution.

By June, the situation in the Barrymore household was so unbearable that Drew moved into a poky West Hollywood apartment with Edie, her ex-ASAP friend. Through connections, Drew got a job as a doorperson in three different clubs and was initially excited about living on her own. But the bubble soon burst when Drew began to dwell on thoughts of her mother and Peter, her broken sobriety and returned mood swings. She sank lower into her depression and gained 10 pounds in weight.

By the beginning of July, things were coming to a head. On 1 July John Barrymore II telephoned out of the blue and left a message for her to call him urgently. When she did so, he was predictably asking for money.

'I flew off the handle,' recalls Drew. 'Everything was coming down on me. I called my mom crying, and she goes, "Oh, honey, by the way, I'm leaving for New York tomorrow." ' Drew was distraught – not only was her mother going away for the Independence Day weekend, but she was going with Peter.

Having fought with Edie, Drew went out shopping with Andie and they bought and smoked some marijuana. They went out clubbing most of the night and Drew spent the night at Andie's.

On 4 July Drew returned to her small flat alone and cried her eyes out. Edie happened to call and Drew sobbed to her for a while. Edie and her boyfriend hurried straight back to the apartment and tried to talk Drew out of her melancholy. But by now Drew was hysterical and they ended up in a slanging match.

What happened next was a dramatic cry for help. Drew knew she was out of control, but couldn't bring herself to articulate the words she wanted to say. In a desperate bid to make Edie understand the gravity of the situation, Drew picked up a kitchen knife.

'I didn't ever intend to take my life,' she explains in *Little Girl Lost*. 'I did, however, think of the knife as a giant exclamation point, something that as I brought the blade to my wrist would allow Edie to hear my cry for help and convince her beyond a doubt that I needed professional attention, and needed it fast.'

Clutching the knife in her trembling right hand, Drew made a faint scratch on her left wrist. Not paying attention due to the fierce argument she was having simultaneously, Drew made two more marks. On the third cut, the knife slipped and the blade sliced cleanly through her flesh. Drew saw the blood pour out and passed out cold.

She was rushed to the emergency room at Cedars Sinai Medical Center where her wrist was stitched up. Finally receiving the attention she desired, Drew told the medical staff that she needed to return to ASAP and a transfer was arranged.

*

While the media blew the incident out of proportion with headlines like '*E.T.* Star, 14, Attempts Suicide By Slashing Wrist', Drew quietly re-entered the ASAP clinic. The addict, who had previously thought she had 'hit her bottom', now rightly knew the meaning of the phrase.

'My counsellors sat me down and said: "You've been close to death before, and you're heading in that direction. This is your last chance, or you can die." I knew they were right,' recalls Drew solemnly.

'It keeps you humble when you think that everyone hits bottom in their life at least once. For me, life is about experience. I want to suck the marrow out of every day of life. I don't want anything to pass me by.'

She knew she had let herself down, but was more embarrassed by the disrespect she had shown to the ASAP staff. In particular, she couldn't bring herself to tell Betty Wyman and Lori Cerasoli that she had broken her sobriety. Instead, she told Jaid, who sighed and passed on the information.

They let Drew settle back in first, but before long raised the issue in one of the group therapy sessions.

'So, Drew, you're the one who got high at six months and eight months. Tell us about the value of being honest with yourself,' challenged Cerasoli.

The relapsed addict was taught a valuable lesson about lying that afternoon.

'The truth is that you are never fully mended,' she acknowledges. 'There is no happy ending because there is no end to the struggle for a clean and sober life.'

Unlike on previous visits, Drew did not rebel at the strict regime. Not only did she know the drill backwards, but she wanted to be there. She was ready to put her past behind her.

Spurred on by her potential brush with death, Drew's spirituality was reawakened and she claims she felt the supernatural support of her ancestors. 'I had other family members whose ghostly spiritual blood was running through my veins, encouraging me to right my wrongs and kick the demons, so that I didn't end up being just a total waste.'

Although Jaid and Drew's relationship had been previously pinpointed and addressed as a source of conflict, it was now suggested that Jaid should seek some individual therapy for her natural drift towards co-dependency. So, while Drew focused on the familiar pattern of therapy sessions, Jaid was sent to The Meadows, Wickenburg, Arizona, for her own treatment. Established in 1978, the four-star rehab centre is situated in the foothills of the Sonoran Desert and boasts mountain views, blue skies, a gym and an outdoor pool. Despite its glorious location, Jaid checked herself out after just six hours.

Drew quite understandably lost her temper – she said that she would try anything to save their relationship, but if her mother wasn't willing then she wouldn't come home. Guilt-tripped into readmitting herself, Jaid endured a gruelling six-week stay.

'I come from a very dysfunctional family,' Drew's mother admits. 'I grew up in a violent household with a lot of anger, so my frame of reference for a solid family structure didn't exist.' At The Meadows Jaid learned to be more consistent in her handling of Drew, and how to be a parent in a constructive way rather than the mish-mash of 'mother, manager, drill sergeant, and friend' she used to complain about. 'When one assumes too many roles, none are done well,' she says.

At the end of August, in a reverse situation, Drew attended The Meadows for a family week. Where previously Jaid had had to sit back and accept her daughter's tirades in therapy sessions, here the tables were turned and Jaid was the patient. Drew was attacked for being insincere and unemotional. However, they both emerged from that week with a positive attitude and hope for the future.

*

Drew's autobiography ended just before her release from rehab for what she hoped would be the final time.

'I'm looking ahead to the start of school, making movies and just being honest with myself,' she wrote. 'I'm feeling stronger personally. And that's me, Drew Barrymore, age fourteen, today. I have to accept this person, frailties and all, for who she is, and not try to be someone else.'

Betty Wyman explains, 'The disease of alcoholism is one based on relapse, so there's no guarantee that next year it won't happen again.' Of this Drew was aware, but knowing where her weaknesses lay was crucial. 'When you find out some horrible news and you almost don't know how to handle it – that's when you're truly put to the test, because you have to overcome your temptation.'

But she was not alone. In September, when Drew was released, rather than going straight home as before, this time she spent the last three months of the year living with David Crosby and Jan Dance.

Theirs was viewed as a halfway house to help Drew readjust properly. Unlike the haphazard schedule with Jaid, here Drew was privy to a conventional household with curfews and a set dinner time. 'Drew tests limits, but if she sees you're unbending, she conforms to limits very well,' explains Betty Wyman.

'I would not presume to try and supplant her parents,' said Crosby. 'But she needed to be around some people who were committed to sobriety, and God knows, Jan and I are. We put a lot of energy into staying straight.'

'When I got out, I realized how lucky I was,' said Drew, who changed her weekend pastimes in accordance with her programme. 'I go to the movies, go out to lunch, go out to an AA meeting,' she said at the time. 'I've stopped going to clubs and parties, so basically I have fun, hanging out with my friends.' Along with her new routine, Drew attended school; but while she could improve her grades, she couldn't control the attitude of the other children. Some things hadn't changed: she was still viewed as an outcast – not only was she a famous actress, she was now also a high-profile recovering addict.

Eventually she teamed up with another oddball, Jenny Brown, and the two soon clicked. 'We were both awkward, then all of a sudden life made total sense because of her,' recalls Drew. 'We ended up being great friends. It's so interesting. I learned so much about human behaviour. Why would people be so cruel? It gets you nowhere. I think it is the awkward person who flourishes in life because of their sensitivity. I don't harbour any resentment, but it was a lonely experience.'

Drew was clearly thriving under the close supervision of Crosby and Dance, and by the time she came to leave, she had even worked through a lot of her complicated issues with men. She had been forced to re-evaluate her attitude because for the first time in her life she was living with another man, a paternal figure. 'At first I didn't know how to deal with it,' she recalls. 'I wasn't used to having to answer to a man, but eventually it was really great.'

She soon realized that her constant need to seek attention from boys, which had seen her jump from boyfriend to boyfriend, was an obvious attempt to fill the void left by her father's rejection. 'Basically, what I was looking for in men or boys was acceptance,' explains Drew. 'You want to feel pretty, you want to feel loved, you want to be hugged, you want to feel adored.' She even began to understand why she was driving partners away. 'You're afraid of losing him, so you start acting crazy,' she continues. 'You can't do anything without him, you're in his face all the time which makes him claustrophobic, so then he pushes you away. Because you're feeling so rejected, you begin to act like someone you're not just to get his approval.'

There was one final piece to fit into the jigsaw. John Barrymore II had asked to see Drew. Although she had agreed, she was shaking when she walked into the Los Angeles restaurant. They sat down together, shared a cigarette and had a chat.

'I want to tell you something,' said John in earnest. 'I want you to know that I love you and that I'm truly sorry that I've never been able to be there for you. I probably won't ever be able to be there for you, but I never take for granted that you are my daughter.'

Drew began to sob silently. She had waited fourteen years to hear those words, and the sincere apology, combined with her current understanding of addiction, began to ease the pain and heartache he had caused all her life.

In December, just before Drew was due to return to her home to live with Jaid, Crosby and Dance took her on holiday to Hawaii. Drew was a little apprehensive about going at first because she didn't want to leave her friends. 'But once she hit the beach and the surfers took one look at her, that was it,' laughed Crosby. 'She spent the rest of the time on the beach with a bunch of guys sitting around her!'

As everyone could see, she was now a much healthier, more rounded human being. At the beginning of 1990 Drew moved back in with her mother and started life afresh. 'It's kind of like watching your baby walk off into traffic,' said Crosby. 'But I have a feeling she'll make it.'

The Barrymore triumvirate: Lionel, Ethel and John, respectively Drew's great-uncle, great-aunt and grandfather.

The romance between John 'The Great Profile' Barrymore and his third wife, Dolores Costello, carried the 1927 film *When A Man Loves*.

Classical good looks and a famous surname enabled John Barrymore II to star in several B-movies, but he was plagued by the family's addictive nature.

John II's third wife, Jaid, was a Hollywood wannabe who became infatuated by his handsome features and star status.

A celebration of the Barrymore dynasty was held in New York in 1982. Drew, a fifth-generation member, was accompanied by Jaid and her half-brother, John Barrymore III.

Drew, dressed as a fairy-tale princess, attended the 1983 Oscars ceremony, at which *E.T.* was nominated for nine Academy Awards.

'She was one of the most remarkable children I had ever met,' says Steven Spielberg, who became Drew's godfather. 'She's wonderfully funny and spontaneous – she just melted me.'

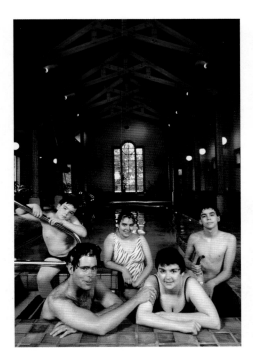

One of Drew's many adopted families: Stephen King, his wife, Tabitha, and their children, Owen, Naomi and Joe, at home in Bangor, Maine.

Top: Anna Strasberg, Drew's godmother, applies the finishing touches before a photo shoot.

Above: David Crosby and Jan Dance provided Drew with a halfway house after rehab.

Drew was an adorable, affable little girl who charmed everyone who met her.

Even before she hit double figures, Drew was at her happiest with a drink in one hand and a cigarette in the other.

Experimenting with a sexy image in a home photo shoot, aged twelve.

The prepubescent Drew was at an awkward in-between phase – heavy, moody and out of work.

Drew's changing boyfriends (*clockwise from top left*): Balthazar Getty, Leland Hayward, Jeremy Thomas, Luke Wilson, Eric Erlandson, Jamie Walters.

Above left: Drew became a spokesperson for the Female Health Foundation in 1997, promoting the use of the Female Condom.

Above right: Drew's affinity with animals dated from her childhood; she has helped causes such as the Wildlife Waystation and People for the Ethical Treatment of Animals (PETA).

Left: Drew considered her photo shoot for *Playboy* in 1995 a 'daring adventure', but her godfather, Steven Spielberg, sent her a blanket with a note saying: 'Cover yourself up.'

PLAYBOY

JANUARY 1995 • $5.95

ENTERTAINMENT FOR MEN

Drew BARRYMORE IN THE FLESH

HOLIDAY
ANNIVERSARY
ISSUE

PLAYBOY
INTERVIEW
Wham! Bam!
JEAN-CLAUDE
VAN DAMME

CLARENCE
THOMAS
RAGE STALKS
THE JUSTICE

SEX AND
PROZAC
THE UNTOLD
STORY

PLUS
BRUCE JAY
FRIEDMAN
DANNY GLOVER
ROBERT JAMES
WALLER

TOM
SNYDER
LATE NIGHT
BIG MOUTH

PLAYMATE
REVIEW
COLLEGE HOOPS
PREVIEW
AND MUCH
MUCH MORE

A RIOTOUS
YEAR IN SEX

After numerous hoaxes and a false wedding, Drew and Tom Green were finally engaged in July 2000 and married a year later.

It was Drew's dog, Flossie, who raised the alarm and saved her and Tom Green from a fire in February 2001 which completely gutted her house.

After an overwhelmingly cathartic experience filming the adaptation of Beverly Donofrio's memoir *Riding In Cars With Boys*, and with Tom Green's support and encouragement, Drew was finally reconciled with her mother in December 2000 after years of estrangement.

'[Drew]'s like a sister to me, somebody I would really fight to protect,' says Courtney Love, one of Drew's famous friends.

Drew made her disapproval of George W. Bush abundantly clear before his election and actively opposed the war on Iraq in 2003.

'I sort of change the shape of my face,' says Drew of the simple trick she employs to disguise herself in public. 'I don't even know that I do it anymore.'

'Fabrizio is a total gift,' says Drew, although she remains otherwise uncharacteristically tight-lipped about her latest beau.

13

INDEPENDENT WOMAN

As 1990 began, Drew was making amends. Her autobiography was published early in the year, putting an end to the scandalous tabloid stories alleging relapses that emerged on a regular basis.

'When it came out, I was very nervous,' says Drew. 'For the first two days I stayed in my house. Then a couple of weeks later my publisher called and said, "I just wanted to congratulate you on being a best-selling author!" I don't give a damn that I'm a best-selling author . . . The point was that I reached tons of people.'

If that was her goal, Drew certainly achieved it. *Little Girl Lost* was a bestseller; Drew continued to receive letters from families that she had helped and people would stop her in the street to thank her for being brave enough to expose her problems. Years later, she still has few reservations. 'Sometimes I want to apologize to people for having to take the time to study me, but that's belittling myself, and it's rude to them,' she says.

'Writing a book was a positive thing, and there are two reasons why: one, if it makes someone feel like they're not alone because they have a weird family or they feel the need to try what is supposedly dark, then that's supercool; and two, it enables me to not have to pretend that I'm perfect. By putting it all out there, I am completely liberated.'

For her fifteenth birthday, Drew was thrown a party at the super-trendy Grotto Room by her friend Ele Keats, the eighteen-year-old actress, with celebrity guests including Keanu Reeves and Scott Baio.

For the time being, Drew had a new beau on her arm. For a change only one month older than Drew, Paul Balthazar Getty descended from J. Paul Getty, the famous oil tycoon. He was currently starring as Ralph in Harry Hook's film adaptation of *Lord Of The Flies* and receiving huge critical acclaim. Balthazar, as he was known, provided Drew with the immense bolstering she required.

'My ex-boyfriend was very supportive during those times and I'll always be grateful to him,' she says. They were often seen at parties and ceremonies, giving rise to claims that they were dating, although such rumours were usually denied, and there was talk of a film called *Ectopia* starring the pair, to be directed by Rene Daalder. 'It's totally a transition because I play the head cheerleader,' said Drew at the time. 'She's very sweet and innocent – Miss Popular.'*

However, not everything in Drew's life was going smoothly; another attempt at cohabiting with her mother was rapidly disintegrating. They were back in each other's pockets and although they had both been through extensive therapy to save their relationship, things clearly wouldn't improve while they were cooped up under the same roof.

There had been too many years where Jaid's role was blurred between mother and manager, and Drew couldn't distinguish between the things she was doing for herself and what was to please her mother.

'If the parent–child role gets reversed and the parent makes the child their partner, the child doesn't really get to be a child,' says Drew. 'It makes the relationship very confusing . . . Not only that, but she was my manager. You could see the disaster coming.'

So, at the worldly age of fifteen, Drew followed in the footsteps of Casey Brodsky in *Irreconcilable Differences* and ex-beau Corey Feldman, submitting a petition to the courts to legally emancipate herself from her parents. She was asking the judge to make her an adult in the eyes of the law, which would mean that she could make all her own decisions, work without child-labour restrictions and live on her own without a guardian.

The case took months to get to court, but after a long wait, Drew was finally free. 'The judge said he couldn't turn back the clock, he could only turn it forward,' she said at the time, elated at her win. But Drew was aware of all that victory entailed. 'It was the hardest decision I ever had to make because I knew I would finally be on my own,' she

---

*It was not long after Drew and Balthazar parted company that the young actor succumbed to the lure of drugs. His father was a drug addict, and Balthazar reportedly only narrowly missed a drug-related arrest in 1998.

says. 'I had to get an apartment and a job. Most of all, I had to figure out what kind of person I wanted to be.'

Consequently, 1990 turned out to be a year of firsts for Drew: a voyage of self-discovery.

Although she had enjoyed her education more since kicking her addictions and half-hearted attitude, the first thing she did was leave school. 'I dropped out rather early, which I don't recommend,' says Drew, who always hoped to make it back to further education.

*

Drew moved out of the Barrymore residence in 1990 and found herself a small apartment. Initially, she wouldn't be sharing with anyone, something which was important to her personal growth.

'I've learned to be more responsible,' she said the following year. 'I have my own house, take care of three pets, two cars. I keep all my appointments. I remind myself to brush my teeth before going to bed. I do my own laundry and shopping. I'm sure people think I eat chocolates in bed all day, and don't I wish that were true. But it's not. I have a housecleaner one day a week, but she only dusts. Some days it's hard because I don't want to deal with reality, but I have to – I've already done non-reality.' And, with a bit of distance between them, Drew and Jaid found that they were able to maintain regular contact and repair some of the damage.

While Drew was waiting for acting jobs to come through, she had to undertake other work to pay for her flat. 'I didn't know how I was going to pay my rent,' she said, 'so I worked at a coffeehouse [The Perk Up]. You have to do everything: clean the bathroom, wash the dishes, meet the muffin man at 6 a.m.' She also took on some part-time work at the music store Music Plus.

These temporary menial jobs gave Drew the time she needed to make firm decisions about her future. 'I thought I would take a break and see how I felt, but I realized I would be lying to myself if I didn't continue to make movies,' she says. 'It's in my soul, it's in my blood, it's my calling and it's everything I've ever wanted to do. I decided to work my way back slowly. I never gave up hope.'

Her goal now was to earn the trust of film studios once more.

'People wouldn't touch me; they just thought I was some loser drug addict,' she says. 'I thought I would never work again.' But knowing that it was her destiny, the actress drew on all her resources and remained resilient. She read endless scripts and attended as many auditions. She tried to keep her spirits up and stayed positive. 'I'm auditioning a lot but there's nothing definite. I just want to keep working and acting – that's my natural drug,' she affirmed in an interview during 1990.

As the studios were still scared to hire the ex-drug user, she failed screen tests for *Cape Fear*, *Edward Scissorhands* and *Bram Stoker's Dracula*. During her audition for Martin Scorsese, who was casting the remake of *Cape Fear*, Drew ruined her chances by trying to overact. 'I never act, I just become people,' she explains, harking back to Steven Spielberg's valuable advice. 'But I really wanted to impress him, so I acted all over the place and it was just the biggest disaster of my life. I remember walking out of there just so humiliated. I don't even know if they responded. And do you know what? They didn't have to.'

The role of the awkward, rebellious daughter flirting with a psychotic Robert De Niro in the 1991 film was won by Juliette Lewis. At just two years older than Drew, this was Lewis's breakthrough performance and it stood her in good stead, earning her an Academy Award nomination.

Winona Ryder had otherwise cornered the market in playing alienated or confused teenagers, starring in a number of films including *Heathers*, *Edward Scissorhands* and *Mermaids*. But Ryder wasn't content just to snatch the role in *Edward Scissorhands* from Drew; she also successfully made the transition from teen roles to those requiring greater maturity. Following a turn as a taxi driver in Jim Jarmusch's *Night On Earth*, she starred in Francis Ford Coppola's lavish adaptation *Bram Stoker's Dracula* opposite Gary Oldman, Anthony Hopkins and Keanu Reeves.

'In the beginning, people at auditions had this attitude of, "You should be so grateful," but I already was,' says Drew. 'They knocked me down over and over again. I would go home and cry.'

Not only was Drew wondering whether she would ever be given the opportunity to act again, but she wanted to make the transition to adult roles, like Winona Ryder.

'There are many who don't make it,' she admits. 'I didn't want to be cast by the wayside, particularly when I had worked so hard in cleaning myself up.'

Fortunately for Drew, she had often played a child in adult films (*Irreconcilable Differences*, *Cat's Eye* and *Firestarter*), whereas her *See You In The Morning* co-star Macauley Culkin, who was finding fame in children's films (*Home Alone* in 1990 and its sequel two years later), struggled to be taken seriously later in life.

Being a teenager, Drew's best hope was therefore to play a teenager in adult rather than teen movies, but in 1990 she would take pretty much anything on offer for someone to show some faith in her once again.

*

While trawling the audition circuit in 1990 to no avail, Drew at last quit the diet she had been on ever since being told to lose weight at the age of twelve. Part of her growing up meant coming to terms with her voluptuous figure and embracing her curves, rather than trying to slim them down.

The day before one of her auditions, Drew really fancied a plate of macaroni and cheese, but held off because of its lasting consequences: 'It gives you cellulite and sticks to your intestines,' she says. 'I was worried because I had to stay thin. But I just said, "I'm gonna eat it and I don't care what happens. I'm just tired of living my life feeling guilty about every single bit of food I put in my mouth."' Since then, she has indeed eaten according to her natural appetite and not concerned herself with Hollywood's penchant for waif-like actresses.

Her pasta and dairy fetish aside, Drew didn't have a problem resisting many sticky, sweet puddings. 'I know it's rich and pure and beautiful, but [chocolate] just tastes like caca,' she once opined, eloquent as ever. 'It's like stomping muddy combat boots that have been through mud and shit-piles on my palate and taste buds.' Instead, she preferred 'strawberry and lime jelly – low sugar, but tastes like it has lots more calories!' Garlic receives a similar response from Drew to chocolate, leading her to suggest that she is even allergic to it. 'It's disgusting, that's how I feel about garlic. It tastes like dirty feet to me.'

Feeling more confident about her looks than she had in a long time, Drew got involved in another romance: this time she was snapped draped all over Carlo Ponti Jr. A far cry from the nights they spent smoking pot and getting stoned together, now the couple appeared in public, clean and happy.

This success in affairs of the heart coincided with a job. Drew was finally awarded the chance to prove herself, winning the lead role opposite Kris Kristofferson in *No Place To Hide*. Kristofferson, both a pop star and an actor, had achieved fame in the 1970s and 1980s, but during this period his reputation was little more than a memory and he fell back on television or straight-to-video B-movies. Unfortunately for him and for Drew, *No Place To Hide* was no different.

The gory thriller shows a troubled ballerina persuading her little sister, Tinsel Hanley (Barrymore), to hide a vital videotape before she is slain on stage during a performance. The detective (Kristofferson) finds the sister uncooperative and sends her to an orphanage until she too is attacked. Determined to solve the case, he takes Tinsel under his wing. The unlikely pair find themselves on the run, trying to stay alive while he tracks down the killer.

Directed by Richard Danus, the adequate cast also includes Martin Landau and O. J. Simpson, but the film is predictable and poorly produced. Worse still, Tinsel was far from the adult, or barely even teen, role for which Drew was searching.

'They bound my chest, didn't put me in any make-up, covered me up in clothes, and put my hair in pigtails,' she recalls. 'I was like, "Wait a minute, when I took this role, she was supposed to be sort of 'coming of age'." And they said, "No! You don't understand – this is a father–daughter thing." But it worked out OK, because I look really young in the film.'

The only consolation was that Drew was shown to be reliable and hard-working, and consequently she went straight from one film set to another. Her role in *Motorama* was marginally better. 'It's a very black comedy,' describes Drew. 'I have a cameo as this fantasy girl. I stand in the ocean in a grass skirt and a bikini.'

The story is a rather twisted version of the classic road movie: 'Motorama' is a promotional road game sponsored by Chimera Gas Company, whereby players have to collect enough game cards from petrol stations all over the country to spell out the game's title, and the winner is promised $500 million. A ten-year-old boy (Jordan Christopher Michael) is fed up of his abusive parents, so he cashes in his piggy-bank savings, steals a bright-red classic Mustang and heads off on a surreal drive through America. His various adventures along the way feature cameos from Jack Nance, Dick Miller and even the pop singer Meat Loaf, alongside Drew.

Directed by Barry Shils, this very bizarre fantasy at least offered Drew the chance to be alluring, but again its greatest input to her career was in showing her dedication and ability.

'I've always felt an incredible pressure to carry on the name,' she said the following year, 'but once I accepted the fact that it was something I didn't have to do, but instead wanted to do, my work became a lot easier.

'People were sceptical about me, which I can understand, knowing what's been written about me. However, I worked hard, went out on zillions of auditions, let people ask the hard questions, and then once I was given the chance to work, I kicked butt.'

*

If *Motorama* was daft and afforded Drew minimal screen time, her next task was a minuscule cameo in the low-budget horror comedy *Waxwork II: Lost In Time*. The sequel to 1988's *Waxwork* starred Zach Galligan and Monika Schnarre as boyfriend and girlfriend Mark and Sarah in a time-travel adventure through a series of interlinking film spoofs, satirizing such classics as *Frankenstein*, *Alien* and *Night Of The Living Dead*. Jumping through time windows as if they've 'stumbled into God's Nintendo game', Mark and Sarah meet monsters, zombies and hunchbacks to the tune of crummy organ music.

Notable performances include a camp cameo from *The Avengers* veteran Patrick Macnee as Sir Wilfred and a literally eye-popping appearance from Spandau Ballet's Martin Kemp as Baron Frankenstein. Completely *un*-notable, unfortunately, are Drew Barrymore's entire three seconds in a minute homage to a black-and-white silent movie. She plays a so-called Vampire Victim, be-wigged and clutching fellow Vampire Victim (Hadria Lawner) in bed as monsters leap around them – 'so-called', because the monsters don't really look like vampires and neither girl is a victim because they are not hurt in any way, shape or form.

It was a shame Drew's part was so small, because there are several other minor female roles in the film with far more screen time – and even lines of their own. Maybe Drew appeared as a personal favour to the director, Anthony Hickox, or perhaps she was attracted to the role because of her strange affinity with vampires.

'The prospect of me being part vampire seems to be an absolute possibility,' she would tell one disbelieving journalist a few years later. 'My mother, Jaid, wears only black – just like a vampire. And I'm positively allergic to garlic, which is used to ward them off.' As Jaid was born in Eastern Europe and the Barrymores can trace their roots back to Hungary, Drew believes she has solid links to Transylvania and should therefore endeavour to avoid wooden stakes, holy water and daylight at all costs.

*

In February 1991 Drew turned sixteen. Free from her vices, she now attended Alcoholics Anonymous meetings four nights a week. Although she had her own place, her own career and a past of which Jack Nicholson would have been proud, for the first time in about a decade Drew at last began to act her age. And she was enjoying it.

A lust for Jason Priestley from Aaron Spelling's *Beverly Hills 90210* was widely speculated on, with tabloids reporting that the actress had written him a fan letter. While that wasn't strictly accurate, she did confess to a crush on actor Johnny Depp.

Meanwhile, in reality, Drew was dating twenty-four-year-old Leland Hayward, an apprentice sound engineer. Like Drew, Hayward was from an established Hollywood family, the grandson of 1930s leading lady Margaret Sullavan.

After the actress was spotted wearing a diamond ring on her engagement finger, it was reported that the two were preparing to marry. Although Drew said, 'I am in love, really in love,' this latest development in her romantic life was also misleading.

'He bought me a diamond ring, and I wore it on that finger, so I suppose I asked for it,' she said later. 'But we were never engaged. I was joking. But what the hell, that's just one more misconception I'll have to live with . . .'

Notably, while Drew was dating Hayward, her resolve was threatened. These days she was far stronger, thanks to her (albeit broken) stints in rehab, but just occasionally she wavered. One of those times was at a party during the summer of 1991.

'Leland drank some soup that had been laced with magic mushrooms,' she recalls. 'He didn't know that the soup was spiked until someone told him. I was tempted to drink some, too, and trip along with him. Instead, I left the party and was fine, though I can't say much for Leland . . .'

Reading between the lines, maybe Drew realized at this point that she seriously needed to shift away from people who were prepared to dabble in what she couldn't, and soon after the relationship fizzled out.

14

LETHAL LOLITA

Shortly after Drew's sixteenth birthday, a role came in that was going to change Drew's professional life for good.

J. J. Harris sent on a script for a film called *Poison Ivy*, in which an attractive teenage girl charms her way into a rich family, seducing each member in turn before her deadly intentions become clear.

It was like no other role Drew had ever considered. 'Ivy', the name adopted by the girl in the film, would have to appear nearly naked, French kiss both men and women, and have sex with the fifty-eight-year-old father of her best friend. There was also a fair amount of murder involved, but that was becoming par for the course for Drew.

'At first when they told me there would be sexual stuff, I went "Hmmmmm . . .",' Drew admits. 'Then I read the script and found that every piece fits together.' Having long searched for the elusive role to effectively break her into mainstream movies, rather than the silly cameos currently on offer, this looked like her best chance yet.

'I had an ulterior motive,' Drew admits. 'It is very difficult for a child actor to make the transition to adult actor. I knew that if I came back as a sexy, evil character, people would be shocked into losing the whole idea of Gertie.

'I felt lucky. It was a daring movie and I liked the idea of shocking a few people. I loved Ivy so much for that and wanted to play her regardless of whether it was a good career move.'

But Drew was concerned to get her agent on board. 'I am very independent and I really want to make my own decisions,' says the actress, 'but it's very important that I have the word "Go" from J. J. – her input has had an incredible impact on my career and I hang out with her too, she's my friend.'

Once Drew had convinced Harris to give her the go-ahead, she then had to persuade the director, Katt Shea Ruben, who also co-wrote the script with her husband, Andy.

'I hadn't thought about Drew for the part at all,' says Ruben. 'But I knew the minute she walked up my front steps she was perfect. She's got this quality – it's kind of the angel and the devil wrapped into one. She's so seductive, she could manipulate anybody into doing whatever she wanted.'

And so Drew was cast in her dream role. She was deeply grateful for Ruben's decision.

'I often thought that my career was over because of all the problems I had,' she recalls. 'It had been hard for me to get good roles because of my past.'

Drew celebrated as only a thrifty teenager with an eye on the rent would: by indulging herself in some much-needed new clothes from her three favourite stores, Benetton, Aardvarks and Gap. 'I did some serious damage,' she laughs, referring to her balking credit card. It was nice to have some money for a change.

*

Filming for *Poison Ivy* began in May 1991, and Drew threw herself wholeheartedly into the role. 'I got to do things like kiss girls, push women off balconies, adulterate with Tom Skerritt . . . what fun to do that for three months!' She was her old self again, loving the cameras, the cast, the crew and lapping up each and every take.

Drew was fortunate to have been cast alongside some experienced and highly credible actors. *Roseanne*'s Sara Gilbert played Sylvie Cooper, the ostracized girl befriended by Ivy; Cheryl Ladd of *Charlie's Angels* played Sylvie's mother – locked away and dying of emphysema; and *Cheers* regular Tom Skerritt (who would receive accolades the following year for his starring role in Robert Redford's *A River Runs Through It*) played Sylvie's father – and Ivy's creepy love interest.

Ivy's sexuality was key to the movie; in many ways, she was a precursor to Mena Suvari's Angela in *American Beauty* (1999). Drew used one of her favourite fictional characters, Vladimir Nabokov's *Lolita*, as her blueprint. Nabokov's novel charts the unlikely relationship between Humbert Humbert, a middle-aged poet, and the twelve-year-old nymphet he calls 'Lolita'. Stanley Kubrick's film adaptation had long been one of Drew's best-loved movies, starring Sue Lyon, then sixteen, in the title role.

'Sue Lyon was so sexy in that movie,' she says. 'Every little detail I totally grooved on. *Lolita* became an idol to me.'

Although Ivy was older and slightly more streetwise than Drew's fantasy heroine, she was equally attractive.

'Ivy was the kind of girl who in reality you would *never* want to become, but maybe when you were younger you knew a girl like Ivy who made you say, "Why can't I be that free? Why can't I just do the things she does, even though what she does is wrong? At least she has the guts to go and do it," ' Drew explains. Of course, the actress herself had embarked on countless 'free' adventures of her own in her time, so she was able to bring a little of that real-life craziness to her character each day on set.

Relishing the lesbian undertones of the script, Drew launched into her odd relationship with Sara Gilbert's Sylvie with gusto.

'We have this friendship, with a twisted sexuality,' she explains. 'We don't have any love scenes, but we have one scene where we kiss, kind of. We were sort of giggly girls about it . . .' For the relatively down-played scene itself, Drew reveals, 'I took Sara's face in my hands and started licking her lips. Suddenly she opened her mouth and I stuck my tongue in – a full-tongue, major kiss!'

'She's intoxicating,' says Gilbert of her challenging co-star. 'She's an absolute extremist: if she does something, she has to live it and be it and consume it.' Gilbert and Drew soon became good friends – Gilbert was the same age as Drew and another Hollywood child who had grown up in the spotlight, thanks to her showbusiness background and ongoing part in the hit ABC sitcom *Roseanne*. She was also the sister of *Little House On The Prairie*'s Melissa Gilbert and would go on to work with Drew again in the future.

Kissing Gilbert might have seemed like child's play to Drew, but getting it on with a man over forty years her senior was something else. She'd had the occasional screen kiss, not to mention the attempted rape scene in *Far From Home*, but this was the first time Drew would simulate sex on screen.

It wasn't easy.

'I was much more nervous kissing Tom than Sara – he's like this elderly man who, you know, is extremely conservative,' Drew said at the time, showing her immaturity. 'I thought he'd just come right out on set and take over and everything would be perfect. But he was really shy, so I had to be the one with the ovaries and say, "OK! Let's go!"

'It's so hard to fake intimacy in front of a hundred people. Afterwards we'd sort of like shake hands, hug, laugh a little bit, and walk in opposite directions.'

And then there was the question of Ivy's nudity. Although, due to her emancipation, the law considered Drew two years older than she actually was, the film's producers ran into difficulties when it came to getting the censors to approve her steamier moments. To her horror, a stand-in was employed for the scene where Ivy's breasts are on display.

'I was really against it because I don't believe in body doubles,' Drew complained in a publicity interview for the film. 'I had to sit there and watch her do it, and I was cringing in my seat. It's difficult to watch someone fake you.'

Perhaps it was the unexpected developments with the body double, or perhaps it took Drew a while to recognize the depth of the character and project she'd taken on, but after the first honeymoon weeks of filming, the stress of being Ivy every day began to show. Her zeal for the troubled teen began to fray at the edges.

'It was really hard for me,' she said. 'I thought I would go insane. I'm a nice person. She's the evilest woman in the world, and sometimes I felt like I was going crazy. It was difficult because after a month I just wanted to be myself, but it was a great working experience because at the same time I loved being her.'

*

The opening scene to *Poison Ivy* is indisputably stunning. Swinging over a ravine on a rope in slow motion, Drew looks at once erotic and trashy in her ludicrously short skirt, leather biker jacket and cowboy boots. Her long peroxide perm trailing behind her in the breeze, her nose piercing, the tattoo on her upper thigh (a cross encircled by ivy) and just the look on her face suggest a wisdom beyond her years. She is otherworldly in her beauty – but has an exceedingly dangerous glint in her eye. Before the scene's close, the real-life animal lover has delivered a fatal blow to a dog which has been hit by a car. Another big clue to the film's content comes when she says she'll die happy if she has a sports car, a nice house and a family . . .

During an argument later in the film, Sylvie says Ivy 'looks like a slut' – and she's right. Drew's overly made-up features are big but scene-stealing, and her sexuality is childishly brazen. Ivy's subtle infiltration into the Cooper family home is ingenious, as she chooses a different method with each member. Even Fred the dog falls under her spell.

On examination, there was far more excitable hype about Drew's lesbian kisses than was necessary, but the sex scenes with Skerritt make for highly uncomfortable viewing. Too tame for true eroticism but too offbeat for the mainstream, there is no escaping the fact that Skerritt has crinkles and wrinkles while Drew looks so undeniably *young*. The worst scene must surely be the second time he approaches her: she masturbates him with her stiletto heel while he stimulates her orally – all on the opposite side of the bed to where his wife has passed out.

Poison Ivy is a very strange mixture of pulpy melodrama and authentic intrigue, made all the more watchable by the sheer beauty of the film (the countryside, the Coopers' mansion with its designer interior, and Drew herself). Skerritt is swarthily odious, Cheryl Ladd's gradual demise provides an interesting subplot, and Sara Gilbert is realistically annoying yet endearing.

In fact, there are solid performances all round – the film is only really let down by its occasional lapses into soft porn, steamy sax solos, clichés and plot inconsistencies (why, for example, doesn't the father notice the giveaway bruise of the steering wheel on Ivy's chest when they're having sex and she's nearly naked?).

If Drew wanted to achieve recognition as an adult, then this was certainly the film with which to do it, although in playing Ivy she also initiated her cinematic typecasting as a 'wild child'. In the movie she drives, drinks champagne, is tattooed and has various forms of sex – all underage, of course.

Poison Ivy is also very much a picture of its time. Released in May 1992, it jumped on the homicidal houseguest/ex-lover bandwagon set off by the success of *Fatal Attraction* in 1987: *Sleeping With The Enemy* (1990), *The Hand That Rocks The Cradle* (1991) and *Single White Female* (1992) were all films with a similar theme.

The video release of *Poison Ivy* sealed its somewhat dubious success, and regular showings on cable TV helped propel it to cult status. Two sequels were inspired by the film: *Poison Ivy 2: Lily* (1996), in which a girl discovers Ivy's diary and starts to mould herself in the image of the teenage temptress; and *Poison Ivy: The New Seduction* (1997), where Ivy's sister Violet takes over as the murderess on a mission. Drew was approached for the first of the sequels, as were Andy and Katt Shea Ruben, and the screenwriters, Melissa Goddard and Peter Morgan, but all declined to participate.

Enough was enough: Drew had made her comeback.

15

MY FRIENDS ARE MY FAMILY

'People were coming up to me on the set, going, "How does it feel to be a sex symbol?" I was like, "Me?!" I might be a sensual person, but I don't look at myself in the mirror and say, "Yeah baby, you've got it goin' on!"'

DREW BARRYMORE

If there was one thing *Poison Ivy* achieved, it was to open the door for casting directors to view Drew Barrymore: Child Star in a completely different light. 'Once people started seeing a little bit of footage, J. J. got all these calls, like, "We've got this role for Drew as a Lolita-esque nymphet,"' she recalls.

For Drew, it led to another form of emancipation. Calling it quits with Leland Hayward, the actress allowed a previously unseen part of herself to come to the fore: she became a born-again lesbian.

'I can totally see how women fall in love with other women, because it's like exploring yourself,' she had boldly declared after her kissing scene with Sara Gilbert. 'I've wished sometimes I could be a man, so I could take a woman.' Rumours began to fly around Hollywood that Leland had been dumped in favour of female model Lisa Reade, and the papers were full of Drew's flirtations with members of her own sex.

Drew positively encouraged the speculation at every available opportunity. It was rare for an actress of any description to be so open about her sexuality, but then again Drew was hungry for work. Judging by the piles of unread scripts on her living-room floor, the wild-child image (in fantasy, if not reality) suited her. She was a perfect pin-up for Generation X: a dangerous girl fitting in effortlessly with heroin chic, sexual exploration and the general apathy plaguing America's youth in the early 1990s.

'Do I like women sexually? Yes, I do. *Totally*,' she emphasized, four years later. 'When I was younger I was with a lot of women. Women are so much more selective with women than they are with men. You really have to like the person.

'I love a woman's body and I think that a man and a man together are beautiful, a woman and a woman together are beautiful and a man and a woman together are beautiful. I don't think there's anything wrong with that.' Drew's fascination with members of her own sex was not exclusive, however, and she continued to date boys as well as girls.

With the money Drew made from *Poison Ivy*, the sixteen-year-old who claimed to still suck her thumb now splashed out on an expensive breast-reduction operation. Ever since her twelfth birthday, Drew had hated the size of her breasts.

'I walked through life with missile tits,' she cringes. 'It was an eyesore in the middle of my body. It made me feel degraded, insecure, it made me slouch. On a small frame like mine, double Ds ain't comfortable.

'When your breasts are huge, you become very self-conscious because men look at them so much. One more Dolly Parton comment and I was about to lose my mind!'

Through the first half of her teens, Drew's resentment of the cruel stares grew until she could stand it no longer.

'I completely lost my identity,' she says. 'People would never look me in the eyes. They'd go, "Boy, you're really growing up," looking straight at my breasts.'

Drew's 34DD chest wasn't overly huge in itself, but the ex-avocado-binger was proud of the petite frame she had worked so hard to achieve. She hated the way that she looked heavy in anything she wore. The backache also got her down.

'The surgery changed my life,' she says today. 'It was the most wonderful choice I've ever made. All of a sudden this thing that was terribly depressing and scary and embarrassing was not a problem any more. I've never regretted doing it because I love my body the way it is now.'

Later in 1991, Drew celebrated her new-found figure – and bisexuality – by posing in a provocative, bosom-to-bosom embrace with model Rochelle Hunt for a glossy magazine.

*

Drew could have had her pick of any number of sexy roles that came flooding in after *Poison Ivy*, but her next work choice was a relatively low-key appearance in a TV film called *Sketch Artist*. She had met the cinematographer Phedon Papamichael on *Poison Ivy* and he became a casual boyfriend over the summer.

Born in Athens, Greece, Papamichael first arrived in America when he was six years old. He studied photography and art in Munich but decided to become a cinematographer, using his family connections and learning on the job. Papamichael would go on to receive much acclaim for his work on movies such as *While You Were Sleeping*, *America's Sweethearts*, *Phenomenon* and the recent *Identity*, but in 1991 he decided to switch focus and try his hand at directing for a change.

His debut as a director came with *Sketch Artist*, a feature for Showtime, the cable TV channel devoted to movies, in which a police artist (Jeff Fahey) realizes to his horror that the likeness he is drawing of a murderer closely resembles his wife (Sean Young). Quickly he changes his portrait and begins his own investigation of the crime.

Calling in a favour, Papamichael cast Drew as Daisy, the eyewitness who first describes the suspect. Drew's part was brief, as Daisy subsequently becomes a victim herself. Although the film was chilling enough and Papamichael received an ACE award nomination for his work the following year, his direction was criticized and he soon returned to cinematography. Similarly to *Poison Ivy*, *Sketch Artist* would spawn another sequel (*Sketch Artist II: Hands That See*) which would see a return to the screen for Fahey, but neither the director nor Drew.

*

Interviewed in September 1991, Drew Barrymore presented something of a dichotomy to her public. On one hand there was the wild child, who had been everywhere, done everything and dated everyone. On the other hand, she came across as incredibly young in print. And why not? She was still only sixteen.

Describing the house which she had bought back in May with some of the proceeds from *Poison Ivy*, Drew revealed she was currently living with two friends. Although her new home was fairly small, with only two bedrooms, the girls were happy to all sleep together in Drew's king-size bed, just like a permanent slumber party. Drew dodged the question of what happened when someone brought home a boyfriend by describing the room-mates' love lives as 'really boring'. She disclosed that, although she was keen to fall in love again, 'marriage is out of the question for the next twenty years. I'd like to have kids while I'm young, but not now – maybe when I'm twenty-three.'

Drew was also enthusiastic about The *E.T.* Adventure – a new, $40 million Spielberg-devised theme-park ride which had just opened at

Universal Studios alongside a similar *Backdraft* tribute. The *E.T.* attraction was a gentle ride with Elliott and E.T., who are pursued on their flying bicycle by government agents. Drew had attended the opening with Spielberg himself.

'We both rode on it. It was actually really cool! You're on this row of bicycles and you cruise through *E.T.*-land. I was really surprised.' During the ride, Drew apparently had time to reflect on how much had changed since she'd played six-year-old Gertie.

'I felt like, "Wow, I've really grown up!" But Steven still sees me as Gertie. It's funny when we go out somewhere and friends of his come up to us and they say, "Look at her! Do you see how grown-up she is?" But he can't get over it, you know?'

It seems incongruous to say that Drew Barrymore was fast developing into a young woman, considering everything that had gone before, but that was how she now alternatively presented herself to the outside world.

Delighting in make-up and beauty products ('I always have lipstick on, I feel naked without it, but I never wear make-up except maybe mascara'), Drew's fashion sense was early-era-Madonna-inspired thrift-shop cheap. 'My style is kind of hard to find in new stores, and if you do, it's, like, a thousand dollars,' she reasoned of her preference for charity shops and markets. 'I like antique dresses, little lace tops, and pyjama bottoms.'

It was all a far cry from the fairy-tale frocks she used to wear for a preteen night out on the tiles with her mother.

*

Since moving out, Drew's relationship with Jaid had markedly improved. Theirs was never going to be a typical mother–daughter bond, but at least they could relate in other ways.

The cross-and-ivy tattoo in *Poison Ivy* turned out to be a near-replica of a new addition to Drew's body art – sometime around Drew's birthday she and Jaid had celebrated by getting 'hers 'n' hers' tattoos on their ankles.

'Drew was desperate for a tattoo so I went with her to have it done,' says Jaid.

Drew designed the picture herself, choosing the juxtaposition of the religious symbol and creeping plant because she loved the meeting of spirituality with nature. As the needle pierced the tender flesh just above her right ankle, she called over to Jaid, 'Come on, Mom, you get one too!'

Her mother hesitantly agreed.

'I thought it would be cool, so I had a matching cross on my left ankle,' says Jaid. 'I didn't have the ivy, though – my pain threshold is much lower than Drew's!'

Although Drew was proud of the new tattoo, especially as it had come from her own drawing, she tended to wear cowboy boots to cover it up. 'No one sees it, just my friends,' she remarked. 'It's funny, the one person who's afraid of commitment has something that's pretty life-lasting!'

The cross inspired Drew to have another tattoo, also during 1991: a butterfly, which is to be found just underneath her navel. 'I love the metaphor of butterflies, that you can actually change and meta-morphose, and grow and become a more profoundly beautiful, capable human being,' she explains.

Famously around this time, Jaid took Drew out to a strip show. Reports have varied as to whether this was to celebrate her sixteenth birthday or was just a girls' night out, but either way it was a slightly different way of socializing with your mum. Apparently, the technically-but-not-legally underage girl was plucked from the audience at the Bar One lapdancing club in L.A. and pulled onto the stage, where the strippers began a more hardcore sex show. Drew was 'introduced' to the transvestite Pippi La Rouge by having her head buried between La Rouge's ample 'bosoms'. The event caused such a stir that the club was closed down the following day by city officials, and later shut for good by an L.A. judge.

As she should have anticipated, Drew found her picture in the papers for all the wrong reasons. The commotion was to haunt her for years to come, becoming synonymous with Drew's 'wild child' era: in 1995 she posed, smiling provocatively, on the front cover of *Premiere* magazine with a copy of a tabloid bearing the headline 'Drew Barrymore Dances At Sex Orgy As Mom Cheers Her On', and it was all revisited again in 2000 when a TV channel broadcast footage from the event.*

Although on the face of it Jaid and Drew had found a way in which they could communicate amicably, this period of getting matching tattoos and living it up in L.A. hotspots was relatively short-lived. Drew felt that she had moved on by moving out of the parental home, and she was beginning to tire of the party lifestyle. But, meanwhile, Jaid didn't seem to have changed at all over the last decade.

'I knew I wanted a different life for myself,' says Drew. 'I wanted to grow beyond that. I had to get free from her. One day, she came to my apartment to give me a TV, and that was it.'

---

*Within the 1995 interview for *Premiere*, Drew claims that the photograph actually came from the premiere party for comedienne Sandra Bernhard's film *Without You I'm Nothing*, where she had been dancing with drag queens.

'We were both screwed up,' admits Jaid. 'We had a huge row one night and Drew just threw all her resentment and pain in my face. She said she was ashamed of me as a mom, that I'd failed her, and that she resented me for living my life through her.'

The old familiar bitterness bubbled up and over.

'Why can't you just be a normal mom, for God's sake?' Drew ranted. 'I never want to see you again!'

'I just cut her off,' says Drew. 'I don't remember how we dissipated the relationship: I totally chalked it out of my memory bank. It was too painful, like cutting off my limbs.'

'I hit the bottle to ease the pain,' says Jaid. 'I didn't hear a word from Drew. The only contact I had was when I would go into dark movie theatres to see my little girl on the screen. I'd sit there and cry.'

It would be four long years before the two spoke again.

*

As was becoming a familiar pattern when Drew went her separate ways with a loved one, she again clung to her idealized view of romance. She now embarked on a relationship with Jamie Walters, an actor from Boston who was six years her senior.

There were no other words for it – in late 1991, Walters was hot property. Having dropped out of NYU film school after two years of study, the aspiring actor-musician had resigned himself to bar work and playing guitar in his spare time with local punk-rock bands. Talent-spotted by an agent, the cute, brown-haired all-American boy made some notable appearances in TV advertisements for Levi's 501 jeans, Gillette and McDonald's. In 1990 he moved to California in the hope of gaining some meatier parts.

There Walters was fortunate to sign up to none other than J. J. Harris. Soon he had a starring role as a teen rebel opposite John Travolta's cool music teacher in the rock 'n' roll musical *Shout*, set in 1955. This was released in October 1991, around the same time as Walters started making waves in the Fox TV series *The Heights*.

It was Harris who matched the two stars together.

'It's corny, but she set us up!' remembers Jamie. 'She'd been talking up a storm to each of us about the other for a long time.'

'But then I was in a relationship and he was in a relationship, so she made us wait, even after we broke up with our boyfriend and girlfriend,' says Drew. 'She was very smart.'

'She wanted it to work out and not be a rebound thing,' Jamie explains.

Drew and Jamie's first date occurred in September 1991. When

Jamie picked Drew up at her house, they were both nervous and painfully self-conscious about agreeing to go on a blind date. They planned to see Drew's all-time favourite movie, the 1946 black-and-white Jean Cocteau-directed *Beauty And The Beast* (*La Belle Et La Bête*), starring Josette Day and Jean Marais. Unfortunately for the anxious couple, 'We couldn't find the theatre!' laughs Drew.

It turned out to be a good thing in the end. The rather conservative 'movie and dinner date' turned into a nine-hour stroll along the buzzing promenade of Venice Beach, chatting and munching fast food.

'We stayed up all night long, sitting and talking,' Jamie told a journalist later that year.

'It was love at first sight,' said Drew. 'Jamie is terrific. I never felt so comfortable and free with someone before.'

Unusually for Drew, who was always extolling the virtues of her latest beau in the press, she and Jamie decided to keep their relationship a secret at the beginning. Too many love affairs hadn't worked out after all the press attention (most recently, the supposed 'engagement' with Leland Hayward still irked), and this one felt special.

'I want to make sure my life and career are together for Jamie's sake,' Drew was to say the following year, when the cat was out of the bag. 'I don't want to throw what we've got down the drain.'

Other than his good looks, Drew was attracted to Jamie for several reasons. Just like her, he knew – or was just beginning to realize – the extent to which fame at a young age could change a person's life. But unlike her, he boasted an attractively stable family background – something that always appealed to Drew. Plus, he was very much into his music; Drew liked rock-'n'-rollers.

A Jimi Hendrix fanatic, Jamie started playing the guitar at a young age and modelled himself on his hero. 'When I was eleven or twelve years old, I had this guitar, a copy of the natural body Strat he always played,' he recalls. 'I'd steal my mother's big silk scarves and tie them around my head, and I had my cut-off army shirt – I thought I was the baddest! I'd just make noise forever. The neighbours went crazy!' It was to be a while before Jamie's music made him as famous as his acting, but Drew for one was happy to play groupie.

*

Drew's professional star was on an ascent to match that of her love life. Towards the end of 1991, she was offered the lead role of Anita Minteer in a feature called *Guncrazy*.

A modern twist on the 1949 Joseph H. Lewis classic film of the same name, *Guncrazy* follows the adventures of Anita, a sixteen-year-old high-school girl born on the wrong side of the tracks. Living in a trailer park with her mother's sleazy boyfriend (Joe Dallesandro), Anita has allowed men and boys to 'use' her since the age of nine, and she is a frequent target for school bullies due to her 'easy' reputation.

When one day Anita is instructed to find a pen pal for an English assignment, she turns the tables on the teacher by corresponding with a prison inmate called Howard (James LeGros). Through their letters they fall in love, and when Howard is released, Anita is instrumental in finding him a job and initiating his readjustment to the outside world. But then things begin to go badly wrong as they explore their shared passion for guns and the two embark on a bloody crime spree on the run from the cops.

'It's been described as a kind of *Bonnie And Clyde* meets *Badlands*, and it is,' Drew sums up accurately.

Totally infatuated with the latest bad-girl role to land on Harris's desk, Drew decided to take matters into her own hands. This was not a part she wanted to lose. She got straight on the phone to Tamra Davis, the film's director.

'This is Drew Barrymore,' announced the actress confidently. 'I read the script and you have to see me. I love this character more than anything. I *have* to play this character.'

Davis was impressed with Drew's conviction and invited her to a meeting. As Drew read for the part, Davis recognized that no other actress could play Anita with such realism.

'I drove home from the interview totally in love with her, just madly in love with her,' Davis would later wax lyrical in a TV interview. 'She completely bewitched me.'

In fact, the two women realized they had much in common, and a lasting camaraderie ensued. They had a similar circle of friends in both the film and the music worlds, and in time would even briefly share a home. Davis's background was actually in directing music videos, although she had served an apprenticeship under Francis Ford Coppola. She had been looking to branch into feature films for a while, and *Guncrazy* seemed the perfect opportunity to hone her considerable talents.

However, it was not long before Drew would test Davis's commitment – even before filming commenced. Just one week before the shoot began that November, Drew and a friend watched the Patsy Kensit coming-of-age movie *Twenty-One*. They were so taken by Kensit's fresh look in the film that they chopped off each other's hair in an attempt to resemble her.

It was a daring move for Drew, whose long blonde curls had

charmed casting directors and audiences alike. Her look had formerly been unkempt but pretty – perfect for *Poison Ivy* and the Lolita-type roles that had been subsequently flooding in.

'The producers freaked out,' admits Davis with a wry smile, 'but I thought it was great, a stroke of genius. It was so messed-up looking, this dorky-looking haircut, it was perfect for the character.'

So the newly cropped Drew was allowed to continue as Anita. And somehow, the rather amateur restyling helped her seem more plausible as a character living in a trailer park. With the short, bleached bob, dark roots and thick, dark 1980s-style eyebrows, in *Guncrazy* Drew's facial features resemble those of Elvis Presley – sensual, striking and intriguingly masculine. Curvy but slim and toned, she is certainly as 'charismatic' as the film's promotion would later claim.

'In *Guncrazy*, I was nude in some love scenes,' says Drew. 'It was done in a tasteful, non-exploitative way, but was still a big step.'

It was the first time Drew would not use a body double in a revealing scene, and perhaps her new-found confidence in her figure after the breast-reduction surgery helped give her the necessary courage. The shower scene – which would be cut down significantly before the movie's release to just a glimpse of wet T-shirt – was filmed on a closed set, with only a handful of technicians present.

'I tried to close my eyes to the fact I had no underwear on,' she continues. 'I tried to keep a sense of humour – if I'd taken myself too seriously I could have ended up looking stupid.'

*

Guncrazy begins with huge promise but sadly goes downhill very rapidly. The fault doesn't lie with Drew; her performance is honest and realistic as she alternates in appearance and demeanour between adult and child. As an actress, her talents are very much to the fore – there are sex scenes, love scenes, murder scenes and even an underage marriage under her belt.

The problems with the film are down to Davis's inexperienced direction and Anita's confusing attitude towards sex.

In the promotion for the film, Anita's background would be described as 'abusive', but in fact she accepts all male attention in good humour, seemingly in total contradiction to any shock factor intended to give her character depth. When Anita finally puts her foot down and is raped anyway by her 'stepfather', because of her previous nonchalant attitude the viewer feels nothing but numbness about her situation.

Sadly, because of this, the viewer remains uninvolved, even when Anita commits her first murder – interest has already been lost and the film fails to reignite any sparks. The plot is certainly explosive but somehow remains wholly unengaging; LeGros's Howard is a particularly brainless character, who is impossible to care for. Unfortunately for all, the homicide theme would be tackled so much more elegantly and thought-provokingly elsewhere, in Drew's own work (*Beyond Control: The Amy Fisher Story*) and in films like 1994's *Natural Born Killers*, where the protagonists' apathy is thoroughly believable and, moreover, frightening.

Where Drew really stands out is in portraying Anita's delusional attitude towards right and wrong. Her misplaced faith in her mother is an interesting theme which ends in dismay. A very mixed bag, if nothing else *Guncrazy* at least highlights the ongoing problems that America faces with its relaxed gun laws.

It was a brave step for Drew, who described herself as 'gung-ho' about it all, but one that looked like paying off in the long run. Initially screened at festivals, *Guncrazy* was a slow-burner, dividing the critics but eventually finding an audience on the Showtime channel.

Through its airing on cable television, the film received enough critical acclaim to merit a later theatrical release in October 1992, and again Drew garnered unanimous praise; she even received a Golden Globe nomination for Best Actress In A Made-For-Television Movie.

'I was shocked when I was nominated,' said Drew. 'It's a real honour and much of the credit goes to Tamra – anyone who gets to work with her is lucky.'

For Drew, perhaps the biggest achievement – other than expanding her repertoire and boosting her profile – was succeeding in completing regular work.

'Now I'm working in films that are shooting back to back, and I've proven that I'm very stable,' she said at the time. 'In the last six months it's gotten easier. There's a lot of complimentary hype about me, which is cool.' Indeed, the actress was on the receiving end of inquisitive phone calls from such acclaimed filmmakers as Spike Lee and David Lynch. 'I'm going to be around for a while,' she affirmed.

16

THE AMALGAMATION OF
TWO SPIRITS

After *Guncrazy* wrapped back in February 1992, Drew was able to concentrate once more on her personal life. She had been dating Jamie Walters for six months, and the two were very much in love. 'We're always trying to be as close as we can,' Drew said at the time, admitting that they drove their friends crazy by incessantly talking about each other, using their joint pet name: Bear-Bear.

Shortly before Drew's seventeenth birthday, the pair couldn't face being apart any longer and so Jamie moved into Drew's place. This was only Drew's second experience of living with a man in the house, but she fully embraced the idea of settling down by finishing the redecorations and getting a new pet together.

'If I wasn't an actress, I'd most likely be an interior decorator,' she said. 'I'm remodelling my house as we speak. I wake up with concrete everywhere, the floor and ceiling ripped up. I'm in the middle of so many projects right now I don't have time to do everything.'

For someone as impatient as Drew, the seemingly endless chaos was unbearable, but, amusingly, she planned to move as soon as the house was finished. 'We're trying to fix up our house for the time that we live there,' she said in 1992. 'Next week we're getting our hardwood floors redone because they're such a mess, but then we want to buy a new place. We have a dog, and we want to have lots of grass for her to run around in.

'I just bought all this really cute furniture. My style is very old, antique, cosy. I want a place where I can drop everything on the floor, jump on the couch, kick off my shoes and put my feet on the table.'

As if living together wasn't commitment enough, Drew and Jamie decided to get his 'n' hers tattoos. Continuing her fascination with angels, Drew's design was of a cherub holding a cross and a scroll which bore the name 'Jamie', inked on the middle of her lower back. Jamie, who already sported an angel on his bicep and a Thunderbird, also had a cross bearing his partner's name.

One of the stranger presents Jamie surprised Drew with was a .357 Magnum. Given that her latest film highlighted America's firearms issues, it was perhaps a little disconcerting to hear the teenager say she used .38 bullets because 'otherwise it gives such a hard kick your arms fly up over your head'.

Drew was clearly enamoured with Jamie, gushing, 'He's wise way beyond his years. He's taught me about love, life – and geography!' When interviewers asked about any future progression in their relationship, Drew was remarkably forthcoming and enthusiastic, if somewhat naïve. 'I can't wait to be a mother. I want three children – a boy, then a girl, then a boy. I want to have a husband who works and has his own life, someone I can talk to and tell him about my day and have him care. I want to cook and clean and be little Betty Crocker at night and a businesswoman-actress by day. *And* be there for my children and get excited about the arts and crafts they did in fourth period.

'Being a mother wouldn't mean I'd have to put my life on hold, the way some actresses think. I wouldn't let it hold me back.'

*

Drew continued to be offered good girl/bad girl film roles, and in 1992 she appeared in *Doppelganger: The Evil Within*. In the horror flick she plays Holly Gooding, a young woman implicated in her mother's death. Leaving New York, she ends up on the doorstep of a young Los Angeles-based screenwriter, Patrick (George Newbern), who is looking for a room-mate.

Once she has moved in, the pair start a steamy affair, but Holly doesn't travel alone: she is accompanied by her evil alter ego. After a few strange events, Patrick becomes confused and then scared when his girlfriend explains what is happening. Finally Patrick discovers – from an ex-nun phone-sex operator (who else?!) – that Holly's 'doppelganger' is a lethal supernatural creature. Stuffed with every cliché in the book, even bastardizing the classic *Psycho* shower scene, the film capitalizes on Drew's sex appeal – although her particular forewarning of evil is to suffer a really unattractive nosebleed.

Until this point, the macabre piece has just been a lame slasher B-movie, but as *Doppelganger* reaches its laughably gruesome ending the plot twists back and forth, leaving gaping holes in the story and manufacturing a painfully contrived double-surprise climax. Newbern is likeable without being false, but neither he nor Drew, with her steamier-than-*Poison Ivy* routine, can carry the film. Even a dedicated Drewbie (as her fans call themselves) would struggle through this one, having to watch their heroine be crucified and morph into a giant maggot. But, if you're so inclined, watch out for Jaid Barrymore's brief-but-bloody appearance as Mrs Gooding – a scene filmed before mother and daughter parted company.

A few years later, Drew wouldn't even discuss the sci-fi fiasco beyond saying, 'You'd stick needles in your eyes rather than watch that.' We second that.

On the back of such an embarrassment, it is hardly surprising that Drew began to wish she had more control over her projects. During this period, she hired a personal assistant, Kim Greitzer, to organize her daily affairs. The two quickly became friends as well as colleagues and discovered that their ultimate goal was much the same. 'We worked together every day and really got to know each other and it was like this amalgamation of two spirits,' said Drew. 'We wanted to work hard and we didn't want our sex or our age to ever be held against us. We just wanted to go forth with our dream and our dream was to have a production company.'

Although Drew dropped out of school early, she was planning some further education to facilitate this other side of her career. 'I'd love to go back to school at some point and learn more about film, because I want to direct a project inspired by a movie I grew up with, *The Red Balloon*,' she said.

*

Poison Ivy was previewed at the 1992 Sundance Film Festival in Park City, Utah, before its premiere in May. The early industry whispers were generally positive, although the movie received a mixed bag of reviews on its actual release.

Variety said '[It] will make audiences itch to get out of the theatre and into the open,' and *Movieline* was no kinder – 'too turgid to even qualify as camp' – while *Empire* was more positive, observing that 'this remains ambiguous and intriguing even when the inevitable murders start'. Fortunately, the one constant was Drew's performance: 'Barrymore is a vivid presence – her fresh-yet-jaded sultriness is alive on screen,' proclaimed *Entertainment Weekly*, while *Empire* wrote, 'A step up the ladder for Barrymore (following interesting work in *Guncrazy*).'

Suddenly, Drew Barrymore was seriously bankable again.

Older and wiser since her early encounter with Hollywood stardom, Drew was flattered, but retained a healthy scepticism. 'Everybody's all over me,' she acknowledged in June, 'but I know that next month the hype might not be there.'

Heavily influenced by the grunge fatigues that Jamie favoured, Drew dressed in flannel shirts and ripped jeans, usually regardless of the occasion. The couple made a joint appearance at the Cannes Film Festival, where their slobbish attire was accepted as trendy, but they received a different response when they tried to shop at Chanel. 'I have these favourite shoes by Karl Lagerfeld – they're little, open-toed, crisscross with thick heel, very Marilyn Monroe – and we went into the Chanel shop looking for them,' explained Drew. 'They just walked us right out because they thought we were going to shoplift. They're very nice to us at Chanel in L.A., but in Cannes, God forbid you should go in there in a pair of Levi's.'

The inseparable pair caused an even greater stir when they appeared on the cover of *Interview* magazine together. Drew had been asked to pose nude for the photo shoot and she agreed, but only if it was done tastefully and strategically composed to preserve her modesty, and if Jamie could appear alongside her – although he was fully clothed.

The image they were presenting was one of unification and befittingly, on 20 June 1992, Jamie Walters proposed to Drew Barrymore. 'She was crying, I was charged – it was really cool,' said Jamie, in his to-the-point fashion.

'We've only been together for a few months, but it seems like for ever,' Drew said dreamily. 'We both have this feeling for the first time in our lives that we want it to be for good. He's my best friend and my lover. I've never been so happy.' With the month of May 1993 tentatively earmarked for the big occasion, Drew started planning early. 'We're going to have a big romantic wedding,' she promised.

*

Jamie was influencing Drew's life in more ways than one. Although she was achieving critical acclaim for her latest film roles, his current success on television in the soap *The Heights* led her to reconsider a similar job, something at which she would normally have balked.

CBS's *2000 Malibu Road* was another Aaron Spelling creation, riding on the back of his popular teen soap *Beverly Hills 90210*. The plot was female-led, focusing on four women who live together at the beachfront residence of 2000 Malibu Road. Jade (Lisa Hartman) is an ex-call girl who owns the property and takes in lodgers to pay the bills; Perry (Jennifer Beals) is a young lawyer trying to escape her past; Lindsay (the part Drew was offered) is an aspiring but timid actress from the Midwest trying to catch a break; and Joy (Tuesday Knight) is Lindsay's two-faced, manipulative sister and manager.

The series opened with the intrigue of a murder and, as with all successful soap operas, the plot twisted and turned, with each character's own complicated actions having knock-on consequences. And of course, being set on the beach, there was ample opportunity for the girls to be filmed frolicking in the surf in swimsuits.

Spelling had enlisted the talents of film director Joel Schumacher (*St. Elmo's Fire*, *The Lost Boys*) to oversee the series, and Drew's respect for him, combined with the explosive script, tipped the balance. 'Our writer is Terry Louise Fisher, who writes women so well,' said Drew in 1992, having signed up for the part of Lindsay. 'Through the course of the series [my character] becomes one of the most famous stars in the world and my sister becomes the biggest agent in Hollywood. Usually, when you watch TV, you see everybody going farther and farther downhill, but in this series they get better. I like transitions, and my character in the show starts scared and then becomes very strong – women aren't usually written that way.

'[Lindsay] doesn't take shit and she speaks her mind – which is very much like me. I want to have real relationships, and I like to see them portrayed.'

Schumacher was certainly pleased with her performance, commenting, 'I think Drew is one of the most honest actors I've ever worked with. With Drew, what you see is what you get. When the cameras are rolling, she starts speaking and you almost think she didn't hear "action" . . . There is a luminous quality to Drew's skin and eyes. The camera just loves her and it has all her life – it's a God-given gift.'

The trial run of five weeks of *2000 Malibu Road* was picked up by CBS, and the series was aired over August and September 1992. The astronomical production costs ran to well over $1 million per episode, and even Spelling was forced to concede it was one of 'the most expensive shows we have ever produced'. In order just to break even, the ratings within the initial period would have had to be phenomenal; although the figures were high, CBS felt they could not justify continuing with such a big-budget show.

Although Drew had accepted the possibility of a permanent role when she signed up to play Lindsay, it would have stalled her film career. As the show was cancelled, despite its good reception, she was excused from her commitment without losing face. More importantly, that Spelling had hired her spoke volumes about her reliability, and Joel Schumacher was equally impressed with the comeback queen: 'Hollywood needs someone like Drew – she's proof that it doesn't kill everybody, that it doesn't eat its young. Someone *can* go through the horror of too much, too soon and really survive.'

The primary drawback of *2000 Malibu Road* was that while Jamie was filming *The Heights* in Vancouver, Drew was stuck in California. The love-struck pair were determined to conquer their enforced separation and Jamie flexed his musical muscles, writing a smoky blues number entitled 'So Hot' for Drew. 'It's easier for me to put my feelings into music than writing or talking,' he said.

In November 1992, Jamie achieved a number-one single with 'How Do You Talk To An Angel?', the theme song from *The Heights*. That series was also short-lived, but it led to his most recognized part: that of guitarist Ray Pruit in *Beverly Hills 90210*. When Jamie's acting career dried up in the mid-1990s, he returned to his music, releasing a couple of solo albums.

*

Over the summer of 1992, while Drew was working in California, she re-established communication with John Barrymore II.

'I started talking to my father on the phone,' she said in June. 'I've never had that part of my life . . . and I never really will. It's really difficult because I've always wanted a relationship with my father, but sometimes I just feel it's too late.'

John remained as elusive as ever, leaving no contact address or number, instead preferring to phone his daughter out of the blue. Since his frank apology and her personal experience of his problems with addiction, Drew had begun to view her father through kinder eyes.

'It's strange, because I see a lot of similarities between us, and I usually groove hard on the type of free spirit he is – someone who travels around with a duffel bag, rides a bicycle, and doesn't wear shoes because he believes it's not right,' she says. 'But he's also tormented and fucked up, doesn't have his life together, and never wants to get it together, and I can't stand quitters. He had an amazing career ahead of him and shitted it all away on drugs.'

While Drew was still unable and unwilling to forge a relationship with her mother, it seemed that she could handle John's sporadic calls with maturity. Drew was also beginning to develop a social conscience: she took part in Rock The Vote. The organization was founded by members of the recording industry in response to a wave of attacks on freedom of speech and artistic expression in 1990, and by 1992 was expanding its reach to politics. The joint aim was to protect freedom of speech and educate the younger generation in affairs of state, encouraging them to participate in elections.

*

Drew's final job in 1992 neatly combined her year's activities: political and social awareness and the role of nymphet.

On 19 May 1992, seventeen-year-old Amy Fisher walked up to the Buttafuoco household in Long Island and shot Mary-Jo Buttafuoco in the head. Despite the point-blank range, Mary survived the attack, but was left with partial facial paralysis. As the press uncovered the history behind the shocking events of the day, it transpired that Amy had already experienced a colourful sex life as a call girl and had recently had an affair with Mary-Jo's thirty-eight-year-old husband, Joey. He vehemently denied the allegations (if they were true, he could be prosecuted for statutory rape of a minor) and Mary-Jo stood by him. Following her arrest three days later, Amy's picture was splashed across the national newspapers, captioned 'The Long Island Lolita'.

The story proved perfect television-drama fodder and by the autumn there were no less than three cable movies in the making – CBS, NBC and ABC, all rushing to beat each other. CBS scored the first coup by securing the rights to the Buttafuocos' side of the story, NBC took the other angle with Amy Fisher's testimony, leaving ABC with little material from which to draw. Instead, they chose to tell the story from the media's angle and, casting Drew in the lead role, decided to capitalize on her current image of dangerous sex symbol, putting all their faith in her name carrying the movie.

Drew was still bewildered to be viewed as a sex symbol and more than a little nervous about the pressure being placed on her to succeed, but hungrily accepted the role and all the challenges the true story presented.

The press image of Fisher was wildly distorted and exaggerated (something to which Drew could relate), and the actress fought hard to discover the driving force behind the girl. Not only did she delve deep into her character's psyche to try and imagine what would possess her to fire a gun at an innocent woman, she also had to perfect Fisher's unique accent – and all in just a matter of weeks.

'It's amazing,' she said, 'there are about fifty dialects from Long Island and I had to study the one from her particular part.' But with the help of her dialect coach, Robert Easton, the dedicated actress developed the accent in time for the start of the shoot on 23

November. Filming took place in Vancouver; ironically, Drew's transfer clashed with Jamie Walters' return to California for the filming of *Beverly Hills 90210*.

For the following three weeks, Drew affected every mannerism of Amy Fisher and embodied the breadth of her emotions over the year prior to and six months after the shooting. As the timing was critical in order to beat the competition, ABC hired Andy Tennant to direct the sixteen-hour-per-day shoot. A former dancer, Tennant had appeared in *Grease* with John Travolta before becoming a scriptwriter and finally an accomplished television director, helming numerous episodes of shows such as *The Wonder Years*, *Parker Lewis Can't Lose*, the popular sci-fi series *Sliders*, and the well-received drama *Keep The Change*.

In the end, the ABC version of events, *Beyond Control: The Amy Fisher Story*, was the second to be released, but was generally considered far superior to the other two, chiefly due to Drew's compelling performance.

The film begins at the end of the story, with Amy Fisher institutionalized at the Huntington Psychiatric Hospital, Long Island, after a suicide attempt. Drew imbues the character with moving realism and added poignancy, obviously drawing on her own familiarity with the situation, if not the exact circumstances that led her there. The whys and wherefores of how Amy came to be locked up in the Huntington are then portrayed in a series of lengthy flashbacks, slowly revealing each situation from different perspectives.

The Fisher family was not particularly happy. Amy was more than a typically rude and temperamental teenager; her mother defended her beyond reason; and she clashed head-on with her father. Still, Amy was given a car by her parents for her sixteenth birthday. Drew expertly executes stroppy adolescence, again not least as she has not long since been there herself.

The actress really excels as she turns from sullen daughter to sultry temptress in the flash of an eye when she is first introduced to Joey Buttafuoco, the mechanic who fixes her car. Her split-second timing in the change of character is uncanny; her piercing stare when she tells her lawyer, 'I love talking about Joey Buttafuoco,' is positively unnerving.

After some well-played coy flirting, Amy and Joey commence an affair, and similarly to the passionate elements of *Poison Ivy*, Drew uses a body double for the steamy scenes. When Joey breaks off the affair in order to be with his family at Christmas, Amy becomes obsessed with removing Mary-Jo from the picture and starts imagining herself in the role of Mrs Buttafuoco.

When Amy is first caught and charged with a string of offences, she pleads not guilty, but after the viewer is made privy to Joey's side of the story, she changes her plea to guilty. On 1 December 1992, Amy Fisher was sentenced to five to fifteen years for assault in the first degree, while Joey was released from statutory rape charges due to insufficient evidence.

The story is put into the context of the media frenzy – overshadowing that year's presidential election campaign – and the only criticism of *Beyond Control* could be that without a particular bias, the film is left a little open-ended. Then again, that is the problem with portraying a true story: the ending can't be fudged or fictionalized for a neat conclusion. Drew really couldn't have been better cast: not only does she add a touching conviction to many scenes, but she also simply oozes the required sluttishness.

Beyond Control received high ratings when it was aired, and caused an even greater sensation when the uncut version was released on video. Drew was less pleased, as although she used a body double for the nude scenes (as per her verbal agreement with Jamie Walters regarding onscreen sex scenes: 'no tongue and no real being naked'), the publicity suggested that it was the actress herself who was seen receiving oral sex from Joey. 'America thinking that I'm letting this man go down on me makes me want to vomit,' she said primly. 'I'm not like that, but they've made me look like an asshole.'

The addenda to the verdict shown in the movie are that Joey eventually served six months in jail for statutory rape (nearly being returned to jail when he later solicited an undercover cop posing as a prostitute) and Amy was released on parole after seven years. Amy publicly apologized to Mrs Buttafuoco, who said her faith in God allowed her to forgive the teenager, and the two corresponded for several months.

Aged two-and-a-half, Drew made her feature-film debut playing a little boy in *Suddenly Love*, with Cindy Williams as her mother.

'[E.T.] was one of the first most important friends of my life,' says Drew, who instantly fell in love with the mechanical alien.

Drew gave Princess Diana a stuffed E.T. doll before the British royal premiere of the film at London's Empire Leicester Square.

'I'm the Firestarter,' declared Drew aged six. 'I'm Charlie McGee!' The stunning pyrotechnics left the young actress with some minor burns.

Drew with the General in *Cat's Eye*; she still missed Gertie, her runaway kitten.

Top: Ryan O'Neal supported Drew throughout the fraught shoot for *Irreconcilable Differences*.

Above: Drew's smiles on screen in *See You In The Morning* hid the reality of her drug-addled life.

One of the steamy love scenes from *Poison Ivy* with Tom Skerritt, whom sixteen-year-old Drew described as 'elderly'.

Poison Ivy was the first of Drew's numerous lethal Lolita roles during the early 1990s.

Drew played another bad girl in *Guncrazy* opposite James LeGros. During the shoot she forged a lifelong friendship with director Tamra Davis.

Drew went to cowboy camp to learn to ride, shoot and lasso a calf for her physically demanding role in *Bad Girls*.

In *Boys On The Side* Drew flexed her emotional acting muscles, alongside firm friend Whoopi Goldberg.

'She's a glitter-dripped Marilyn Monroe,' says Drew of Sugar, her character in *Batman Forever*, seen here with Tommy Lee Jones (Two Face) and Debi Mazar (Spice).

Drew, a great Woody Allen aficionado, was staggered to be cast in the musical *Everyone Says I Love You* in spite of her refusal to sing.

Although her role was short-lived, Drew was certainly memorable as the first victim in Wes Craven's *Scream*.

Drew didn't believe in love at first sight until she met Luke Wilson on the set of *Best Men*.

Drew had so much fun filming *The Wedding Singer* with Adam Sandler that they have recently reunited to star in *Fifty First Kisses*.

Drew Barrymore and Anjelica Huston in *Ever After*, combining two great acting dynasties in a fairy-tale film.

Achieving a total transformation as the perfect Southern belle in *Home Fries*.

With Bill Murray, Lucy Liu and Cameron Diaz on the set of *Charlie's Angels*.

Top: As Beverly Donofrio in *Riding In Cars With Boys*, with best friend Fay (Brittany Murphy).

Above: Jake Gyllenhaal was impressed with Drew's dual role as actor and producer in *Donnie Darko*.

Confessions Of A Dangerous Mind was George Clooney's directorial debut, and Drew frequently turned to him for advice.

Dylan's wild past unravels in *Charlie's Angels: Full Throttle*.

Flower Films' Nancy Juvonen and *Charlie's Angels* producer Leonard Goldberg.

Lucy Liu, Drew and Cameron Diaz demonstrate their genuinely close friendship for the cameras while promoting *Charlie's Angels: Full Throttle*.

Top: Drew and Ben Stiller taking direction from Danny DeVito on the set of *Duplex*.

Above: 'He makes me laugh so hard that I unfortunately might have ruined a few of his best takes!' says Drew of co-star Ben Stiller.

17

EVEN COWGIRLS GET THE BLUES

The aftermath of filming *Beyond Control: The Amy Fisher Story* wasn't so positive for Drew. Having spent so much time away from her fiancé, Jamie Walters, the couple were naturally drifting apart. On 13 December 1992, just days before filming wrapped, Jamie called to say that the engagement was off and he was moving out. Drew begged him to wait until she returned, but he had made up his mind.

'He was the first big love of my life. I was head over heels, but he didn't want to be with me as much, so it failed. And yes, it hurt a lot,' she later confessed.

When she arrived in Los Angeles, she persuaded him to try dating again while living apart. 'We're trying to work on it,' she said at the beginning of 1993, 'one of our strongest points is we're the best of friends.' But it was not long before she had to admit that it was completely over.

'I think what hurts the most when you get out of a relationship is all the security and comfort you give up,' said Drew honestly. 'Jamie was the best friend I've ever had, and I miss that friendship. I hope after some time has passed we'll be able to be friends again.'

Two years later, Jamie offered, 'That relationship got so much attention and I'm not exactly sure why,' forgetting that the celebrity lovebirds thrust themselves into the public eye as a couple at every given opportunity. While Jamie was left a little confused, Drew became cynical. 'I've never been in love before except for Jamie,' she said, belittling her previous boyfriends. 'I don't even know if I could be in love again after him.

'It's not just sex you need protection from – it's everything else that goes along with a relationship. Maybe what I need is an emotional condom!' There was one last drop of pain to be extracted from the break-up: having Jamie's name blocked out in her tattoo.

During the first few months of 1993, Drew needed some TLC and while her mother hardly fitted the bill, she turned to her good friend Justine Baddeley.

Drew felt it was too painful to live in the house she had once shared with Jamie and so moved in with Baddeley, whom she'd known since she was thirteen. From the start, Drew openly agreed she was a monster to live with – switching suddenly from soft, gentle tones to a tirade of expletives or floods of tears. The same was true of her behaviour with boyfriends. 'One minute I'd be all over a man, whispering sweet words of love in his ear. The next, I'd be raging at him, shouting four-letter words and kicking him out.' Perhaps she needed to work more on her mood swings.

Sharing the same interests, Drew and Baddeley were usually only parted with the use of a crowbar. 'We're like an old married couple, we really are,' laughed Drew that summer. 'I wish I could find a boyfriend like Justine, and she wishes she could find a boyfriend like me.'

Their life became one giant slumber party: they would have friends over, watch movies, muck about with arts and crafts and even play dressing-up. It was like being a kid all over again. 'I'm so lucky,' Drew regularly repeated, 'my friends are my family – I adore them so much.' Baddeley was often present during press interviews and would reciprocate with her own expressions of adoration.

Confusingly, while most of Drew's friends tend to call her 'D' or 'Daisy', Baddeley nicknamed her 'Lulu', after trying to get her attention in public and not wanting to shout her real name, which would have caused a stir. During this time, Baddeley presented Drew with a T-shirt she had painted of two stick women smiling, with 'I Love You Lulu With All My Heart' written underneath.

'My friendships are the only relationships I've ever known,' says Drew, 'and I have the greatest respect for them. They've been a tremendous influence on my life and helped me figure out who I am. I think friends make your dreams come true.' Their dreams in 1993 included Baddeley becoming a casting director and Drew moving on to be a writer, producer and director.* 'We would have these great

*By 1998, Baddeley had reached her goal of becoming a casting director.

fantasies of what our life would be like, even though we were nowhere near it at that point,' she says.

Along with a change of address and renewed interest in her friends, Drew altered her image in 1993. The previous year she had clearly adopted Jamie's fashionable grunge look, but starting afresh after the break-up, she burned all her unisex flannels and 'started to dress like a girl again – I took all my old Agnès B. suits, bought some new dresses, and started wearing bell-bottoms with vintage jackets. I think my look is 1940s meets 1970s,' she said at the time, 'and since I rarely go out at night anymore, I dress up wherever I go.'

The actress celebrated her eighteenth birthday sedately at a mini-golf course, with a few close friends. While the celebrations were fun, Drew felt the milestone was a bit of an anticlimax – after all, she had been viewed as an adult in the eyes of the law for three years, although now she could *legally* buy cigarettes (which of course she had been doing for years).

One of the few clubs Drew still attended was Manhattan's Sound Factory. 'I usually go there when I'm in New York,' she said. 'It's fun because everyone is in their own world, and nobody bothers me there. It's a place I can do my own thing and release about a year's worth of tension in six hours of dancing.' After three years of sobriety, Drew was careful not to give in to temptation.

*

With financial security and critical acclaim under her belt, Drew was afforded the luxury of picking and choosing her next career move. She was bored of horror and trailer-trash murders, and after *Poison Ivy* and *Amy Fisher*, she was particularly concerned that she didn't get stuck with the Lolita stereotype.

'I'm moving away from playing nymphets,' she explained in 1993, 'and for now, I don't want to do anything sexual on screen. I'm grateful to have the opportunity to be selective, and I'm going to choose wisely.'

That was easier said than done, as the studios insisted on sending her bad-girl roles. Drew stood her ground, saying, 'That's nice, that [they] think that I do that well, that's a compliment in itself. But it's not the only thing I can do and it's not the only thing I want to do.'

While she had successfully made the transition from child to teenage actress, Drew had yet to break into adult roles – but then again, she was only just eighteen.

The first job she accepted in order to break the mould was therefore an unusual choice. As Drew waited patiently for the perfect part to fall into her in-tray, she was offered a cameo in *Wayne's World 2*, the zany sequel to *Wayne's World*.

Mike Myers and Dana Carvey had found big-screen fame and fortune in 1992 with a film based around their alter egos from a popular *Saturday Night Live* sketch, Wayne Campbell and Garth Algar. *Wayne's World* was a top-grossing hit comedy, particularly successful with teenage boys, which introduced the world to a brand-new cult vocabulary. It was time for Wayne and Garth to return in a new feature packed with pop-culture references, cool music and celebrity cameos.

Although Drew was trying to edge away from sluttish roles, her tiny part as Swedish receptionist Bjergen Kjergen involved her wearing a see-through crochet top and being willing to drop her knickers for Wayne by the end of their banal dozen-line exchange. Still, it was all in the name of humour and placed her alongside the other big names happy to send themselves up, including, among others, Charlton Heston, Harry Shearer, Heather Locklear, Jay Leno and the whole of the rock band Aerosmith. The leads were suitably silly in their quest to put on a mammoth rock festival, Waynestock, and Kim Basinger and Christopher Walken also turned in good performances, helping 1993's *Wayne's World 2* become a respectable – if not as wildly successful – sequel to a well-loved favourite.

If nothing else, Drew hoped the association at least would help ease her way into the world of comedies, a genre she had always fancied but had yet to crack.

*

In the spring of 1993, Drew Barrymore received a telephone call from Paul Marciano, co-owner of Guess? Inc. Being a lover of fashion, the actress was well aware of the stylish French company's attire and, more importantly, their strong visual identity.

The clothing company was founded by two brothers, Maurice and Paul, in the early 1980s; while Maurice oversaw the company's design direction and expansion, Paul conceived the Guess? image and created some of the most innovative and ground-breaking adverts. The campaigns for their jeans in particular had launched numerous household names. It was this coveted role that Marciano was offering to Drew, taking over from model Anna Nicole Smith.

Although clearly viewed by the public as a sex symbol, Drew remained modest and unsure of her appeal. At first, she didn't believe the request, assuming that all Marciano wanted was to send her a free pair of jeans. When it dawned on her that he was serious, Drew found it faintly ridiculous.

'I was wondering, "Why me?" I mean, I'm not like the other girls, Claudia Schiffer and Anna Nicole Smith, who've modelled Guess? jeans – I'm only 5 foot 4,' she laughed at the time. 'I was thinking, "People are going to take one look at my ass in those jeans and they'll be wondering why I was chosen at all!" '*

Accepting the honour, Drew took her mission seriously, if only to prove that she was dedicated in all fields. 'It wasn't easy to discipline myself,' she confides. 'I had to diet and look after myself better than I'd done since I was in junior school.' She added, 'I also needed to get all the ghosts from the past out of my head,' by which she meant the years of insecurity she felt about her body and being fat.

Unfortunately, the day that she was due to meet the photographer, Wayne Maser, to discuss his ideas, Drew broke out in unsightly blotches due to an allergic reaction to eating a large chunk of garlic. 'I blew up like a red blowfish,' she joked, putting a brave face on her disappointment, 'a puffer fish that has acne.' Blemishes aside, the week-long shoot was arranged for July in Miami.

The results were striking, due in equal part to Maser's style and Drew's imagination. 'I was in a bikini posing like Brigitte Bardot,' she explains. 'I ended up persuading myself that I just had to be as free as possible, like I was doing a character, not thinking, "I'm so ugly. I'm not right for this. I'm not thin enough, not pretty enough." I got down to 7 stone for those ads, because I pictured the girl as a waif, petite with blonde curls everywhere.'

When the campaign was launched in October 1993, Drew was unprepared for the impact the pictures of her svelte semi-naked figure would have.

'The campaign changed my life,' she says. 'It was on bus shelters right by my house, on the most huge billboards I've ever seen, on the first page of every magazine for six months. It was in so many places, I said, "If I see myself one more time, I'm going to vomit!" '

The promotion was so effective that bosses at Prada jumped on the bandwagon the following year, asking Drew to model for their Miu Miu offshoot. 'To be absolutely honest, I've done it for the money,' she confessed on accepting the second contract, reported to be worth $1 million. 'I live in a big Spanish-style house in Hollywood that costs a fortune to run, and I was beginning to wonder where I'd get the money.'

*

*Amusingly, another Guess? jeans model was Tom Skerritt, the 'elderly' man with whom Drew had recently been seen in *Poison Ivy*.

While negotiating the contract for Guess?, Drew had been planning her next movie and was due on location straight after the photo shoot in the summer of 1993.

Although she had been wary of accepting any roles which could reinforce her pigeonholing as a bad girl, Drew could not turn down the opportunity to work with director Tamra Davis again. Admitting no doubt about the content, the film was actually called *Bad Girls*, but the appeal of working with her friend was matched by the acclaimed cast. Also, the genre was different: Drew was entering the world of the western.

Andie MacDowell had joined the Brat Pack brigade with *St. Elmo's Fire* in 1985, but became recognized as a 'serious' actress with her riveting performance in *sex, lies and videotape* (1989). She retained notoriety in the early 1990s, appearing in the romantic hit *Groundhog Day* and Robert Altman's *Short Cuts* (both 1993), and went on to star in 1994's smash comedy *Four Weddings And A Funeral*. Madeleine Stowe's film career during the 1980s and 1990s was solid, if less memorable, but she was riding high on the back of 1992's *The Last Of The Mohicans* and had also appeared in *Short Cuts*. Mary Stuart Masterson had started well in *Heaven Help Us* and was another Hollywood darling following her role in *Fried Green Tomatoes* (1991) and her portrayal of Johnny Depp's mentally ill girlfriend in *Benny & Joon* in 1993. The three women were in turn supported by *Young Guns* star Dermot Mulroney and James Russo, the ultimate baddie.

Westerns were uniquely American and almost exclusively male-dominated, extolling the virtues of cowboys and settlers pioneering the western frontier in the 1800s. Westerns had undergone numerous bastardizations over the decades, and increased social awareness in the 1970s led to a series of so-called 'revisionist westerns', which attempted to present historical events and attitudes in more realistic terms. These films found little success at the box office, but a series of blockbusters in the 1990s rekindled the form. Still, women were only ever portrayed in a negative light, and few movies made them heroines.

Cue *Bad Girls*. The female answer to *Young Guns* and *Young Guns II* was to be a movie about four gun-toting cowgirls.

'I never had to audition for the role, I just had to meet with everybody,' marvels Drew. 'I couldn't see how they could tell if I could do the part just by meeting me but, thank God, they were incredibly gracious.' Surely with Davis's urging, Drew was offered the role of fourth bad girl, Lilly, in the small project by the independent company New Line. Drew was excited and honoured to be involved in the film.

For three weeks prior to filming, the four women went to 'cowboy camp' to learn the ancient arts of gun-slinging, calf-roping and wagon-driving, with the aim of doing most of their own stunts.

'I was completely uncoordinated and totally pathetic when I arrived,' she says. 'I couldn't twirl a gun and, even though Lilly is supposed to be a trick rider, I wasn't very familiar with horses. By the time we'd finished, I wanted to do all my own stunts and was ready to take the falls from a horse. Everyone thought I was crazy. But it goes to show what you can do with determination.' Although Drew was almost twenty years younger than MacDowell and Stowe, and a decade Masterson's junior, her guts and willpower showed her to be a worthy contender.

*

While the actresses had been preparing physically for *Bad Girls*, they also learned their lines, identified with their characters and embraced the plot. Behind the scenes, however, trouble was brewing.

'Twentieth Century-Fox just bought *Bad Girls*,' Drew's agent told her over the phone.

'What do you mean? We were all contracted to make a small movie,' said Drew in disbelief.

'Your contract's out the window,' came the blunt reply.

Having not had to audition in the first place, just as Drew was ready to start filming she was now faced with the indignity of proving herself in front of seven different executives at Fox before they would agree to recast her alongside MacDowell, Stowe and Masterson.

Finally, filming got underway in Sonora, Texas, but rather than enjoying themselves as before, there was a sour taste left after the Fox takeover. Even Drew's previous enthusiasm for the physical aspects of the job waned.

'In the first week, we shot a scene where I'm riding this horse on railroad tracks, but the horse didn't like it and kept trying to buck me off,' she explains. 'When the studio people saw the footage and said, "You've got to get more into it," I said, "What the fuck do you mean? The horse was trying to kill me!"'

Then, after a week-and-a-half of filming, the cast and crew were dealt a second blow: the film was closed down, Tamra Davis was fired and the script was scrapped. Fox put the actors on hold while they hired a replacement director and rewrote the dialogue.

Drew's immediate thoughts went to Davis. 'She's one of my dearest friends, and what happened was really terrible – she was put in a very shitty position,' says the actress, who offered to walk out in support of her buddy, regardless of the threat of a lawsuit. Davis insisted that Drew stayed, particularly as *Bad Girls* had turned into her first opportunity to star in a big studio picture for a decade.

Eventually, Jonathan Kaplan of *The Accused* fame was brought in to save the film and a revised plot was produced. 'I love Jonathan Kaplan's movies, but when he first came onto *Bad Girls* it all got incredibly confused, like, who are our characters? Where the fuck are we? Does this movie have an ending?' explains Drew.

From there on in, things progressed from bad to worse. 'There was not a single ounce of unity on the set,' she continues, 'which was terrible because in the movie, the four women are supposed to be acting like we're the most loyal people in the world.' Drew tried her best to stay out of the on-set politics, but found herself inadvertently drawn in. Furthermore, she was struggling with her own battles: 'It was very hard because I was the youngest by far. I was treated differently on the set and it was disappointing. I was looking forward to getting to know the other girls, but I ended up feeling like an outcast at times.'

The revised screenplay shifted the focus, throwing the whole emphasis of the film off balance. Rather than just being the survival story of four whores-turned-outlaws, *Bad Girls* became more of a battle of the exes as Cody (Stowe) fights for one-upmanship over her former boyfriend, his father, also a one-time client, and her old gang. Her current crowd, Anita (Masterson), Eileen (MacDowell) and Lilly (Barrymore), are little more than hangers-on.

The film is embarrassingly formulaic, with horse chases, tender moments, quick-draw gun battles and, when you have four beautiful women together, the obligatory nude bathing scene. The action is littered with cries of 'Hy-ah!' and even boasts a few hurried history lessons. Ultimately *Bad Girls* is pulled in too many directions, cliché-ridden, slow in the middle section and lacking in atmosphere or tension. Both *Maverick* in 1994 and *The Quick And The Dead* in 1995 were better attempts at revisionist westerns.

Drew was undoubtedly given the smallest role and, other than showing off her horse-riding skills, says and does little until the final section of the film, where she is brought to the fore. However, as MacDowell and Masterson are weak, even miscast in their roles, it is Stowe and Barrymore who carry much of the film, along with their male supports.

Having lost weight for the Guess? adverts just prior to filming, the slimline Drew looked fantastic, her 7½-stone figure enhanced by long peroxide tresses and flawless skin that positively glowed from her outdoor pursuits.

Acknowledging that the four women did manage to have some laughs, Drew later praised her character, which was undoubtedly her saving grace throughout the gruelling schedule. 'Lilly was great. She's so strong,' she said, 'so at one with her body. So completely without fear . . . I've always wanted to regain that sense of freedom from fear and, for the first time in my life, I'm having it. I'm really not afraid – and that's one of the best feelings I've ever had. I came back from doing the movie a totally changed person.'

However, if anyone were to suggest another all-girl cast, the response would have been curt. 'I was terrified to do another female ensemble after that.'

*

As with *Beyond Control: The Amy Fisher Story*, Drew experienced another split when she returned from the set of *Bad Girls*. Stuck out in the Texan desert for five months with three older women, the actress gave a lot of thought to her struggling relationship with her mother. Since their almighty row in 1991, Drew had been plagued by questions from nosy journalists about the state of their relationship.

'We're like oil and water, we just don't mix,' she explained in 1994. The biggest conflict lay in their attitudes. 'I think we differ in the fact that she seems to love Hollywood and I hate Hollywood. It's a shallow, inconsistent, cruel world.'

Indeed, Drew was coming across in interviews as the most un-Hollywood star around. She made no bones about her dislike of celebrity pomp; she was just a happy-go-lucky, kiss-the-sky kind of gal.

It already seemed a lifetime ago that Drew was cooped up in rehab. Although she generally avoided the clubbing scene, she drank beer and wine occasionally, didn't attend AA meetings anymore and flitted in and out of therapy when necessary. Instead of drugs, she said she went 'up into the forest, down to the ocean' to find her release. However, in 1993, she was still a chain-smoker – two packs of Camels a day – and felt seriously wheezy when she climbed the four flights of stairs to her friend Melissa Bochco's flat, whom she'd known since she was eight.

Drew claimed variously to suffer from anaemia, claustrophobia or insomnia, and was unabashedly proud of her maladroitness. 'I'm geeky. Silly. Extraordinarily uncoordinated. Pretty basic,' she beamed. Her love of butterflies, daisies and all things yellow became synonymous with her sunny attitude, as she flaunted them wherever she went. 'There's an old Swedish movie called *I Am Curious Yellow*, and that's what's on my car licence plate: Curious.'

She was pretty much a recluse, avoiding Tinseltown's glittering parties, preferring to stay at home, painting, reading and writing. Alongside her cupboard full of journals were her poems, many of which resembled Anaïs Nin's erotica: 'It's sort of embarrassing,' she giggled, 'they're really dirty, actually!'

Drew also loved indulging in regular girly nights with Baddeley and Bochco. 'I never go anywhere, except with my friends to see bands play,' she said. 'Tonight is girls' night and, for about two years now, we've always done the same thing – cook dinner and watch *Melrose Place* and *90210*.'

The striking change of pace from Drew's youth was a result of having crammed so many experiences into her first fifteen years. 'I always used to think that I would never live beyond the age of twenty-five, but as the years go by I just get happier and happier,' she said. 'For the first time, I realize that I can take things slowly, I can stop and admire things; that life is not about going out and partying.

'I find it really amazing that I have so much ahead of me, yet I seem to have done so much already.' Despite her youth, Drew had already considered her options after life. 'I don't want to be cremated,' she stated. 'I want to be buried underneath an avocado tree. And I want the roots to grow right through me. I want my friends to eat avocados and see how I'm tasting this year.'

18

1-800-I-MARRY-U

In February 1994, Drew Barrymore turned nineteen and started dating Jeremy Thomas. She had known Jeremy for the best part of two years – he was a thirty-one-year-old ex-merchant navy Welshman who owned a Los Angeles bar called The Room.

Five weeks into their relationship, they were hanging out in Jeremy's bar and chatting about nothing in particular. At about 2 o'clock in the morning, Drew asked him to marry her. Although it seemed slightly unconventional, he readily accepted.

The excitable pair couldn't wait a moment longer and so called a twenty-four-hour wedding hot line (1-800-I-MARRY-U). They were connected to Patricia Vander Weken, a minister-cum-private-detective-cum-psychic, who agreed to appear at the bar as soon as she could. Weken was convinced that the happy couple had in fact known each other in a previous life and Drew for one agreed, 'Everything about us is like fate.'

So, at 5 a.m. on 20 March 1994, Drew wore a white slip dress and combat boots while she exchanged wedding vows with Jeremy in the bar's basement.

Although the ceremony was as private, spontaneous and secret as they come, the press soon found out. And when they did, they had a field day.

Whereas most people can laugh off a quickie Las Vegas-style wedding with the excuse of being drunk at the time, Drew and Jeremy were stone-cold sober. 'I married because I was totally in love and not confused about my feelings,' Drew defended herself. 'This is definitely for life. Jeremy is just what I need – he's strong, supportive and not at all wild. I know this stuff about marrying in a bar sounds strange, but that is just how we felt about each other. I'm very lucky to have met him and he's going to be a big influence on what I do in the future.'

But Drew was only able to spend the wedding night with her new husband. She was immediately required on the set of her next film.

Jeremy, suddenly a celebrity by marriage, was left to hold the fort. 'Yes, it was crazy, but it just felt right,' he repeated to the press. 'We'd been dating only a few weeks, but we loved each other. Why wait for something to go wrong?' That in itself sounded ominous . . .

*

'I always pick a film strictly because of the characters,' Drew insists. 'I don't think I'm a good actress, so I have to fall in love with the character. That always sparks my interest in a project. Who's on the page? Can I see myself being them?'

Boys On The Side gave Drew Holly: definitely one of those characters. Perhaps the closest Drew has ever come to playing herself, Holly is a radiant, romantic and ditzy wild child who is running from her drug-filled past. Through the course of her travels with two female companions, she will find strength she never knew she had and charm everyone with her infectious *joie de vivre*.

Unhappily for Drew, the casting for this latest film was not as straightforward or as pleasant as she would have liked. For the second time in a row, she really had to fight for her role.

'Nothing in my life comes easy,' recalls Drew through gritted teeth. 'Jim Brooks, one of the producers, believed I was the person to play this. And I'm grateful he was in my corner . . .'

When the part of Holly was announced to Hollywood agents, the director, Herbert Ross, and the producers chose to hold an open audition, instead of having someone in mind from the beginning. Still smarting from her experiences on *Bad Girls*, Drew was the first in line to read for the role.

'You're sitting there in a cold room with two pages out of a script and you're as nervous as hell,' she said the following year. 'It's so degrading. I want to be at a point where I don't have to do it.' Nothing was guaranteed. 'It's hard watching everyone else go in after you,' she continued. 'I heard rumours that other people were going to get it. That lasted three months.'

Fortunately for Drew, alongside Jim Brooks, the already-cast Whoopi Goldberg was also campaigning in her name. The two had stayed in touch since their encounter on the set of *The Color Purple*, becoming close friends.

'They brought in a lot of different actors, including Drew, who was wonderful,' says Goldberg. For those three long months the decision-makers wavered, much to her annoyance. 'I said, "Pleeeease, you *have* to hire this girl!"'

Finally, they relented and Drew was relieved to get the part, saying, 'The struggle made it all the more rewarding.' But, again as with *Bad Girls*, the schedule kept changing. At first she was due to shoot immediately after the cowgirl caper wrapped, but then it was delayed for four months. Goldberg was then committed to another film and after all the waiting, Drew decided to pull out. 'I felt like I was going in a different direction,' she says.

Apart from anything else, Drew was nervous of repeating the experience of being the youngest actress in a group of women. 'After *Bad Girls* I was scarred,' she elaborates. 'I just didn't want to subject myself to anything like that again. I just wanted to do the most mellow film-shoot possible, so I decided I'd back out of the movie as discreetly, kindly and professionally as I could.'

Drew was surprised with the response. Herbert Ross had taken long enough to be convinced, but now he was, his faith would not be shaken.

'He wouldn't take no for an answer, which scared me at first, but then I took his dedication as one of the biggest compliments I'd ever received,' she explains. 'I went in and talked to him and realized that my first instinct was right, that he really did like me.'

And so Drew Barrymore, Whoopi Goldberg and Mary-Louise Parker relocated to Tucson, Arizona, for three months to shoot *Boys On The Side*. The relatively unknown actor Matthew McConaughey (who was to play Drew's love interest) came too – legend has it that, quite unlike Drew, he had apparently won the role of the ludicrously named cop, Abraham Lincoln, hands-down in his very first Hollywood audition.

The story of *Boys On The Side* was previously charted territory for the director, whose successful 1989 film *Steel Magnolias* tackled many of the same themes, in particular the unshakeable bond of female friendship.

There are three strong characters in the movie, each of whom begins her journey with a secret: Jane (Goldberg) is a lesbian lounge singer; Robin (Parker) is the straight-laced woman who hires Jane to take her on a road trip to Los Angeles, but in truth she is dying of AIDS; and the effervescent Holly (Barrymore), whom they pick up for the ride – simultaneously saving her from the abuse of her stoned boyfriend – is Jane's one-time girlfriend and also eight weeks pregnant.

Throughout the course of the tale, the unlikely bond between the women deepens and becomes more complex. WASP-ish Robin has trouble coming to terms with her friendship with the abrupt black lesbian; Jane's reciprocal feelings create problems of their own; and Holly is arrested 'for her own good' by her policeman fiancé when he discovers the threesome had left her ex for dead. There are many plot elements to cover (AIDS, sexuality, birth, death, marriage, murder, love and hate), but generally the film succeeds without becoming too soppy or over-emotional.

'This movie makes people aware of how closed off they are to these issues,' explains Drew. 'The issues in this film are so contemporary, but the story is so timeless. The deep core of the film is about friend-ship . . . For those of us who aren't fortunate enough to have a family, you create it on your own with friends.'

There were obvious comparisons to be made to the ultimate girly road movie *Thelma & Louise*, the 1991 Ridley Scott classic starring Geena Davis and Susan Sarandon. Although *Boys On The Side*'s road trip is prematurely halted in Arizona when Robin becomes ill, the strong characters and feminine camaraderie mixed with the elements of abuse, murder and running from the cops are clear parallels.

This was a particular attraction for Drew, because *Thelma & Louise* was the one movie which she always named when people asked her what film she would have liked to have starred in. The connection is made explicit when, early in the film, Jane comes out with the wry aside: 'I am *not* going over the cliff for you two . . .'

*

Regrettably for Drew, although Holly was her onscreen embodiment, it was by far the lesser of the three roles in *Boys On The Side*.

Parker gives a fine performance in her difficult role as Robin gradually comes to terms with her approaching death, Goldberg provides the film's emotional backbone (although it has to be said she stretches the audience's imagination as a singer), and it is left to Drew to bring some light and humour into proceedings. Fortunately, her part, although smaller, allowed her to develop on screen in her own way.

'Holly's definitely different from any of the characters I've played,' she says. 'She's like this flower and you see her open up and blossom and metamorphose . . . The truth of the matter is, I am the silliest person on the planet. I am really, really goofy. And it was so great for me to put my goofiness to productive use through Holly. She takes life seriously but doesn't take herself seriously. She has humour.'

Herbert Ross agreed with Drew and was delighted that his eventual faith in her was paying off.

'I had no idea she was an actress of the quality she is,' he admits. 'She brought humour, wit and bravery – in addition to sweetness and goodness.'

For Drew, *Boys On The Side* and, more importantly, Holly provided the perfect antidote to *Bad Girls*. Although on the face of it, it must have been quite straightforward to portray someone so similar to herself in real life, Drew's acting abilities were stretched along the way. She was required to do two topless scenes (one of which involved audaciously pulling up her top to perform a half-naked shimmy to the boyfriend she had tied to a chair and gagged), she was brutally thrown against a wall during a fight scene and had to retaliate convincingly with a baseball bat, and she had to simulate giving birth. Of course, at the movie's close she also has to come to terms with her friend's inevitable demise, although admittedly the main focus is on Goldberg by this point.

A pleasing bonus for Drew was that she would go on to appear in the promotional music video for the award-winning country singer Bonnie Raitt's song 'You Got It'. The Roy Orbison original is covered touchingly in the film in one of the closing scenes, sung first by Jane as a farewell to Robin, and then during the credits by Raitt herself.

Later, when it was released, reviews for *Boys On The Side* would lavish praise on all three actresses. Drew's honest performance was widely lauded as audiences lapped up a very different turn from the newly married artiste.

'I think this picture has done her a great deal of good,' said Ross proudly. 'She'll be taken seriously now.'

Goldberg was equally smug, especially as she'd been instrumental in keeping Drew in the picture.

'She walks off with the movie!' she gleefully exclaims. 'This child was like a diamond – her performance was wonderful. And now everyone pats themselves on the back, and I laugh . . .'

*

'My marriage was about a life lesson to trust your instincts, and that the stomach is as important, and vital, as the heart and mind, soul, and all the things we sort of rely on for our instinct and intuition,' explains Drew.

Basically, within days of leaving for *Boys On The Side*, the actress realized she had made a hideous error in marrying Jeremy. But a week later, she was booked on Jay Leno's *The Tonight Show* to promote *Bad Girls*, and of course everyone wanted to know about her spur-of-the-moment wedding.

'I think that was probably one of the most painful moments in my life,' she confesses. 'Jay Leno asked me, "Are you happy?" And if you got a videotape of it you can probably look at me and see me look down at the floor as I say yes.'

Drew could not go on living the obvious lie that she told that night. 'There was no avoiding reality anymore,' she says. 'Anyone who knows me knows that my heart was beating slower every day. It was the first time in my life that I had truly been dishonest to myself.'

When she returned from the shoot, she told Jeremy it had been a mistake.

'You know what the situation is,' she said cryptically. 'You've gained everything from this and I've lost everything. I have to get out of something that was never right to begin with, and if you don't see that I'm terribly sorry.'

It later transpired that the situation she was referring to was giving Jeremy legal status to live and work in America: a green card. 'We were friends,' she explains, 'he needed something and I thought, "OK, I can be a hero and save this person, and that will be that." I couldn't tell anybody because of the green card. I had to lie.'

Six weeks after the whirlwind wedding, Drew filed for divorce, claiming 'irreconcilable differences'. The sham newlyweds didn't even go on the honeymoon they'd told everyone they'd planned in Hawaii.

But rather than settle for an equally quickie divorce, Jeremy made Drew's life a living hell.

'Retaliate is *exactly* what he did. He tried to sue me, for anything he could,' she says. It took a year of legal wrangling and a sizeable payoff before Drew was free of her first husband.

She celebrated by going on holiday with her girlfriends – ironically, to her honeymoon destination. 'I had to sign my divorce papers on the sand in Hawaii,' she laughs. 'I'm sitting there with a frothy beverage in one hand and divorce papers in the other.'

Admitting the whole fiasco was a mistake meant Drew had to bare her soul to the public again. 'It's the only thing I've ever done in my life that was untruthful to myself,' she said at the time. 'It's really ruined marriage for me.'

Adding insult to injury, who should choose this moment to call other than John Barrymore II? He got Drew's voicemail and delighted in leaving a message. 'Daughter! It's father!' he crowed jubilantly. 'I'm glad to see your marriage lasted as long as your mother's and mine did!' Click.

*

While Drew was contemplating the breakdown of her marriage in her Tucson hotel room, she also had to deal with the predictably poor reviews of *Bad Girls* when it was released in April.

Variety noted that the film 'drinks from an empty trough of wit and style,' while the *Chicago Sun-Times* attacked the cast: 'the failure of *Bad Girls* is all the more poignant because the actresses are at the top of their forms right now'.

Back in the spring of 1994, Drew was fed up. She knew that she wanted more out of life than to just be an actress. To that end, she set up a production company called Flower Films with her assistant, Kim Greitzer.

'It's two girlies wanting to make good movies, with people who are passionate,' Drew said. 'We're very much on the same wavelength in a business sense. We sit down with our iced teas and cigarettes at our desk and we just plough through the day. We do it together and it's really great.'

Drew, who had always been frustrated with the fickle profession of filmmaking, saw Flower Films as a way to change the industry from within – a perfectly natural progression. 'I still had so much to learn,' she confesses, 'so a lot of the job was about research – learning about filmmakers, meeting with an agency and getting to know who they work with, building relationships.'

As Greitzer was heavily involved in the direction of the company with Drew, the actress needed a new assistant. Drew had been introduced to twenty-seven-year-old Nancy Juvonen at the beginning of the year, when Juvonen had helped the saxophonist Clarence Clemons from the E Street Band start his own business. 'A few weeks later, Drew called me and said, "I dare you to come to Los Angeles and work with me",' recalls Juvonen, but there was a catch. 'The first three months was getting groceries, picking out tiles, redoing her house and cleaning the pool.'

With the company in full swing, Drew was asked in interviews how she coped with giving orders. 'I'm not very good at that,' she confessed. 'I have an assistant and I let her do her own thing – I can't even tell her what to do!' Alongside her chores, it was Juvonen who took it upon herself to read *Variety* and *Hollywood Reporter* to keep abreast of all the industry developments.

While the women behind Flower Films had a lot to learn about the other side of the business, Drew had a clear idea of her ultimate director. 'Woody Allen – I think he's kind of a genius,' she said at this time. 'Unfortunately I don't know if I'd be right in any of his films, because his casting is so specific and he tends to use the same people in his movies.'

While waiting for Allen (or similar) to call, Drew was content to accept another bit part, although her motive for signing up to *Inside The Goldmine* remains a mystery. The grim psychodrama tapped squarely into the Generation X attitude, a posture that she had since dropped. Josh Evans was the screenwriter, director and co-star of this disturbing profile of modern youths from wealthy backgrounds living aimless lives. Drew appears as Daisy in the story based in Los Angeles, highlighting the unwarranted despair of Hollywood youth. Stylish and elegant, yet utterly depressing, the small film did nothing to enhance, or harm, Drew's career.

19

MACARONI-AND-CHEESE GIRL

Over the summer of 1994, Drew met Eric Erlandson, guitarist with the rock group Hole.

Twelve years her senior and a foot taller, Erlandson was a sweet, soft-spoken man with blond hair. He grew up in a religious household and initially became an accountant for a major record label. In 1989 he answered an advert in the music magazine *Recycler* for a guitarist to join a band. The group was in its infancy, just a girl singer and her neighbour on bass. 'I stood there playing whatever noise I could think of and they were strumming their guitars, screaming at the top of their lungs. I thought, "Wow, this is gonna be interesting!" ' recalls Erlandson.

The singer had wanted an all-female band to avoid any sexual tensions, but was enamoured by Erlandson and so gave him the job. The band was Hole and the frontwoman in question was Courtney Love.

Born in the mid-1960s, Love was a wild child from the start, getting in trouble with the law at an early age. She used her maternal grandmother's trust money to see the world, and when that ran out she became an exotic dancer. Love tried her hand at acting (*Sid And Nancy*, *Straight To Hell*) before founding Hole.

In 1990, as Hole was beginning to get noticed, Love married Falling James Moreland, the punk transvestite frontman of a band called Leaving Trains, for a dare. Shortly after that fiasco, she broke all her own rules by dating Eric Erlandson on the quiet for a year-and-a-half.

'It's weird that no one asked, but we kept it pretty tight,' says Erlandson. For that brief period, he managed to tame the shrew a little and the duration of their relationship was perhaps the calmest period of Love's life. After Love, Erlandson went on to court Hole's bassist, Kristen Pfaff.

Meanwhile, Love became involved with Kurt Cobain, the lead singer and guitarist of Nirvana and notorious user of heroin, something with which Love would also experiment. The volatile partnership culminated in Love's pregnancy in 1992, during which time the pair tried desperately to clean themselves up. '[Eric] totally saved our lives during that whole time,' Cobain told *Rolling Stone*. 'He was the only piece of reality, the only calm person who was there as an example of what life could be like afterward, once this crazy shit was over.'

Love and Cobain's child, Frances Bean, was born in August 1992 and for a while the bizarre family were happy. But Cobain sank into drug-induced paranoia and depression, finally committing suicide in April 1994 after a triple dose of heroin by firing a shotgun into the roof of his mouth. Two months after that tragedy, Kristen Pfaff also took her own life, injecting herself with heroin and slipping into a full bath, to be found later by Erlandson.

It was during this troubled time that Drew entered Eric's life.

*

The scene is Los Angeles, end of 1993 (before the Jeremy Thomas saga).

On one of Drew's rare nights out, she goes to see her friend Anna Waronker's band, That Dog, in a rough area of east Los Angeles.

Suffering from claustrophobia, Drew needs to get some air and escapes the club. Standing in the doorway, the actress rather unglamorously brings up the contents of her stomach. Suddenly she feels a cool hand on her shoulder.

'Ex-*cuse* me,' Drew gasps between heaves, 'I don't think you want to be here right now!'

'This is a really dangerous neighbourhood, so if you don't mind I'm just going to stand with you to make sure you're OK,' replies the mystery man.

Drew, feeling particularly vulnerable to be seen vomiting, asks him to leave her alone.

'You don't have to be embarrassed,' he reassures her, 'this is what we do. In fact I've thrown up a couple of times myself!'

He refuses to move, she continues being sick and soon enough his shoes are splashed with yellow goo. There is a long pause. Drew is nearly crippled with embarrassment.

'Did you have pasta tonight?' he finally enquires.

Surprisingly enough, Drew had indeed eaten macaroni and cheese before she left home that evening. The peculiar chain of events led to a half-hour chat, when eventually she introduced herself as Drew Barrymore, famous actress – but of course, her knight in splattered armour already knew that.

The next scene takes place a fortnight later.

Drew goes to meet photographer Ellen Von Unwerth at Ma Maison hotel in Los Angeles (the photo shoot that ensues is another story entirely). When she knocks on Von Unwerth's door, fate intervenes.

As the door opens, Drew screams, 'No way!'

'Macaroni-and-cheese girl!' replies Eric.

They say actions speak louder than words and, as Drew is speechless, it seems somehow appropriate for her to kiss him fully on the lips and thank him for his previous kindness. But, although Drew is well aware she has a crush on Eric, she confusingly agrees to marry Jeremy Thomas, who turns out to be a rat.

The final scenario is almost half a year later. Drew is in Seattle, Eric's hometown, on a film set (which we haven't even got to yet). Attending a concert by 7 Year Bitch (the band that features in the film we haven't yet mentioned), Drew hears a familiar voice whisper in her ear: 'Eat any macaroni and cheese lately?'

After a reunion chat, they agree to meet up for coffee the following afternoon. The date lasts nine hours, involving a long walk and oodles of kisses.

'Kissing, and I mean like, yummy, smacking kissing, is the most delicious, beautiful and passionate thing that two people can do, bar none,' drooled Drew at the time. 'It's better than sex hands-down.' The relationship, seemingly contrived by the gods, progressed and it was not long before Drew moved into Eric's apartment.

*

The reason that Drew was in Seattle in the spring of 1994 was to film *Mad Love*. She was teamed up with A-list hunk Chris O'Donnell, who had earned his stripes playing opposite Al Pacino in *Scent Of A Woman* and consolidated his heart-throb status as D'Artagnan in the 1993 adaptation of *The Three Musketeers*.

Mad Love was directed by British filmmaker Antonia Bird, who had started her career in British television on *EastEnders*, *Casualty* and *Inspector Morse*, and was renowned for dealing with the complexities of human pain. Bird's last film for Miramax had been *Priest*, which was yet to be released but was set to cause consternation with the League for Religious and Civil Rights. In the meantime, however, Bird had been offered her first 35mm feature film by Disney (owner of Miramax) and she completed *Mad Love* before the uproar over *Priest* arose.

It was no surprise, then, that the subject matter of *Mad Love*, although essentially a teen movie, was not just sex, drugs and rock 'n' roll. Drew's character, Casey Roberts, moves to Seattle, where she meets and falls in love with Matt Leland, an intelligent and sensible student at her school. Matt is captivated by Casey's effervescent free spirit and is soon caught up in her high-jinks.

But Casey is not all she appears to be. After a prank at school she is grounded and subsequently tries to commit suicide. It then transpires that she is bipolar – suffering extreme highs and lows – and her father wants to commit her to a mental asylum. Matt knows that Casey cannot be caged and together they break out. Hitting the road, the pair head for Mexico and enjoy their freedom until Casey, not on her medication, begins to break down again. After another suicide attempt, Matt takes Casey back to her parents at the hospital where she agrees to receive medical help.

While Drew always relished the challenge of a meaty role into which she could sink her teeth, playing someone who was fighting institutionalization was daunting due to her familiarity with the situation.

'When I read the script it made me cry because I felt so much for this girl, because I understood her so well,' she explains. 'I know that not many young actresses have been through that. I knew I had the experience to pull from and make it real rather than a *sturm und drang* schmaltzy crazy weird movie.' Drew had previously undertaken physical preparation for her roles, but this was only the second time (other than for *Beyond Control: The Amy Fisher Story*) that she did extensive research into unknown territory, studying the bipolar disease at great length.

Her co-star, Chris O'Donnell, was five years Drew's senior, and was staggered by her maturity. 'Drew is not self-conscious at all,' he said. 'She's very sure of herself – opinionated, even. She doesn't sit and think about things. She knows what she likes and where she wants to go with her character. That makes her seem much older than she is.'

It seems that Bird was similarly impressed with Drew's ability and *Mad Love* was originally shot as a hard-hitting R-rated film. Drew was hugely affected by the hardest scene, when she's in hospital being held in a five-point restraint.

'It's a strap across your waist and your arms are handcuffed to each side of the bed and then your legs are handcuffed to each side at the bottom. I had to kick everyone out of the room, because it was so hard to get back into that, because I've been there.'

Drew had never spoken before about the extent of her suffering in the rehab facility's Intensive Treatment Program, and this new revelation came as a shock to most of her fans, as well as the cast and crew.

'I tried to hold back in the scene and stop myself from crying, because it was so close to home. But then I felt like I'd got to use one of the scariest things of my life for something productive, and somehow the pain had been lifted, and not only the pain but the fear.'

However, Disney wanted the teenage road movie to be accessible to adolescents and therefore cut it considerably to produce a PG13-rating, losing much of Bird's urgency and effectiveness. Moreover, the actual term 'bipolar' is never used in the film, leading the viewer to believe that Casey is clinically depressed, which seems to be disproved by her moments of elation. Ultimately there is not enough intrigue to make the viewer really care. Without being able to see the original version it is difficult to comment, but the end result – the released edition of *Mad Love* – is frustrating.

While Bird's usual directorial approach was realistic, aggressive and visceral, *Mad Love* is slow to get going, clichéd and ultimately loses focus, brushing over the real issues. The first third establishes Matt and Casey's growing love, crassly depicted with a formulaic day of fun and soul-searching. The middle section wanders off into the realms of the teenage road movie, with little drive and one too many prolonged scenic panoramas – was the film in fact an advert for the American national tourist board?

The conclusion, finally getting to grips with Casey's diagnosis, is far superior. Drew magnificently portrays the scared confusion of her character as she loses control, while O'Donnell equally expertly tries to hold everything together. Casey's downfall begins when she focuses on the conversations of strangers talking about control – here the direction is edgy and Drew is entrancing. Similarly impressive is the bedroom scene where Casey rips out pictures of people's eyes from magazines and pastes them over the walls to protect her (one can only imagine how good the film could have been with more commanding images of this ilk).

Sadly, while the scenes concentrating on Casey's illness are incredibly powerful, they are far too few and far between, undoubtedly due to Disney's heavy-handed editing. Herein lies the greatest problem: the director wanted to deal with some tough issues, but in doing so

Mad Love required a high rating; on the other hand, by thrusting the problems onto teenagers, the plot has limited appeal for adults.

Other irritating points worth noting with regard to *Mad Love* are the intrusive grunge-rock soundtrack featuring 7 Year Bitch, Nirvana, Luscious Jackson and Grant Lee Buffalo, and the various criminal activities which have no repercussions whatsoever, including stealing, leaving the scene of a car crash, GBH and hijacking – certainly not the moral message one would expect Disney to send to teenagers in such an otherwise desensitized film.

*

Although the end product was unsatisfactory, there is no doubting the emotional work Drew put into creating Casey's trauma onscreen.

'To be in that mentality constantly for three months – I must say, it drove me nuts,' she admitted. 'It killed my spirit to play this character. But when it was over, the cathartic aspect of it kicked in, and I felt freer than I've ever felt. To go through all that and come out the other side is a revelation in the highest sense – without question.'

But it was not as simple as Drew made it sound. Firstly, she had some on-hand help throughout filming. 'Eric was with me every day,' she said. 'He got me through. He would have to wake me up in the morning because the movie was so emotionally debilitating and strenuous.'

Then there were the numerous issues that were brought up regarding institutions, control, authority and restraint, and Drew needed professional guidance to process these resurfaced feelings. Drew had previously said that she drifted in and out of therapy; she recognized that now was a time to recommence her counselling.

'The first step towards solving problems is to realize that you're not alone,' she said at the time. 'I still have my own counsellor and therapist – she's been like a fairy godmother at the times when I might have felt like going back to my bad old ways.'

The most frightening aspect of the movie for Drew was being locked up in cuffs, a method of control that was used on her in ASAP. 'Sometimes you'd just not want to take your vitamins and you'd throw them, and all of a sudden you'd have five men on you, *boom*! It was insane,' she said, shedding new light on the treatment she had always publicly extolled.

'I couldn't understand why I was in a place where you couldn't go outside and if you dared try to, you'd be shut in a four-by-four room with no windows. You get so frustrated you start acting out, and then you get even more in trouble and more scary things happen to you . . .'

The secondary issue was that both Casey and Drew were institutionalized by their parents, supposedly for their own good. 'Nobody deserves that. *Nobody*,' stressed Drew in an interview promoting the film.

Although the actress always acknowledges that ultimately the rehabilitation experience enhanced her appreciation for life, this was the first time she had confessed that it almost broke her spirit. She clearly still bore tremendous resentment towards Jaid for the action, and there would be no foreseeable reconciliation.

*

Eric Erlandson turned out to be Drew's rock in more ways than one, providing the same stability he had given his ex, Courtney Love. During the filming of *Mad Love* in Seattle, Drew's bag was stolen from Eric's car. She wasn't concerned about the money she had lost (several thousands of dollars), but there were some sentimental photos and her personal journal. Drew's innermost thoughts would have proved priceless if sold to the tabloids and the actress would have suffered unwarranted humiliating attacks.

Drew immediately telephoned both her lawyers and the police to try to rectify the potentially devastating situation. But it was Eric who played detective, vowing to find her bag. His was a close-knit neighbourhood where everybody knows everybody, and Eric had an inkling about who the culprit might be. When he finally tracked the woman down, the bag was right where he had envisioned it, in her wardrobe.

'When I walked into Eric's place after work he wasn't there,' recalls Drew, 'but all the contents of my bag were spread on the floor. I burst out crying!' In professing her love for Eric, Drew, as always, forgot her previous declarations. 'I don't know if I've really been in love before,' she said, as was her curious habit of repeatedly discrediting her past feelings for her substantial string of exes, 'but this is the most beautiful thing I've ever experienced.'

When not filming, Drew's relationship with Eric threw her into a rock-'n'-roll fantasy world, as she attended Hole's concerts, studio sessions and backstage parties. Thrust into this new arena, Drew came face to face with Courtney Love. The rock chick, still deeply affected by her husband's suicide, was then best friends with ex-*Word* presenter and fellow grunge queen Amanda de Cadenet. The singer bristled at the prospect of her very dear ex dating a wacky former child star.

Touring with Nine Inch Nails during the summer of 1994, Love told the audience that she had been offered the Guess? jeans ad campaign, saying, 'That's so retarded, those stupid pants.' Whether or not this was a dig at Drew, there was no love lost between the pair.

Fortunately, although Drew admitted there was some tension at first, the two women rarely came face to face and so nothing was made of it. 'I feel like I relate to this person so much, and yet in other ways we seem so opposite,' she said at the time of the compelling feelings she had for this virtual stranger. 'But then I think that we're the kind of people who don't feel like we need to try and be best friends. We just don't mind each other's presence, and sometimes I respect that as much as I do friendship.'

20

COVER YOURSELF UP

Shortly after filming on *Mad Love* was completed, Drew was reunited with Chris O'Donnell. This time he was wearing a rubber outfit.

Batman Forever boasts a first-rate cast: since the departure of Michael Keaton as the caped crusader (rumour has it because the supporting characters had more scenes), Batman/Bruce Wayne was to be played by Val Kilmer (*Top Gun*, *The Doors*); O'Donnell was the new boy, Robin; Jim Carrey (*Ace Ventura*, *The Mask*) beautifully overacted as the Riddler/Edward Nygma; Tommy Lee Jones (*JFK*, *The Fugitive*) portrayed both aspects of Two Face; and Nicole Kidman (*Dead Calm*, *Far And Away*) provided the love interest as Dr Chase Meridian. Some said the star-studded cast carried the show.

Along with the change in Bruce Wayne, another difference from the previous two *Batman* films was the director. Joel Schumacher took over from Tim Burton and replaced the latter's very dark approach to Gotham City with something lighter and camper, ultimately steering it back towards the tone of the 1960s television show (O'Donnell even utters the immortal line, 'Holy rusty metal, Batman!' as he scales the corroded foundations to the Riddler's lair).

It was Schumacher who brought Drew Barrymore into the mix. Although she was only offered a small cameo in the third adventure of the flying comic-book hero, she couldn't refuse the director with whom she had worked on *2000 Malibu Road*. 'He was there for me,' Drew explained, 'he's always been a strong, supportive friend.'

Batman's original enemy in the film is Harvey Dent: a former district attorney scarred on one side after an acid attack, with two personalities to match his divided face. Drew plays one half of Two Face's totty duo, Sugar 'n' Spice. 'She's a glitter-dripped Marilyn Monroe,' says Drew of Sugar, her peaches-and-cream character. Some besotted critics even suggested that Drew was the Monroe of the new generation. Drew was extremely flattered. 'I'm a complete fan, a total sucker,' she says of the legendary sex symbol.

No matter how gorgeous Drew looks all dolled up as Sugar, she wasn't allowed much screen time. Not only was she just a moll, but the Lycra-clad, rubber-bodied Jim Carrey steals every scene, and so Two Face is little more than an accessory himself. 'There are certain times when I'm baffled. I think I'm so little and insignificant in the big picture, it shocks me that other people find something to talk about in that,' laughs Drew.

That said, and although her role is limited, she does have some great moments: she is far more eye-catching than Debi Mazar as Spice; she smoulders on Edward Nygma's arm at the ball; and she tricks Bruce Wayne into entering Nygma's mind machine.

Drew was overawed to work with such big stars, not least Jim Carrey. 'He's my hero,' she said. 'I got to be in *Batman Forever* with him, which was the biggest thrill of my life!'

At the ball, Sugar fancies Bruce Wayne and when he asks her name, she huskily purrs, 'Oh – you can call me anything you want.' But Kilmer's then wife, Joanne Whalley, was more concerned by some real-life rumours that were filtering back from the set about her husband and Drew.

Whalley, who was pregnant with their second child at the time, was apparently used to hearing reports of her husband's womanizing, but this was the last straw, and she reportedly cited Drew as 'the other woman' in the divorce proceedings.

Both Drew and Kilmer refuted the claims, saying they were 'just good friends'. Drew admitted, '[Val]'s one of those people you can run off in the corner with and smoke cigarettes,' but considering that she was madly in love with Eric Erlandson at the time, that anything more happened seems unlikely.

Kilmer unfortunately seemed to rub everyone up the wrong way. Allegedly Nicole Kidman's offscreen friendship with Kilmer was almost as unpopular with her then husband, Tom Cruise, as the two actors played rivals in *Top Gun* and it is said the onscreen friction was reflected in reality. Meanwhile, Kilmer, who had clashed with director Michael Apted during filming for *Thunderheart*, now disagreed with

Schumacher, eventually to the point where he broke his contract, refusing to appear in another *Batman* film.

Drew kept her head down and steered clear of all the office politics.

*

When Drew finished filming *Batman Forever*, she began to concentrate more seriously on her own company, Flower Films.

While Nancy Juvonen had assumed control of many aspects of the business during her trial period, Drew was well aware that she was overdue a promotion. As Juvonen had turned out to be very perceptive about scripts and development, Drew took her on a surprise trip, leaving the office in the capable hands of Kim Greitzer. 'We drove cross-country in a Winnebago,' says Juvonen. 'We left from Los Angeles, drove for about three weeks and ended up in New Hampshire.' Armed only with their Dictaphones, the pair spent their time tossing ideas around and learning to predict each other's next creative move.

On their return, the women began a steep learning curve, educating themselves about all aspects of the industry. Drew became more and more serious about her goals. 'You can stand around and complain at Hollywood, with all of its hurt and bullshit, or you can do something about it,' she explained. 'I want to produce films, not to make more money or to become powerful, but just to have some control over my working life and future.'

Just as Drew was trying to become more businesslike, her photo session with Ellen Von Unwerth was published. It had been a shoot for *Playboy*.

Drew had been a huge fan of Unwerth's work and hadn't thought twice about shedding her inhibitions and clothes for the top-shelf publication. The results were spread across twelve titillating pages of the notorious magazine's January 1995 issue.

'I was intrigued about working with *Playboy* and I thought [it] would be a daring adventure,' explains Drew. *Playboy* had in fact been courting Drew for years, and she finally felt happy enough about her looks to accept. 'I've grown more and more comfortable in [my skin] and I'm at a point now where I could live my life stark, raving naked and I wouldn't care,' she said. 'I thought, "This is fun. It's an interesting, daring, controversial adventure, and a little controversy never killed anybody, especially me!"'

But what did her boyfriend think?

'There is definitely a side of Eric which liked that I did it,' she says. 'But how he complimented me on it meant the most to me. He's the one person I aim to please that way.'

However, there were several people within the industry who were less impressed and Drew was back on the defensive. 'Posing naked in *Playboy* was a fun thing for me, because when my breasts are down at the floor, I'm going to be able to look at it and remember that gravity was once my friend,' she joked, making light of the criticism. 'You just have to express yourself when the moment arrives, because there may come a day when you won't want to do that again. You have to live for the moment and not care what people think.'

Godfather Steven Spielberg, for one, clearly disapproved. For Drew's twentieth birthday in February 1995, he sent her a special package. When Drew opened up the big box, she found a giant quilt accompanied by a note saying: 'Cover yourself up.'

Tucked in the blanket was a magazine. *The* magazine – Drew's issue of *Playboy*. But Spielberg's art department had been busy . . . airbrushing clothes onto all the pictures!

'I love that,' she said, 'because it's funny and it's fatherly and it says something, but it doesn't make me feel bad.'

*

In February 1995, Drew was once again pictured naked, this time when *Boys On The Side* was released. Again, not a good move for an actress hoping to be taken seriously, but Drew in fact received great reviews for her role as Holly.

The *Chicago Sun-Times* heralded her as the 'catalyst of the group'; the *San Francisco Chronicle* writer comments on her comic finesse, accurately describing both Drew's performance and appearance as 'about the closest thing to Jean Harlow since Jean Harlow'; the *News Of The World* said, 'Barrymore is very good as the slightly mad, boy-crazy Holly, but the other women give strong performances as well'; and critic Julian Ketchum said, 'The acting is flawless, the principals fleshing out their characters far beyond their hastily sketched stereotypes.'

But Drew was beginning to take the theme of being at one with her body to extremes. She had discovered a new hang-out: a bar called Blue Angel. 'It's sort of burlesque,' she described. 'There's naked women with angels on . . . then this woman pees in this litter box . . .'

One night at the club, Drew's comedian friend John was doing his stand-up routine when suddenly the actress interrupted by bounding up on stage and performing an impromptu striptease. She refused to *completely* disrobe until boyfriend Eric jumped up to assist her – which he promptly did.

'It was really fun and totally free – we didn't think some

spontaneous move of normal people would ever make headlines,' laughs Drew naïvely. But then Drew is not your average Jane Bloggs.

What better way to divert the public's attention than with another extreme escapade? Shortly after the Blue Angel incident, Drew was invited to appear on *Late Night With David Letterman* and was told that he wanted to discuss her recent nudist activities.

Drew agreed and was particularly excited as she had always harboured a crush on the chat-show host. 'I think that the most attractive combination a human being can contain is intellect and humour,' she says, 'and he's got that. I was just drawn to him.'

When Letterman steered the conversation onto her striptease act, Drew took everyone (including herself) by surprise and offered to re-enact the dance. Letterman didn't need to be asked twice, so Drew leapt up on his desk and started gyrating and stripping before she even knew what she was doing. While the audience went wild, Drew flashed Letterman her breasts and dropped her jeans to shake her bare ass.

The cameras could not actually see her in all her glory, but Letterman certainly could: 'I can't thank you enough for that,' he managed to splutter when she finally climbed off the desk.

'That was one of the funniest moments of my life,' said a flushed Drew. 'I *love* being naked!'

Capturing her exhibitionist streak, photographer David LaChapelle took some striking pictures of Drew to illustrate an extensive interview in *Premiere* magazine that June. The provocative poses show off her curves in some bizarre, cheeky scenarios, including one in which Drew holds half a grapefruit topped with a bright-red cherry in one hand, while the other is left free to pull her shirt down, revealing a vibrantly rouged bare nipple.

*

When Jaid was asked what she thought about all of Drew's nudity, she commented: 'Drew is an adult now. Who am I to shake a finger at her? I trust her boundaries and respect her choices. Besides, there was nothing sleazy about it. It was spontaneous, uncontrived and sweet.'

But there was more to Jaid's blasé attitude than she was letting on. Having not spoken for years, she wrote her daughter a beautiful letter for her twentieth birthday. Drew was touched by her mother's well-wishing and correspondence between the pair ensued. Then Jaid told Drew that she had been writing a book recently, and that it was dedicated to her. Of course, it wasn't just any old book.

'It's sort of a *Joy Of Sex* for the 1990s. It's called *Secrets Of A World*

Class Lover,' says Drew. According to *Playboy*, the guidebook 'covers everything from the thrill of public sex to kinky ways to masturbate,' but Drew remained remarkably unfazed: 'She is such a sexual person, and very into the art of sexuality. That's where I get my lack of inhibitions from – physically from her and spiritually from my father's side of the family.'

Jaid was pleased to have finally achieved fame in her own right (although it seems unlikely the book would have been commissioned without the Barrymore name), and the reconciliation with her daughter was the icing on the cake. 'The book saved me and got my daughter back,' she says. 'For the first time, I'd achieved something for me.'

Over the summer, Jaid and Drew maintained contact and even met up a few times. Drew told her mother about Eric, and in turn Jaid mentioned that she too had a boyfriend, a twenty-seven-year-old musician (for those keeping track, Eric was then thirty-two).

But in the autumn, the reconciliation ground to a halt.

Aged forty-nine, Jaid appeared in a full-frontal nude spread for *Playboy* magazine with a male model. Drew was horrified, and the cold war resumed.

'She was posing in *Playboy* and going out with young musicians, and I thought, "Gee, *I'm* posing in *Playboy* and going out with young musicians, too," ' said Drew. ' "Why are we still living parallel lives?" I realized it still could not work between us.'

*

Back in May 1995, *Mad Love* was released to mixed reviews. As predicted, Drew's performance was credited as being one of her best yet, but the film itself was seen as a let-down.

Batman Forever came out the following month to a whirl of media frenzy. Warner Brothers took over two cinemas in West Hollywood for a grand premiere, causing great excitement. All the stars turned up: Val Kilmer, Tommy Lee Jones, Jim Carrey, Nicole Kidman with hubby Tom Cruise, and Drew, among others.

'I won't say it's better than the other *Batman* films because that can be misconstrued as snotty,' she said during the surrounding hype, 'but I think it's very different from the others. It has a genius screenplay that takes you into this realm of total imagination, and I love the fact that Joel played that up. He really went for the comic-strip idea and the surrealism of that.'

Drew then took some time out to think long and hard about her next project. She had been offered the lead in *Showgirls*, but wisely turned it down (the 1995 release starring Elizabeth Berkley was universally slated). Instead, she had another project with Tamra Davis up her sleeve. 'Both of us hate the norm and just want to do what we want to do,' she said. 'Fuck money, fuck politics, fuck Hollywood.'

Sorrow Floats was a screenplay (based on the book of the same name by Tim Sandlin) about a messed-up alcoholic young mother who travels across America with a pair of recovering addicts. It sounded frighteningly similar to a combination of *Mad Love* and *Boys On The Side*, as Drew acknowledged: 'I'm going to be branded queen of the road movie!'

Unfortunately, *Sorrow Floats* was put on the back burner almost as soon as Drew mentioned it in interviews (a bad habit she would soon learn to break the hard way), and Drew began sifting through other potential material.

When not worrying about work, Drew enjoyed some rare time alone with Eric. He had recently moved into her Spanish-style home and they spent some time redecorating, just as she had done with Jamie Walters previously.

Drew was particularly comfortable with Eric's stable home life. 'I never thought I'd have a traditional family until I had one of my own – I know what all the fuss is about now,' Drew said of the Erlandsons. 'Everything else dissolves around you and you're lost in a really safe world.'

Along with Eric's circle came Courtney Love. The two strong-willed women in his life were beginning to tolerate each other. By the autumn of 1995, Love had changed; her love of music had waned while her passion for acting had resurfaced, which she described as 'a whole new way to kick ass'. Having turned down *Tank Girl* in the wake of Kurt Cobain's death, Love provided the film's soundtrack, and she had a successful, if small, role in *Feeling Minnesota*.

It so happened that Oliver Stone was casting a new movie based on the life of Larry Flynn, the *Hustler* publisher who was shot and paralysed by an opponent of pornography. With Woody Harrelson as the lead, Stone was looking for someone to play his drug-addict wife, Althea, who had AIDS. The gritty role was coveted by A-listers from Julia Roberts to Patricia Arquette, but the producers were intrigued by Love.

To secure the role in *The People Vs. Larry Flynt* (for which she later earned a Golden Globe nomination), Love was subjected to several drug tests, something to which Drew could relate. Drew's recent flair for nudity probably also appealed to Love, who regularly flashed her breasts on stage. Having fallen out with her usual crowd, Love was low on female friends and turned to Eric's actress girlfriend for company, advice and support.

The two quickly found they shared much in common and a strong bond grew between them; Love went on to name Drew as godmother to her daughter, Frances Bean. '[Drew]'s like a sister to me,' said Love, 'somebody I would really fight to protect. She brings that out in all sorts of people. She has really taught me to simplify my life a little more, to take pleasure out of stupid stuff that's just fun – having barbecues, having picnics, going to the movies, having sleepovers.'

Drew was equally enamoured of her new pal. 'She's part of the group that lives inside my heart,' said Drew. 'I really love her. She's so smart, she blows my mind. I think she's such an eloquent person, and if she wants to go out there and be crazy . . . let her.'

21

YOU SCRATCH MY BACK AND
I'LL SCRATCH YOURS

Having previously cited Woody Allen as a genius, Drew was staggered in 1995 when he asked her to audition for one of his films.

'I am an absolute Woody Allen aficionado,' she declares. 'I have seen every single one of his movies at least twenty times. I can quote them all. This man has the best emotional provocation of any director in the world. He allows us to relate to people of love and relationships and human circumstance. He's so smart.' To prove the point, she ranks *Annie Hall*, *Manhattan* and *The Purple Rose Of Cairo* as some of her favourite films of all time.

Although all are greats, the three pictures she names represent only the tip of the iceberg as far as the prolific writer, director and actor's body of work is concerned. Allen redefined comedy during the 1970s, adding his unique combination of sophistication and psychological complexity. His movies were often more like vignettes on recurring subjects such as art, religion and romance, tapping into the anxieties of contemporary audiences.

His new project was called *Everyone Says I Love You*, and the role offered to Drew was that of Skylar, the moneyed New York debutante. Although she proved that butter wouldn't melt in her mouth as Sugar in *Batman Forever*, Allen was concerned that Drew had always been linked with unstable screen characters, but he was open-minded enough to invite her to read.

'I was *so* nervous,' she admits. 'I didn't know he knew I was even *alive.*' Drew became even more passionate about securing the role when she heard the list of names also involved: Goldie Hawn, Alan Alda, Julia Roberts, Edward Norton, Tim Roth and Woody Allen himself.

'We have some similarities,' she said of the character she longed to play. 'We're dreamers, philanthropists . . . we believe in the good people. But she's also very graceful and collegiate and coordinated with a very interesting fashion sense. I'm not any of those things!' But it was obvious that she was drawn to the part for another reason. 'I have a love triangle with Tim [Roth] and Edward [Norton] in the film. Ha! I'm *the* luckiest girl in the world!'

But she still had to convince Allen.

'I auditioned many times,' Drew recalls. 'It was really hard for Woody to see me as a debutante – and I could completely understand that – but I knew I could do this character.'

Fortunately, Allen could see past Drew's lingering wild-child image and felt she was the perfect Skylar. '[She] has the kind of gift that can't be taught. She's just naturally interesting, believable and sexy and is capable of a wide range of performances,' he said, echoing the thoughts of many directors dating back to Steven Spielberg on *E.T.*

Miramax, the company who would eventually release *Everyone Says I Love You*, felt that there was one last thing Drew could do to ensure she was cast. It was a case of you scratch my back and I'll scratch yours.

Co-chairman of Miramax Harvey Weinstein suggested to Drew that signing her to Woody Allen's film would be infinitely easier if she would just help him out on a small matter. Writer and director Adam Park had signed to Miramax for his feature-film debut, *Wishful Thinking*, a project which Harvey felt would be significantly more successful with a big name – like, say, Drew Barrymore – attached.

Drew had no interest in yet another Generation X romantic comedy, but was so desperate to work with her hero that she would have jumped through any hoops put in her way.

*

During the autumn of 1995, Drew lived in New York, filming *Wishful Thinking* with co-stars James LeGros (*Guncrazy*, *Bad Girls*), Jennifer Beals (*Flashdance*, *2000 Malibu Road*) and Jon Stewart (a comedian and talk-show host).

The plot follows the troubled relationship between Max (LeGros), a projectionist in a revival theatre, and Elizabeth (Beals), a veterinarian. When the couple first meet, sparks fly and romance blooms as they move in together. But, when Max produces a small box, Elizabeth excitedly assumes it is an engagement ring and is somewhat disappointed to discover that it is in fact a prototype for his toothpick/flosser invention. Tensions build between the couple and Max becomes convinced Elizabeth is having an affair. Mounting insecurity provides Max's co-worker Lena (Barrymore) with the perfect opportunity to act on her secret desire for him.

The film is intriguing at the outset: Max and Elizabeth meet unconventionally, Park makes good use of quirky camera angles and sound effects, and bringing the black-and-white movies in Max's theatre to life is an inspired dramatic device. It transpires that the story is to be told in three parts, each from a different character's viewpoint. While this would normally maintain the viewer's attention, it seems that Park concentrated a little too much on the ground-breaking style and not enough on the plot or characters, as the film quickly loses any sense of direction.

The middle third is Lena's story, where Drew does her best to rescue a doomed script. Pasty-white, with short blonde hair, Drew is great as the quirky friend, a regular at tarot readings and a believer in destiny. Slim and attractive, she is particularly sexy during one black-and-white film section where she strips seductively.

But despite Drew's magnetism, the film is excruciatingly slow and, considering it is a fairly mundane tale of jealousy, it is truly unforgivable to show it three times. *Wishful Thinking* should also be pulled up under the Trade Descriptions Act for being billed as a comedy – there isn't one funny line in the whole hour-and-a-half.

Drew hated the pressure she was under from Miramax during filming and did not mince her words after the movie wrapped. 'I was really unhappy on that movie, because I got manipulated into doing it,' she told *Harper's Bazaar*. 'Gwyneth Paltrow had the same deal with Miramax and had to make *The Pallbearer* to make *Emma*. And it's so funny, because she totally busted Harvey Weinstein in an interview. So I'm like, not only hats off to Gwyneth Paltrow, but I'm going to do it too! I got fucking manipulated into doing a goddamn movie I hated!'

*

The saving grace after *Wishful Thinking* was that Drew safely secured the role in *Everyone Says I Love You*. As her second film was also based in New York, Drew gave up her hotel suite and rented an apartment in Manhattan's trendy West Village. Unfortunately, Eric was still based on the West Coast and so the two resigned themselves to a lengthy period apart.

Drew's optimism about *Everyone Says I Love You* came screeching to a halt when Woody Allen leaked a bit of information he had carefully omitted during her auditions.

It was a musical.

Drew was singularly unimpressed.

'I have to be honest – I wasn't a big fan of musicals,' she said, 'but I thought, "The one person who could pull this off is Woody Allen." The thing he does in this movie that I love the most is he allows you to laugh when people break into song and dance. I think that's important, because I want to laugh at people who start doing that!'

Once she got over the initial shock, Drew went into panic mode.

'I've got a really deep, raspy voice,' she says, a result of her two-packs-a-day cigarette habit, 'but my character's voice was pretty and pure, so I couldn't sing like that.'

Woody insisted that he 'wanted to do a musical for people who couldn't sing', but Drew was even more adamant that her voice was unsuitable. 'It was hard, because I didn't want people to think I didn't take my job seriously,' says Drew, who refused point-blank to contribute musically. At the end of the day, Drew remained resolute and she is the only person to be dubbed in the finished product.

Make no mistake that it's a musical as Holden (Ed Norton) opens the film singing to Skylar (Barrymore), but it is also pretty tongue-in-cheek stuff as he is joined by three mothers pushing prams, an elderly lady and her carer, and a beggar on the street. Teenage D.J. (Natasha Lyonne) narrates the story of her family's disastrous love lives, introducing her mother (Goldie Hawn), stepfather (Alan Alda), sister Skylar and her boyfriend Holden, stepsisters (Gaby Hoffmann, Natalie Portman), her real father (Woody Allen), and finally Von (Julia Roberts) a patient in therapy initially unconnected to the rest of the characters.

The songs are beautiful standards from the 1930s and 1940s, including 'Just You, Just Me', 'My Baby Just Cares For Me' and 'I'm Thru With Love'. Fortunately Drew only has one number, which is reasonably well dubbed. The real fun lies with the unlikely romance between Allen's and Roberts's characters. Drew's line, 'I've never been kissed by a sociopath before,' said to Tim Roth playing an ex-con, is quite brilliantly delivered and she competently handles the rest of her reasonable-sized role.

Everyone Says I Love You is characterized by typical Woody Allen traits such as extensive hand gesticulations and 'real' conversations where people talk over one another. Although at first it doesn't seem to be a style that blends well with spontaneous bursts into song, it does become more comfortable, particularly as the numbers become increasingly bizarre – the dancing dead, the French Marx Brothers production and Goldie Hawn's flying acrobatics. The changing image of New York through the seasons is another nice Allen touch, and although the story itself ends up pretty much back at square one, it's a gently pleasing stroll through numerous relationships.

*

Having caved in and got into bed with Miramax to land the part in *Everyone Says I Love You*, Drew was rewarded with another film offer.

The proposed role was the lead in a high-school horror movie called *Scream*. Drew's childhood love of such films made her curious, but the actress feared the thriller genre had passed its peak and didn't especially want to be tied to a movie that died a death, if you'll excuse the expression.

Drew felt the compromise would be to play Casey Becker, the film's first victim, instead of the heroine, Sydney Prescott. Her reasoning was simply 'because that was really my favourite part of the movie'.

The script was the debut for writer Kevin Williamson, but having secured Wes Craven (notorious for the 1980s *Nightmare On Elm Street* series) as director, it was set to reinvent slasher films for the 1990s. However, Craven had signed up to the film believing that Drew was to be the star. When he discovered her crazy proposition, he called her up.

'I think I can take this picture and kick it off in a way that you'll be happy with,' Drew said, to try and convince the bemused director. 'Think of how astonishing it will be if my character dies after fifteen minutes – the audience will be totally flummoxed!'

Begrudgingly, Craven agreed that to kill off the movie's biggest celebrity within the first scene might just be a stroke of genius. If the audience saw Drew's name had top billing, it wouldn't occur to them that she could be the killer's starting point.

'She came in, gave us absolutely everything she had and just kicked that picture off into [the] stratosphere in the first fifteen minutes in a way nobody's been able to forget,' marvels Craven about Drew's resulting performance as Casey.

Drew's total screen time was less than twelve minutes, but the camera is on her alone for the vast majority of the shot. Casey casually walks around the house, making popcorn for a regular evening in. When the phone rings repeatedly, she is naïvely coy at first, but soon refuses to play along with the caller. The stalker is persistent and when she realizes his darker intentions, she is terrified. It is clear that she is not a resourceful person capable of fighting back, and her demise is therefore inevitable.

Drew was paid a cool $500,000 for a couple of weeks' work, but she earned every penny, putting herself through the emotional wringer. Although a fan of the more laughable slasher movies herself, Drew wanted to grip her audience with pure realism for her short but memorable appearance.

'The psychopath is strangling me, and I like the way my character reacts the way one imagines you would in such a situation,' elaborates Drew. 'You'd fight for your life, no matter what. But I would be so scared. Unfortunately, you have to take yourself into some pretty dark, sad places to scream about.

'I was acting out hysteria for days on end, shouting and shrieking. It was exhausting, and brutal on my throat, but extremely cathartic.'

Drew spoke very highly of the director. 'I would have never done the job if not for Wes Craven. Wes is the most amazing director. He's really talented.' Craven was equally complimentary, saying of his first victim, 'There is an emotionality and vulnerability. She knows what is of value and what is not. And for another thing, she's a legend in her own time.'

The nature of her single scene meant that unfortunately Drew didn't get to work with her co-stars, Neve Campbell, Courteney Cox, Skeet Ulrich and David Arquette, although she had been friends with David since they were teenage actors mixing in the same circles.

22

PRINCE OF THE REFRIGERATOR

In the spring of 1996, having not seen each other for several months due to Drew's extended stay in New York, it seemed preordained that Drew and Eric Erlandson would part company. The amicable split was sad, but Drew maintained, 'There are relationships that end and you not only remain close, but get closer in a different way.'

As was her way, though, Drew did not have to wait long before plunging headfirst into another full-on relationship. It all happened on the set of her next movie.

Tamra Davis, who had by now achieved mainstream success with 1995's *Billy Madison*, starring Adam Sandler, looked for a new project after *Sorrow Floats* was shelved. She became involved in *Best Men*, and as the male-dominated flick was cast with mostly TV actors and unknowns, she called upon Drew to provide not only the female interest, but also the star quality.

The quirky black comedy gets straight to the point as it opens with four tuxedoed men meeting a fifth at the penitentiary on his release after three years in jail. Jesse (Luke Wilson), the ex-con, is on his way to marry his girlfriend Hope (Barrymore), who has waited patiently all this time. En route to the church, one of the lads, Billy (Sean Patrick Flanery), asks to be dropped off at the bank so that he can get some money for a wedding gift. Although he says he'll catch them up, one by one they join him in the bank. Of course, when he said he wanted to pick up some money, none of them thought he would be robbing the place.

It turns out that Billy is a criminal known as 'Hamlet', currently topping the FBI's Most Wanted list. He's not nasty, though: he makes regular drop-offs at charities and orphanages. The problem with knocking off the bank in his hometown is that his cover is blown as the hostages recognize him.

Eventually, Hope hears of the fiasco and, in her full wedding regalia, breaks *into* the heist. In trying to resolve the situation, the boys receive help from their hostages, but the FBI are not willing to play fair.

The low-budget film is a gem, with several plot twists to maintain intrigue, great one-liners and many farcical situations. Although Quentin Tarantino takes the credit for reinventing the heist-gone-wrong genre with *Reservoir Dogs* (1991), *Best Men* is a slick follow-up. Without conforming to a neat Hollywood ending, this well-cast and ably directed film impresses and entertains.

For her part, Drew was more than adequate. Her appearance, however, was a shock. Since her waif-like days of getting down to 7 stone for the Guess? adverts, her weight had increased to a healthy 8½ stone, but she had recently put on a further stone-and-a-half. With over-dyed dark hair she doesn't look her best, but it hardly matters as she isn't the film's main focus.

The change of hair colour was a calculated decision on Drew's behalf. 'It's important for me to change for each role – dramatically,' she explains. 'That's one of the best things about acting – we get to be chameleons. I think you should change your hair, your make-up, your clothes all the time. It's so lame when actors look the same in every movie.'

More importantly for the actress, *Best Men* introduced her to Luke Wilson.

Tall, dark and handsome, Luke was three-and-a-half years older than Drew and for a while became better known as her boyfriend than as an actor. The third of the Wilson acting brothers (after Andrew and Owen), Luke came to prominence in Wes Anderson's acclaimed indie film *Bottle Rocket* (1993). Starting with *Best Men*, Luke made a name for himself in several romantic comedies over the next couple of years, but preferred not to attract too much attention to himself. The Texas-based Wilsons are a tight, supportive unit, as Luke verifies: 'We have a very good, close family. My parents are still together, and me and my two brothers are very close.'

Luke had been a fan of Drew's for a while; the actress fell for him in an instant. They first met in Tamra Davis's kitchen.

'He was the prince around a silver refrigerator,' laughs Drew. 'I didn't believe in love at first sight before I had met him, I kind of had to be clobbered over the head to get it. When I looked around [the refrigerator], Luke was on the other side. That was it, and my life changed.'

Although Drew realized the attraction immediately, the actors played it cool at first and took time to get to know one another. Towards the end of filming, Luke made the first move.

'I just kind of asked her out,' he recalls. 'It seemed natural. She makes you feel that at ease. She's so smart and funny and ready to laugh, she has a way of making you forget all the stuff you may have heard or read [about her].'

Wary of the pressure of media attention on a new relationship, they were careful to keep it secret. Rather than shout their new love from the rooftops as Drew was so often inclined to do, no one knew they were more than friends.

*

Over the summer of 1996, Drew had a house guest – one Courtney Love. She stayed with Drew after a spell in rehab, allegedly to break her dependency on Valium after being given an ultimatum by her then boyfriend, Edward Norton (also a friend of Drew's after *Everyone Says I Love You*). During this time, Love returned to music and worked on Hole's new album, *Live Through This*, which was steeped in the pain and anger of the losses of Kurt Cobain and Kristen Pfaff.

Drew was also forging ahead with work, and turned her attentions once more to nurturing her baby, Flower Films. During 1996, Kim Greitzer had flown the nest, and Drew and Juvonen were very much a close partnership by this stage. They were offered a vanity deal by Twentieth Century-Fox – this common practice sees the studio covering the company's overheads in return for the star producing and appearing in films, which go straight to video at best. Although a popular device in the past for struggling production companies, Drew was determined that Flower Films was going to be a legitimate entity, and should they succeed, it would be their own doing.

But she hardly had time to concentrate on either her company or her romance with Luke Wilson; Drew had a quick tonsillectomy and started a new film. When she was approached by Adam Sandler to co-star in his new venture, a romantic comedy called *The Wedding Singer*, she jumped at the chance.

Sandler's unique brand of comedy, a winning combination of tasteless vulgarity and innocent charm, had gained a loyal following. *Saturday Night Live* was going through a 'dead' phase and the show seemed to have run its course when Sandler joined in the early 1990s and proved instrumental in turning its fortunes around.

Sandler was enough of a cult figure by the time he left *SNL* to successfully branch out into films, receiving good support for early features such as *Billy Madison* (1995), which was directed by Tamra Davis, and *Happy Gilmore* (1996).

Although the new project meant that Drew didn't move forward with her own company, she was extensively involved in the script development with Sandler and Tim Herlihy (head writer of *SNL*). 'It was so exciting, and it made a huge difference,' says Drew. 'I like to be involved in films from the ground up. It's a whole different process. You get in there and get your hands dirty. It takes more out of you, but it's much more fulfilling when you get to be a collaborator.'

The story is set squarely in the mid-1980s and from the first frame of Adam Sandler singing Dead Or Alive's 'You Spin Me Round (Like A Record)', the viewer is thrown in at the deep end. The script is full of nostalgic references, from the shooting of J.R. in *Dallas* and the appearance of the Rubik's Cube to Michael Jackson gloves and moonwalking, all backed by a soundtrack to die for.

Julia (Barrymore) is a new recruit to the team catering for all aspects of a wedding, and she becomes friends with Robby (Sandler), the wedding singer.* Julia's fiancé, unfaithful yuppie Glen, finally sets a date for the wedding and she needs help organizing everything. She turns to Robby for help and it turns out to be just what he needs to get over being jilted at the altar. Julia and Robby make a lovely couple; the question is, will they realize this?

'Julia is the kind of woman men want to be with,' explains Drew. 'She's not a nag, she's fun, optimistic, confident and lacks vanity, although her glow makes her pretty attractive.' Robby was also an almost-too-good-to-be-true, likeable soul. 'I like playing guys who catch a lot of crap, and end up doing all right for themselves,' says Sandler. 'It's fun. Those guys always made me laugh, my whole life. I like people who get grief, and aren't sure how to respond to it.

'I felt comfortable playing this guy. And it felt good being with Drew – she was fun to work with, because she's so relaxed, and she makes acting look so easy.'

Sandler tends to bring with him a regular crew, which leads to a happy on-set atmosphere. 'In the morning, people were smiling when they came to work,' Drew says. 'People would clap when everybody came on. Adam kept everybody laughing all day long, every day. It just was one of the most incredible working experiences I have ever had.'

*Adam Sandler was actually in a high-school band in real life and even played at his sister's wedding.

The Wedding Singer is primarily a showcase for Adam Sandler to prove his versatility; Drew's is more of a supporting role and her charming, giggly character doesn't seem a million miles from the actress herself. But although it's not a great acting challenge, Drew's performance as the hopelessly romantic Julia is thoroughly engaging.

The love story falls down a little with the corny ending, although the singer Billy Idol makes an amusing cameo. 'Oh, he's the best!' raves Drew about the Sultan Of Snarl. 'He's awesome. He is the 1980s, of course, but he's also very timeless.' Other comedic input is provided by Jon Lovitz (*Saturday Night Live*), Steve Buscemi (*Reservoir Dogs*), and Alexis Arquette (*Threesome*), but perhaps the funniest moment is Robby's Cure-inspired song which was written both before and after his break-up with his fiancée.

On its release over the summer of 1998, most critics expected the worst from the film and were instead pleasantly surprised.

'*The Wedding Singer* aims low, and tries to be both Meg-Ryan cute and *Dumb-And-Dumber* funny; the big surprise is that it works,' said *Total Film*, while *Film Review* wrote, 'This is neither a film that holds its secrets for long, nor one that works on more than one level. Instead it is a good-natured romp, a pantomime for grown-ups that has more charms and more laughs in its ninety-seven minutes than some other comedies can muster in a whole series of sequels,' giving it four stars.

For her part, Drew received three award nominations (1998 MTV Movie Award For Best Onscreen Duo with Adam Sandler, 1999 American Comedy Award For Funniest Actress In A Motion Picture, and 1999 Blockbuster Entertainment Award For Favourite Actress In A Comedy).

She also made a friend for life. Sandler says, 'She's funny and smart. Can get goofy at the drop of a hat, can stay up late, can listen to me and not yawn. And just plain old-fashioned cool as hell.' He gave her a jukebox for her twenty-fourth birthday.

In return, Drew comments, 'Adam is amazing. I'm really close with him. We travelled the world [promoting] *The Wedding Singer*, and we became really good friends. My relationship with him is unique and profound.'

*

Drew's romance with Luke Wilson was still under wraps when they were cast opposite each other in a new film, *Home Fries*.

Producer Mark Johnson had first stumbled across the script by Vince Gilligan while judging a screenwriting contest back in 1988.

'Here was this offbeat comedy that was really original,' recalls Johnson. 'It was darkly funny and touching at the same time. In the years that followed, I always kept the script in the back of my mind as a project I wanted to produce.'

The black comedy centres on Sally, a nine-months pregnant fast-food restaurant employee. She ended her affair with the baby's father when she discovered he was married, but after his death she becomes a wanted woman pursued by his two stepsons – Angus wants to kill her, while Dorian wants to marry her.

Johnson commenced work on the project some eight years later, searching for a director whom he felt would respond to the edgy plot. That person was Dean Parisot, an award-winning director of shorts and episodes of *ER* and *Northern Exposure*. Once on board, Parisot took his time in casting the offbeat ensemble.

'It is very seldom in this business that you get your first choice for a particular role,' says Johnson. 'I know it sounds clichéd, but Drew Barrymore was the actress all of us had tagged as Sally.'

As soon as she read the script, Drew knew that this was a project in which she wanted to be involved.

'Sally is an extraordinary young woman,' she says. 'She has the optimism of a genius. There is something about her that's like a prodigy, someone with really high intelligence – and I don't mean intelligence from education, I mean intelligence from the heart.'

Parisot had seen Luke Wilson in *Bottle Rocket* and had him in mind for the role of Dorian. He has the ability to 'portray an ordinary character who, at the same time, has to be engaging,' says Johnson.

Comedy actress Catherine O'Hara had in fact read the script a few years previously and was still interested in playing the distressed widow and manipulative mother. And it was Drew who picked the fourth lead character, Angus, the borderline psychotic brother. She had spotted Jake Busey's picture in a magazine and, as he happened to be filming in Texas, where *Home Fries* was to be shot, he auditioned.* Parisot noted, 'Jake stretched the character of Angus into some deeply disturbing places. That is just what we were aiming for.'

As filming began in the Texan town of Bastrop, where they were welcomed by the locals, Drew turned to Dolly Parton for her inspiration. 'I'm not a good actress,' she volunteers. 'If I tried to "act" I'd probably really stink. I just have a good ability at adapting characters and becoming them.'

---

*Jake was also the son of Gary Busey, with whom Drew had partied as a nine-year-old at Helena's.

Less easy to master was the physical aspect of Sally's condition. 'I've played pregnant before,' she says, referring to *Boys On The Side*, 'but this time I was weighted down with a 40-pound stomach. It was very heavy and uncomfortable – you walk differently, it's harder to move around, but it made me more real.' Although Drew had professed to want children since she was just a teenager, she was vocal about the relief she felt every evening when she could remove the cumbersome suit: 'There wasn't a day that went by that I didn't wonder what it would be like if I couldn't unstrap that demon.'

*

'I didn't know they were an item when I cast Luke,' insists Dean Parisot of the lead couple in *Home Fries*. In fact, he didn't find out until an awkward lover's tiff occurred.

'I don't think I'll ever forget the day we shot the scene where Drew's very pregnant burger waitress takes Luke's befuddled stranger to her Lamaze class,' he says of the moment the two are supposed to fall in love. 'Dozens of crew members came rushing to me, saying everything from "they were fighting" to "they'd broken up". [When] I saw them together on set, I knew my stars were in major break-up mood.'

As Drew and Luke patched up their differences, the director and crew watched the pair fall for each other all over again. 'The more times they did that scene, the more it was obvious to them, and us, that they felt something very special for each other and it's captured on film forever,' he concludes.

Drew was particularly appreciative of Parisot's delicate direction. '[He's] our wonderful, wonderful fairy godfather,' she says, disregarding poor Spielberg. 'He is more a parent to me than my own parents. Luke and I love, admire and worship him. He did so much to help us understand our feelings for one another.'

Thus it finally emerged that she and Luke were an item. Drew still wanted to keep media interest to a minimum and often refused to name him, instead stating that she was 'a loveaholic now, and of all the holics you can be, that's preferable'.

Home Fries itself is a wonderfully quirky comedy of the darkest nature possible. Drew takes on a whole new look – whether it's the extra weight, short ringlets in her dyed red hair or clever make-up, she is hardly recognizable as the perfect Southern belle.

The film sparks intrigue from the beginning, carefully revealing all the pieces of the jigsaw and building progressively to the climactic ending – to say too much would be to spoil the film's charm. The slowly gathering suspense is aided by some interesting camerawork, humorous visuals and an infectious soundtrack, permeated by Chris Isaak's 'Baby Did A Bad Bad Thing' (which was later used equally effectively on *Eyes Wide Shut*). All the characters are extremely well cast and played, the only criticism being that Drew seems remarkably sprightly for a lady about to give birth.

The critics were suitably impressed by the unusually complicated story. 'Wickedly funny with superb performances,' said Jeffrey Lyons of *NBC TV*, while Bill Bregoli of *Westwood One* commented, 'A cutting edge romantic comedy.'

*

At the end of 1996, Drew was seen on the big screen in two movies. The first release was her terrifying ordeal in *Scream*.

The movie was a huge success, both at the box office and with the critics (a vast improvement from her last attempt at horror with *Doppelganger*). Many reviewers picked out Drew's brief opening scene in their praise, but the film's biggest achievement was perhaps in relaunching the entire genre for a new generation. And, if imitation is the greatest form of flattery, then *Scream* received the highest accolades with its own sequels (*Scream 2* and *Scream 3*), copycats (the *I Know What You Did Last Summer* and *Urban Legend* series) and take-offs (the *Scary Movie* series).

The first of the take-offs featured Carmen Electra as Drew Decker in a spoof of Drew's own scene. 'We had a television monitor and we watched the scene over and over, and we just went beat by beat to try to imitate that scene perfectly,' recalls Electra, who achieved the complete image of Casey Becker. 'Basically, we just took a picture and then the stylist went out and tried to recreate the same look. They even made my hair blonde and a little shorter for the film.'

On the back of the horror hype, Drew was conversely seen in Woody Allen's romantic musical. Bordering on workaholism, Drew could not help but become intrigued by an interesting new opportunity that arose at the *Everyone Says I Love You* premiere.

'I'll never forget hearing about that project,' Drew says about the proposed remake of the classic Cinderella story. 'I was going nuts for a month after that hoping that I would get an offer. It's every girl's fantasy.'

Drew spent Christmas 1996 at the Wilson homestead in Fredericksburg, Texas. She was somewhat nervous about meeting the whole family, such gatherings not being her strong point.

'They are classy, smart, intellectual people,' she said of her boyfriend's family. 'I found it intimidating. I spilled a plate of food all over my chest in the process, because I was so anxious to make a good impression.' When she settled down, Drew felt more at home than she ever had in her life. She had filmed in Texas on numerous occasions, and the ranch seemed an ideal family setting.

On her return to Hollywood, a place about which she'd never hidden her disgust, Drew spoke of an imminent move. 'I think I'll be living in Texas soon,' she said. 'Fredericksburg, Texas: it's this beautiful little town. I want to be far away from all the bullshit, and Texas reminds us that we're little. I like being so close to nature there.'

23

CONCERNED ABOUT A WASHCLOTH

'The thing I love about Elizabeth Taylor is that she made her fame matter, you know? Whenever I feel showbusiness is shallow, I remember I can use my fame to do philanthropic work.'

DREW BARRYMORE

Drew's social conscience had been awakened in 1995 and, over the past two years, had been growing in fervour. While she was crossing her fingers for the Cinderella role in 1997, she turned her attentions once again to her good deeds.

As she had always surrounded herself with pets, it was no great surprise when Drew began donating to and volunteering at Wildlife Waystation. Founded in the 1970s by Martine Colette, the non-profit organization runs an animal sanctuary situated on 160 acres of California's Angeles National Forest. The internationally recognized charity has a dual purpose: to rescue, rehabilitate and relocate wild and exotic animals; and to educate the public about the global plight of wildlife. Other celebrity contributors to the sanctuary include Brad Pitt, Keanu Reeves, Bruce Willis and Johnny Depp.

Drew also associated herself with an animal rights organization called People for the Ethical Treatment of Animals (PETA). They stand by the slogan that 'animals are not ours to eat, wear, experiment on, or use for entertainment'. Consequently, Drew became a staunch vegetarian and refused to wear animal products such as leather, suede or fur. She stuck to her guns – and proved that passion is the only fashion – when she turned down a lucrative photo shoot for the cover of *Vogue* magazine. The editors wanted her to model clothes by a company that worked with fur and leather, but Drew refused, offering instead to do the shoot wearing cruelty-free designs by Stella McCartney. An agreement was not reached.

'I love animals and I don't want to eat them or wear them,' she explained. 'I can't even eat fish because I snorkel and I'd feel guilty.' A few years later, she began to take her beliefs a stage further, inciting much ridicule. 'I'm an animist, someone who believes that everything has a soul – inanimate objects too,' she stated. 'Like a salad or a washcloth. So I'm going to be concerned about a washcloth.'

It was hard to locate, but there was some logic behind her reasoning.

'I make sure I treat everybody and everything I come into contact with respectfully,' she said. 'I mean, I don't eat burgers, but I don't judge others because they don't believe what I believe. I'm concerned with people's feelings.' Drew was also particularly conscious that the 1980s were a very selfish time for the human race and, admitting she was guilty of such an attitude, was now committed to saving the planet in the 1990s.

They say charity begins at home and, along with her work at the Waystation, Drew took in stray dogs. When she was in New York filming *Wishful Thinking* and *Everyone Says I Love You*, Drew bought two puppies, Flossie and Templeton, at a flea market. She later rescued a third stray pup from the streets, whom she called Vivian. A few years later, Drew even saved three turtles from being sold for soup in Los Angeles' Chinatown market.

As Drew approached her twenty-second birthday, she also adopted a mature stance on the issue of safe sex, becoming a spokeswoman for the Female Health Foundation (FHF). Established in 1996, FHF is a not-for-profit company dedicated to improving awareness of women's health issues worldwide, focusing in particular on education about sexual and reproductive issues. The related business, Female Health Company (FHC), is the maker of the FC Female Condom®. This new barrier method of contraception empowered women by giving them control over their health. Agreeing to promote the Female Condom, Drew visited colleges to educate students about safe sex and sexually transmitted diseases.

'Women have to take control and communicate with their boyfriends. It's empowering that women can take that into their own hands,' she said. 'I'm thrilled to be part of the Female Health Foundation. It funds clinics all over the world because it's associated with the United Nations, and it's distributing hundreds of thousands of female condoms to women all over the world.' Drew also gave several interviews in teenage and women's magazines advocating the cause and saying that the Female Condom was her own preferred method of birth control.

This new-found philanthropy and compassion even extended to her family. While the last attempt at re-establishing a relationship with Jaid had failed as soon as it began, her sporadic phone contact with John Barrymore II suddenly evolved into something deeper. The actress saw her homeless father in Hollywood from time to time and during one of his unexpected calls, she made an equally surprising proposal. Drew had a guesthouse in her new home and wondered if John would like to stay there? He readily accepted and temporarily swapped sleeping rough for the luxury of Drew's solar-heated home in Coldwater Canyon, complete with 2½ acres of land riddled with streams and ponds, a tennis court, a yoga studio, a screening room and a swimming pool with a man-made beach.

'It is the irony of the century, because we never lived together when I was growing up,' she laughs. 'He told me: "I cannot be a father. You have to understand that." He did not want a kid, but can now handle dealing with me as a friend.

'I've had to get over feelings of resentment that he never took care of me, [but] he's my father and even though he's crazy, I didn't want to read about him dying on the streets.'*

*

'I like to feel I'm mature, responsible and really together,' said Drew in 1997, 'and then I look in the mirror and see a totally ridiculous nerd, silly in every way!'

While Drew may have had difficulty viewing herself as a sensible grown woman, the rest of the world was beginning to take her quite seriously. Having refused the vanity deal Twentieth Century-Fox offered Flower Films, vowing to remain self-sufficient, in the summer of 1997 Drew and Juvonen were in a position to consider a new offer from a different branch of the company. They signed up for a two-year first-look development deal with the Fox 2000 Pictures division. Drew had particularly impressed a senior vice-president of Fox 2000, Carla Hacken, when she discussed potential scripts and simultaneously dealt with adoring fans during their initial lunchtime meeting.

The screenplays on Drew's table were varied: *Frigid And Impotent* never got beyond preliminary talks; *Born To Shop* was a tale about shopping for the perfect parents; *Like A Lady* was described by Drew

---

*It was not long before Drew and John Barrymore II were again fighting and he left. Drew currently refuses to see her ailing father but continues to pay for his healthcare.

as 'Pygmalion meets The Wizard Of Oz', in which a tomboyish jockey is taught how to act like a lady by a drag queen; All She Wanted was the true story of Brandon Teena, a young woman who lived her life as a man, but was brutally raped and murdered as a result; and Beyond The Sea was a proposed biography of the legendary 1950s crooner Bobby Darin, to star Johnny Depp with Drew as his widow, Sandra Dee.*

'When we deal with people on a business level, I just try to be direct,' says Drew. 'A lot of people like to sweep things under the carpet and not discuss them. I pull the carpet out of the room. I talk about the elephant in the corner. I don't like lies, I don't like power plays, so I just don't do it.'

It was this mature attitude that so impressed Fox, despite her youth. 'Drew has deep-seated ambitions,' says Bill Mechanic, former chairman of Fox Filmed Entertainment. 'Not like her teeth are fanged, but she wants to do more with her life than simply act.'

But Drew was soon to be away for several months, 'simply acting' in her next film – the project was in fact a dream come true which she wouldn't miss for the world – so Juvonen busied herself with organizing the Sunset Boulevard offices. She decorated the walls with a photographic wish list of people with whom they'd like to work, hired a few staff and oversaw the ten projects that were in the development stage (three of them with Fox). Drew kept in regular contact with Juvonen, not to check up on her but because she was so excited about the way Flower Films was leaping forward.

*

Perhaps it was because of her relatively unique status as former child star, or perhaps it was the kid in her that refused to grow up, but twenty-two-year-old Drew Barrymore wanted to try something different. It was quite simple: 'I want to make movies for children,' she said. And not just any old movie would do – it had to be a fairy tale.

'I just worshipped fairy tales growing up,' she explains today. 'I loved Alice In Wonderland and The Wizard Of Oz, they were my favourites. But they were a little bit psychedelic to me, whereas Cinderella was more about romance.'

According to Twentieth Century-Fox's research, about 500 versions of the Cinderella story exist all over the world, alongside the

*Kevin Spacey has since bought the film rights for Beyond The Sea and wants to play Darin, but the film is still stumbling in negotiations as Dee reportedly doesn't approve of casting Drew, preferring instead Reese Witherspoon – although then the age difference between the leads would be laughable.

traditional telling by the Brothers Grimm. *Ever After: A Cinderella Story* was to be a new twist on the tale – not in a modern setting, but with modern values. And most importantly: a modern heroine. On the back of the success of *The Wedding Singer*, Drew accepted $3 million to play the lead.

'The story was such a calling to me in my heart and soul, that I had to do it,' she says. 'Even though it's a fairy tale, there is a lot of truth in it.'

Drew was to play Danielle de Barberac, the only daughter of a French nobleman. Her father dies suddenly when Danielle is eight, but as he has recently remarried, she is brought up by his widow, Rodmilla. But Rodmilla – the archetypal evil stepmother – is snobbish and selfish, and reduces Danielle to servitude. Constantly covered in ash from cleaning the fireplace, she is given the nickname 'Cinderella' by her two stepsisters, Marguerite and Jacqueline. But this is about as far as the similarities to the popular fable went.

Although Baz Luhrmann's retelling of *William Shakespeare's Romeo + Juliet* had been undeniably successful the previous year, studio executives were initially unconvinced as to the feasibility of rehashing an old tale. 'It didn't seem new or interesting until Drew came along,' says Bill Mechanic. But Drew knew that with the right production, director, supporting cast and, of course, a brilliant effort from her in the lead, this could be a chance of a lifetime. So, with her usual boundless enthusiasm, she set about convincing the financiers – and that meant putting her money where her mouth was.

After *Everyone Says I Love You*, Drew had been offered a part in Woody Allen's forthcoming satirical comedy *Celebrity*. The shooting schedules (beginning in September 1997) clashed, so something had to give, and sadly that was the chance to work again with one of her greatest heroes – a heart-wrenching decision for Drew. Her coveted role of waitress/actress Nola was taken over by Winona Ryder, the actress whose career had so closely mirrored Drew's own.

Still, Drew's unshakeable belief in *Ever After* was further strengthened as it would mean a reunion with one of her other favourite erstwhile directors: Andy Tennant. After *Beyond Control: The Amy Fisher Story*, Tennant had progressed to directing feature films for the big screen with 1995's *It Takes Two*, followed by *Fools Rush In*, released in 1997. Tennant was Drew's own choice as director, but in turn he was allowed to pick the evil stepmother: Anjelica Huston.

'I felt that if you had Tyson, you needed Holyfield,' he explains, using a heavyweight-boxing simile. 'It was Barrymore–Huston, these two acting dynasties put together.'

Indeed, Oscar-winner Anjelica Huston was the ideal choice for Rodmilla. Although belonging to a different generation of actresses, Huston, like Drew, hailed from Hollywood royalty. The daughter of director John Huston (himself the son of actor Walter Huston), half-sister of director Danny Huston and long-time partner of Jack Nicholson, Anjelica was so much Tennant's idea of perfection as Rodmilla that he and co-writers Susannah Grant and Rick Parks tailored the script especially to her. 'It's nice to be wanted!' Huston affirmed at the time.

Drew was thrilled. 'Anjelica is so wonderful, incredible,' she enthuses of the actress she first met in the nightclubs of Los Angeles. 'To work with her was an honour and a gift for many different reasons. I got so into the idea of Huston and Barrymore working together – our ancestors looking down on us . . . I was like, "Let's go!"'

Dougray Scott was to play the dashing Prince Henry, Danielle's love interest. This was the handsome Scottish actor's big Hollywood break after appearing on stage in the West End, starring in British TV series such as *Soldier, Soldier* and in smaller parts in feature films including *Princess Caraboo* and *Deep Impact*. Scott was attracted to the part because he thought the story as a whole was romantic without being overly sentimental, a trap it could easily have slipped into.

'The Prince is such a famous character, but when I read the script I didn't see him as a fairy-tale figure,' he explains. 'He's a realistic and flawed character who has a life, a history and his own agenda.' Scott relished the thought of adding a new depth to the previously one-dimensional character.

Ever After's cast was bolstered by some other famous faces willing to give Anjelica Huston a run for her money. Celebrated French actress Jeanne Moreau played the Grande Dame of France – the great-great-granddaughter of Danielle herself – who opens the film with the intention of setting the Grimm brothers straight. The prolific Moreau surprised the rest of the cast by mingling freely with them, happy to chat and pose for photos.

The Dutch actor Jeroen Krabbé played another brief role, that of Danielle's father; British stalwarts Timothy West and Judy Parfitt appeared as the King and Queen of France; *The Rocky Horror Picture Show*'s Richard O'Brien played alternative villain Pierre le Pieu; and Patrick Godfrey was genius-in-residence Leonardo da Vinci. With American Megan Dodds and New Zealand-born Melanie Lynskey as the not-so-ugly sisters, it was an international cast to rival no other.

The filming of *Ever After* took place over just three months starting in September 1997, at a breathtaking medieval fortress and in the countryside of the splendid Périgorde region in southern France. Drew missed Luke Wilson terribly, consoling herself with nightly phone calls, but couldn't help being swept away by the sheer beauty of her environs.

'It was wonderful being surrounded in nature, which is absolutely my temple,' she says. 'I felt right at home and really lucky to be there. The level of concentration that derives from being in the middle of nowhere, working six-day weeks is incredible. People just lived and breathed this movie, rather than forgetting about it each night or going off on the weekends.'

Drew resourcefully ingratiated herself by throwing a Hallowe'en party in the second month of filming. 'Everyone was sort of segregated in their groups, but I did my best to bring people together,' she explains.

*

Ever After was set in the sixteenth century. 'When I heard that this was going to be a period piece, I wondered if it would be stiff,' Drew recalls. 'I had a few problems with Cinderella.' As a thoroughly contemporary actress, Drew thought to herself: why does Cinderella wait to be rescued? As Tennant and co. were keen to update the fairy tale, they allowed Drew's personality to infiltrate Danielle's, and the actress was instrumental in many of the changes to her character.

'I felt it was important that she wasn't sitting around, waiting for life to happen,' she says. 'She's a person who fights for what she believes in, crusades for the people she loves, tries to do right in the world. She's taken the pain in her life and turned it into her strength, yet she's not patronisingly perfect. She's still human and vulnerable.'

So instead of the traditionally passive heroine, Danielle was well-read and intelligent, and could match any man in running, jumping, horse-riding and swordplay. Drew's role became ever more physical and she insisted on performing all her own stunts. 'You get beaten up, but you know, this is a Cinderella that is very physical,' she smiles. 'She climbs trees, rides horses, she runs a lot. I was excited to play a Cinderella that not only didn't want to be rescued, but also rescued other people!'

Sword-fighting in particular was one stunt she attacked with great relish. 'I've seen a lot of really great movies where men do it, and they make it look really easy – it's not,' she admits. Drew was also relieved that her real-life hobbies included horse-riding, so she was already prepared for many of the scenes, unlike Dougray Scott, who had to take several months' of lessons before filming commenced: 'It was worth it, because I was really looking forward to working with Drew,' he says.

Interestingly, Drew also campaigned for Danielle to be a brunette. Having most recently appeared peroxide-perfect in *Scream*, either Drew felt it was time for a change, or she realized that the hair colour itself could present a clever twist. Convincing the studio, however, was hard.

'I wanted the evil sister to be the beautiful blonde,' she says. 'Cinderella should have long brown cascading hair. That was a tough battle for me.' Drew, of course, could be very persuasive when she tried, and the Danielle the audience sees on screen is indeed a brunette, the actress looking astonishingly young and fresh-faced with very little of her usual make-up to hide behind.

Other than the major changes in the protagonists' personalities, *Ever After* dispensed with many other details from the conventional *Cinderella* tale. There was to be no pumpkin turning into a glass coach, no Buttons, and the fairy godmother was imaginatively replaced by Leonardo da Vinci.

'I thought it was time to set the record straight about a few things,' says the director. 'I have two daughters and I did not want them growing up believing you have to marry a rich guy with a big house in order to live happily ever after. If you dig a little deeper and ask yourself why *Cinderella* is the most popular fairy tale of all time, it has to do with self-worth, mother–daughter relationships, sibling rivalry, things that everybody can relate to.'

'I think one of our main goals going into it was to abolish clichés and to answer questions,' agrees Drew. 'For instance, why is the stepmother so mad at Cinderella? In our version, it's because the father, when he is dying, reaches for Cinderella instead of the stepmother – and she's pissed! [She] resented Cinderella for it for the rest of her life and made her pay for that one moment.'

Of course, Danielle's complex relationship with Rodmilla all too easily brought to mind the pain Drew had endured over the years of dealing with her own mother's jealousy. Tennant's favourite scene was when the two of them are talking about the past while Danielle brushes Rodmilla's long black hair. 'It was really important for me to let them just play that scene,' he says. 'It sums up the mental abuse that goes on, but you also understand what Anjelica's back story and pain are all about.'

In another, similar scene, Danielle asks her stepmother if she had ever loved her at all. As Danielle's own mother had passed away years before, Rodmilla was the only maternal figure she had ever known, and she misguidedly hopes that their shared love of her father could one day bring them together. But the cruel, heartbreaking reply is, 'How can one love a pebble in one's shoe?'

Reading the script, Drew balked. Often in her roles she was forced to confront the reality of her relationship with Jaid, but this might be pushing it too far.

'You have no idea how close to the truth this is,' she told the director in a small voice.

'Do you want to talk about it?' he asked her, surprised.

'No.'

'Do you want to use it?' For a $3 million performance, Tennant didn't want to risk unduly upsetting his leading lady.

'Yes,' came the assured response.

'I had to hold back because I didn't want to be bawling,' said Drew of that scene, speaking after the film's release. 'When I'm dealing with the pain of my stepmother, I totally think of my own life and how much I need to have that conversation with my own mother.'

This is where the genius of casting two actresses from such high-profile chequered pasts really took effect. Huston was also a child of divorce and had never fully recovered from her mother's death in a car crash when Anjelica was just seventeen.

'There was a sense of tumultuousness that we've experienced with our families that we were able to draw from,' says Drew. 'Certain scenes became so emotional to us that we had to *hold back,* versus pushing ourselves to get there.'

Huston realized how important the moment was to Drew, and supported her accordingly. 'I'm a stickler for going the distance, but when you're around someone like Anjelica, it's a different distance you travel,' says Drew. Apparently, her performance in the couple of confrontations between Danielle and Rodmilla was so moving that the older actress was reduced to tears.

*

Ever After turned out to be just the breath of fresh air the world needed in 1998. In the wake of that year's fascination with disaster movies like *Armageddon* and *Deep Impact*, it was an upbeat, quirky diversion providing escapism, adventure and a hearty dose of morality.

'It's good to be doing this kind of movie at a time when there are so many films being made about tough, evil subjects,' said Huston. 'Being involved with something sweet and tender was a delight.' Drew extolled the strong message Danielle sent out to young women, and indeed teenage girls became the movie's biggest audience. 'She's a great role model,' she said, 'it was inspiring playing her.'

Visually, the film was stunning. 'Andy knew how to do a period piece, but also how to give it contemporary attainability,' Drew continues. 'I loved the sense of humour he put in it, and the historical references.'

Although Tennant only had a comparatively small budget with which to make *Ever After* – a mere $29 million – he chose his tools and crew exceptionally well. His first decision was to photograph in the more expensive Super-35, which gave the film an otherworldly, panoramic, theatrical feel. Then, cinematographer Andrew Dunn (*The Madness of King George*), designer Michael Howells (*Emma*, *Orlando*), and Oscar-winning costume designer Jenny Beavan (*A Room With A View*) all lent their experience to creating the gorgeous look of the film. Veteran film composer George Fenton's lush, swirling soundtrack added that extra touch of magic. The most eye-catching scene and rightful highlight of the picture has it all: the grand masked ball towards the end is spectacular, watched over by an angelic Danielle, festooned with glitter, chiffon and fairy wings.

But, somehow, all of the film's components were eclipsed by its star. Drew turned in an exquisite performance and proved she was worth every cent of her paycheck.

'After seeing the movie, and this is my opinion, it's one of the best performances I've ever seen her do,' praises Tennant. 'It felt to me that *Ever After* was her real shot at carrying a feature, and she kicked ass.'

The luminous actress 'has a wonderful relationship with the camera,' agrees Huston, 'not so much as a chameleon, but she has that star quality.' And moviegoers the world over agreed. The only fault critics could find with Drew's performance was her rather distracting accent – somewhere between Californian twang and upper-class English aristocracy.

Ever After opened in America at the end of July and found its way to British shores in early October. As thoroughly committed to the movie's promotion as to the work itself, Drew attended a plethora of premieres and press junkets, helping the film stay in the charts for months on end and gross over $60 million at the box office.

Drew's infectious gusto lends a spirit to the movie that transcends the usual 'feel-good' blandness of many lesser imitations. And the actress was amply rewarded too, receiving the Blockbuster Award, the Saturn Award and the Crystal Award for Best Actress in 1998. The following year, her success was still resonating with the Young Artist Award – Former Child Star Lifetime Achievement and Actress Of The Year at the 1999 Hollywood Film Festival.

The player was on top of her game.

*

Although Drew had spoken to Luke Wilson almost every day during their enforced separation while she was filming *Ever After*, the pair had longed to be together again. Thanksgiving 1997 was spent at the Wilsons' ranch in Fredericksburg. 'I don't eat meat, but I know they do – and that'll be great. I'll eat stuffing! I love stuffing!' enthused Drew, just thrilled to be in a loving environment.

'Most of the people I know have very close-knit families and I really like that. I get so excited when I get invited to their homes – I'm like the crazy orphan,' she explained. 'If I have a big family someday, I would love to bring people into it, because I know how good it feels.'

As Drew reached her twenty-third birthday, she was still prone to gushing about her new love, but, with age, her vocabulary was expanding. 'When you're happy and in love and you're just dripping in mellifluous perfection,' she enthused. 'I'm absolutely quixotic, it's pathetic. I love romance, I'm a sucker for it, I just love love so much, I'm crazy for it, I'm nutty for it!' She was clearly still a little repetitive, however.

During interviews, Luke cheekily added that he was amazed the relationship had lasted so long: 'She doesn't exactly have the best track record as far as relationships are concerned!' Drew was quick to defend herself. 'I used to think when I was young that it had to be really heavy in order to be deep – but it's the opposite. I think the glue in our relationship is that we enjoy spending time together and we always seem to be laughing,' she said of her current flame, suggesting that mirth was missing from previous liaisons. 'It would be really wonderful if some day Luke and I could show our grandchildren *Home Fries* as some kind of home movie. It's a sweet, romantic movie and for us it was a sweet, romantic time.'

Drew was freely talking about the likelihood of the pair becoming parents. 'I would love to have children with Luke. I am sure he would have a cool, athletic, interesting girl. I even have names I dig, like Lucy or Violet.'

Such bold statements naturally raised the question of marriage, but after her fiasco with Jeremy Thomas, Drew was understandably wary. 'Marriage is just a ceremony,' she dismissed. 'Then comes the pressure. I'm into an almost two-year relationship with my boyfriend – why mess that up? To tell the truth, I don't think that the institution of marriage has endured as well as society has.'

Wise words from one so young. But while on the subject of relationships, romance, affairs and – well – men, interviewers tended to bring up her past. Wasn't Drew a lesbian? Or at least bisexual?

At the beginning of 1998, the actress appeared as the cover girl on the launch issue of *Jane*, a New York-based magazine produced by Jane

Pratt. The ex-editor-in-chief of the controversial publication *Sassy* wanted to give women in their twenties and thirties a new-look magazine combining behind-the-scenes fashion, beauty and health tips, relationship advice, gossip, celebrity interviews, travel information, music, book and film reviews, and recipes.

As a result of the shoot, Drew and Jane were linked as a hot new item.

'I've always been bisexual,' responded Drew bluntly, 'but right now I'm very much in love with my boyfriend and I haven't been with a woman in three years.'

24

ON TIME AND UNDER BUDGET

In March 1998, Drew attended the Academy Awards, looking the perfect picture of wholesome happiness. Long gone was her dyed-black hair and dark make-up, replaced with a blonde pixie hairdo adorned with daisies and simple make-up highlighted by strident red lipstick; completing the look was a simple off-the-peg dress, which revealed her tattoos.

Even *Time* magazine were impressed with her new image, claiming she had undergone the best transformation since Courtney Love went glam. 'I think it's fulfilling to constantly reinvent yourself,' says Drew. 'Who I am as a person is very different than when I was younger.'

The public also noticed that the twenty-three-year-old had proved herself to be respectable both in her personal life and as an actress. 'Young girls come up to me all the time to ask for advice. I think they see me as a survivor,' she acknowledged. 'I experienced way too much as a child, although I believe that was out of a misguided conviction that I wasn't going to live very long. There are very few people who can claim to have got it all out of their system at my age!'

Despite her ditzy image, Drew's head certainly wasn't in the clouds. She was deeply involved in difficult negotiations for Flower Films' first production. Having made great headway in setting up the administrative side of Flower Films during 1997, while Drew was away filming *Ever After*, Nancy Juvonen had also been ploughing through the screenplays with which they were inundated. It was she who first stumbled across *Never Been Kissed*, knowing instantly that it was right for both Drew and the company.

The romantic comedy centres on Josie, a geeky twenty-something copy-editor at the *Chicago Sun-Times* who hopes to one day become a proper journalist. Then her boss gives her an undercover assignment: to enrol in high school posing as a teenager to research a piece on the youth of America. Josie is thrilled, but is reminded of her hideous experience of education the first time round, when she was nicknamed 'Josie Grossie'. Accepting the task on the assumption that as an adult she can handle the teenagers, Josie is mortified as she is ridiculed from her very first day. She quickly becomes friends with the calculus nerds (who call themselves 'The Denominators'), but must infiltrate the cool clique for the sake of her story. Therein lies her greatest challenge.

Juvonen was particularly taken by the idea of 'finding your inner self'. 'There are times in all of our lives when we tried to fit in somewhere, whether it was at camp, in school, or in the workplace; most times we at first don't succeed,' she elaborates. 'Josie has to go through many levels of discomfort before she finally finds that acceptance from within.'

Without further ado, she pitched the story to Drew, who was similarly hooked. By the time the actress had finished reading the script, she connected fully with the main character. 'I wanted to make this movie because it taps into an emotion everyone can identify with: the awkward moments of our high school years,' says Drew. 'Josie completely lacks in social skills, and now, when she has to relive those years by going back, she again misses the mark by a mile.'

Flower Films took the script to Fox as part of their first-look deal at the end of 1997. The studio executives were equally enthusiastic about the screenplay, but had serious reservations about Drew playing the lead. While Drew could obviously relate to the uncomfortable school years, Josie was also supposed to be a virgin in sex, drink and drugs – something to which Drew could hardly lay claim. 'No one believed I could play such an innocent role,' laments the former wild child.

But Drew was not giving up that easily. She persisted for weeks and then months, convinced that the film could work, and with her as the star. 'Drew kept talking about a caterpillar who turns into a butter-fly, which is a story she connects to,' recalls Fox executive Kevin McCormick.

Drew explained that it was much deeper than a plain-Jane trans-formation movie: 'All the beauty, all the ugliness, and the outside is just the shell that you work with. High school was the perfect venue for that self-exploration, self-examination and how to learn to love yourself.'

Eventually, by the spring of 1998, she had won the battle. The Fox execs were willing to take the gamble of putting Hollywood's current darling up on screen as a dork.

*

Drew was ecstatic. Not only had she won the role of Josie, but she was finally about to try her hand at producing, having worked without credit behind the scenes on *The Wedding Singer* and *Ever After*.

With the shoot of *Never Been Kissed* scheduled for the summer of 1998, Drew felt under stress during preproduction – not least as Flower Films' first foray *had* to be a success. 'Producing is so much fun, but it's really hard, because you want to make sure everything's right,' she says. 'I was involved in every aspect of making the film: casting, production, design, costumes.

'It can be a lot of pressure, but producing gives you another [creative] outlet. I like being in control of my life, and I really like trying to be a problem solver.'

One of Drew's primary tasks was to choose actors and actresses for the lead characters. Handsome French-American actor Michael Vartan had appeared in several European and independent films, but was still a relative unknown. Drew wanted him to play her love interest in the film regardless of his lack of star appeal. Again Fox voiced their reservations, but again Drew won them over.

'I heard through the grapevine that she really fought to get me in this film,' said Vartan gratefully on getting the role. 'To a studio, I'm still a nobody, so this is a great opportunity.'

The mutual attraction between Josie and her English Literature teacher, Sam Coulson (Vartan), poses an amusing dilemma for both parties. 'She really can't say anything to him about her real purpose there, for fear of losing her job,' he explains. 'At the same time, he may be falling in love with someone he thinks is a seventeen-year-old student.'

LeeLee Sobieski (*Deep Impact*) was put forward to play the most popular girl in school by Fox, but they were thwarted once more. This time the challenge came from Sobieski, as she insisted on portraying the antithetical role of Aldys, 'Queen of the Nerds'. Sobieski's choice reflected her desire to take on more unconventional roles, and was also influenced by the chance to work so closely with Drew. 'There's no other actress I look up to as much as Drew. I'm so amazed by her, because she's had a hard life and she's still become the sweetest person in the world,' she said.

Drew looked to her old friend David Arquette to play her cool older brother, Rob, which proved a natural role for him. 'I feel very close to

Drew; I've seen her grow up, so we've built a trust and now it's very comforting to work with her,' said the actor. 'I feel like she's my sister; she's an incredibly sweet, warm-hearted person.' Arquette, also from a family of entertainers, was currently well known for reprising his role in the *Scream* sequel – and dating his co-star Courteney Cox.

Josie's promiscuous best friend, Anita, is played by *Saturday Night Live* cast member Molly Shannon, while her boss, Gus, is played by John C. Reilly (*Boogie Nights*).

'We've put together a wonderful cast which, to me, was the most difficult experience,' recalled Drew after all the contracts were signed. 'You never want to compromise – you just want to get the best people who are right for the film.'

The director for *Never Been Kissed* was another newcomer: Raja Gosnell had worked as a film editor since 1975, with credits including *Pretty Woman* and *Mrs Doubtfire*, but waited until 1997 for his directorial debut with *Home Alone 3*. This was his second experience at the helm – one up on Drew as producer – and the pair rallied together.

'It's very empowering to have the opportunity to make so many decisions, but it's still a democracy and majority rules,' says Drew of the artistic hierarchy of moviemaking. 'You choose your battles and stick to certain things that you're passionate about.'

Gosnell was praising of her ability and attitude as a producer. 'Drew's very creative and brought a lot to the process,' he says. 'She lived with this story for so long that she knew it inside and out.'

With the bulk of filming taking place at two schools in southern California and in downtown Los Angeles, where the *Chicago Sun-Times* office interiors were shot, Drew was always keen to maintain a happy, positive environment. 'It's a great thing to be able to create an atmosphere where actors are free to do what they want and improvise a little,' she says.

'We were like a barrel of monkeys, constantly laughing and hanging out. David and I have known each other for eleven years. He's gorgeous and effervescent and giving of himself, and he's fun. And LeeLee is someone who just jumps out at you because she's so charismatic and unique. I believe that I'll know her for the rest of my life.'

Once she had conquered many of the initial headaches, *Never Been Kissed* proved an enjoyable first project as producer for Drew. 'Producing is hard work, and my ambition is to write and direct movies, which is even harder,' she says. 'I wanted to make a good first impression – I was on time and under budget.'

*

The film's plot was straightforward enough, but Drew had to be careful that she didn't alienate a large part of her potential audience by making a teen flick. Establishing a strong grown-up work environment at the start of the movie really helped, and also allowed Josie to be portrayed as a nitpicking control-freak. Far from Drew the glamorous Hollywood star, Drew as Josie looks exceptionally frumpy, almost to the point of being unrecognizable at first.

'I wore the ugliest hair, make-up, and wardrobe in the history of movies,' she laughs. 'I remember the studio would get dailies and it was very hard for them. I wanted to make myself look so ugly that people didn't like me, to be so goofy that people felt uncomfortable. I wanted to make choices that were so repellent for such a nice person that you would have to get to the root of what the movie is about: the outside is bullshit, and it's the inside – the heart, the kindness – that matters.'

Worse still is the image of Josie in high school first time round (viewed in a series of flashbacks), with long, unkempt mousy-brown hair, braces, spots and very square outfits. Humiliated from the word go, Drew makes Josie so excruciatingly embarrassing that it is sometimes hard to watch.

During the course of her trials and tribulations, Josie progresses from being the office geek to a popular prom queen. But while that would normally mark the end of a teen movie, her problems are only just beginning.

'It's a slice of life, with a lot of humour, and the adults in the audience enjoy it as much as the kids,' says Drew. Unfortunately, that meant that there would have to be a moral to the story, and it is here that *Never Been Kissed* borders on being overly sentimental, but with a splash of comedy it just about scrapes through. With a fine cast, a good script, and a healthy combination of slapstick, romance and emotion, the film is a worthy addition to the romantic-comedy genre.

*

Proving that she really had been working hard over the last few years, Drew went from one premiere to another. *Ever After* stormed the box offices over the summer and autumn, and then *Home Fries* was released in November 1998.

Unfortunately, the reviews, like the box-office takings, were mediocre: 'The sheer lunacy of it all is half the charm, with the chubblicious Barrymore and squeeze Luke Wilson (dating on and off set) making a captivating odd couple,' said *heat* magazine, while *Video Movie Guide* wrote, 'The amiably offbeat premise and the sweet, vulnerable performances of Barrymore and Luke Wilson help to offset the meandering contrivances of the script and Dean Parisot's uneasy direction.'

The second film to star the lovers attracted considerable attention to the pair, who hadn't really spent much time together due to Drew's hectic schedule. The cracks were beginning to show.

Luke admitted that, 'Drew and I are lovers, but we need our space,' and Drew confessed that she found it hard to maintain a mutually respectful relationship when she didn't see her boyfriend. 'How do you keep it going?' she questioned tellingly. 'How do you keep a consistent healthy relationship going that's communicative and has compromise, yet allows you to remain the individual [he] fell in love with?'

Tongues began to wag when Drew was seen stepping out with Jeremy Davies. Having made his debut in Drew's film *Guncrazy*, Jeremy went on to play a series of damaged and offbeat characters before achieving kudos and fame in *Nell* and, in 1998, *Saving Private Ryan*. The pair were reintroduced by Steven Spielberg at a party after the Golden Globe Awards to celebrate the success of *Saving Private Ryan*. Drew insisted that she and Jeremy were just good friends . . .

Drew hardly had time for Luke, let alone anyone else, as she couldn't let her career stand still, not even for a minute. The day-to-day running of Flower Films was ably handled by Nancy Juvonen: 'I thrive on systems and organization, while Drew is so creative. A lot of the business stuff doesn't interest her, so we both enjoy doing what we excel at.' Meanwhile, Drew employed a new personal assistant, Chris Miller. 'We refer to ourselves as an old married couple,' jokes Miller. 'I spend more time with her than anyone. Also, I'm interested in producing and I'm gaining a lot of experience.'

Although her business was flourishing, Drew was left smarting a little at the 1999 award ceremonies. She had been so caught up in her obsession with the true-story film *All She Wanted* that she had neglected to find out if any other companies were interested. As with *Sorrow Floats*, Drew boldly told reporters about her plans and was quoted as saying, 'Playing a boy would be the biggest challenge of my life.' She even credited the movie in her filmography on the DVD of *The Wedding Singer*.

However, while Flower Films had been in production talks with Diane Keaton's Blue Relief Productions, Fox Searchlight Pictures eventually purchased the rights, stealing the project from under their noses. It was Hilary Swank who portrayed the young woman killed for posing as a man in the film, renamed *Boys Don't Cry*.

Drew was bitterly disappointed, not to mention hugely embarrassed.

'I really wanted to do the Brandon Teena movie – I wanted to produce and star in it,' she said. 'I had such a great interest in the film and told everyone long before I should have. I have learned to keep my mouth shut.'

Swank swept the board at all the award ceremonies the following year, winning an Oscar and a Golden Globe for her riveting performance.

*

Still smarting from losing out on the pivotal Brandon Teena role, Drew instead immersed herself in another project, lending her vocal talents to an animation.

On the back of Disney's phenomenal success with *Beauty And The Beast* in 1991 and *Aladdin* in 1992, the heavyweight company delved into Greek mythology to produce *Hercules* in 1997. Although the film featured the fabulous vocal talents of James Woods, Danny DeVito and Tate Donovan, it was surprisingly not a box-office success. The spin-off TV series was already in production and had secured a host of famous names; regulars joining DeVito and Woods included Sandra Bernhard, Eric Idle, Lisa Kudrow and most of the cast of *Frasier*.

Then, without even waiting to see the audience response to the series, Disney made the shock decision to cut the episodes to just sixty-five – sadly, Drew had signed up for one of the programmes that never made it.

Instead, she reunited with Twentieth Century-Fox for their apocalyptic sci-fi feature *Titan A.E.* (working title *Planet Ice*), which combined traditional cell animation with state-of-the-art computer-generated imagery. Drew voiced the role of Akima, opposite Cale (Matt Damon), Korso (Bill Pullman), Gune (John Leguizamo) and Preed (Nathan Lane).

Set one thousand years in the future, aliens have destroyed the earth as they feared the construction of a spaceship called Titan. Shortly before the final destruction of the planet, Titan is hidden by its inventor, who gives his son, Cale, a map to find it. His reluctant quest to save humanity is aided by Korso and Akima, a spacecraft captain and pilot respectively, and a crew of friendly aliens.

Despite the impressive technical credits and aesthetic polish, *Titan A.E.*, directed by Don Bluth (*Land Before Time* and *Anastasia*), ultimately falls flat due to a clichéd script, underdeveloped story and weak characters. Bluth, usually influenced by Disney's strong, winning style, instead chose to reference several live-action classics, including *Star Wars* and *Independence Day*, which does not work. Furthermore, serious stories such as saving the earth are not particularly well suited to animation, as the 'actors' are unable to portray the range of emotions required. *Titan A.E.* tried to appeal to both adults and children, but even with a big-name cast it failed; Disney was similarly stumped with their more adult version of *Hunchback Of Notre Dame* (1996).

The summer release did nothing for its stars, and in fact *Titan A.E.* was so financially disappointing that Fox scrapped plans for a full-time animation studio to rival Disney and DreamWorks SKG.

*

A few minor hitches aside, little could hold Drew back, and in March 1999 she made her second appearance hosting *Saturday Night Live*. For the popular sketch show, 1995–2000 was known as 'The Era of Talented Women' as *SNL*'s audience embraced a female ensemble of Cheri Oteri, Molly Shannon and Ana Gasteyer. That *Never Been Kissed* not only co-starred Shannon, but was also written by head *SNL* contributor Tim Herlihy (*The Wedding Singer*), undoubtedly led to Drew's invitation.

It had been almost seventeen years since Drew's first appearance, and this time she was willing to tackle the opening speech. 'All I want to do in my monologue is two things: I want it to be a musical number because to me those are so funny. And . . . I really want to make fun of myself, but I don't want it to be so mean that I get a bad taste in my mouth,' she told Herlihy. It was set to be a cathartic moment.

Although Drew does not have the best singing voice, she bravely opened with a ditty detailing her wild adventures to date, including her years as a child star, drug addict, teenage vamp, quickie bride and *Late Show* flasher. She amply succeeded in her goals: the audience laughed with gusto – *with* her, not *at* her.

The following week, Drew accompanied old friend Edward Norton to the Academy Awards, sparking further gossip that she had split with Luke Wilson and started a new relationship – with another of Courtney Love's exes. 'We've been friends since the Woody Allen movie, like best friends,' Drew asserted, but dismissed the tittle-tattle.

Just a few weeks later, *Never Been Kissed* was released and Drew was once again required for promotional events, meaning even more time away from Luke. Determined to help her first production in any way she could, Drew attended endless interviews, junkets, chat shows and any other appearances offered. The result was a respectable $55 million domestic gross, a handful of award nominations for Funniest Actress, and the ShoWest 2000 Comedy Star Of The Year award – which Drew was the first female to win.

When the reviewers looked beyond the teen-movie façade, they were generally impressed. 'But despite the almost painful predictability of the plot, *Never Been Kissed* breathes new life into the ugly-duckling-makes-good scenario,' commented Jonathan Ross. 'Barrymore revels in being clumsy and unattractive.'

Drew was on top of the world. 'A few years ago I'd have gone into a deep depression, thinking I don't deserve success because I'm frivolous and worthless,' she said proudly. 'Today I can look at myself in the mirror and feel happy to be me.'

25

GOOD MORNING ANGELS

Drew Barrymore had always been a big fan of the 1970s television series *Charlie's Angels*, about three former policewomen who work for an anonymous boss, Charlie, who is heard, but never seen. It had been Drew's girlhood fantasy to play Jaclyn Smith's Kelly – 'she had this great confidence about her that I always thought was so sexy' – but Drew particularly related to Charlie's ethos of giving people opportunities. Fortunately, so did the original producer, Leonard Goldberg.

When Drew first heard rumours on the Hollywood grapevine of the movie version (following recent adaptations of the 1960s shows *Mission: Impossible* and *The Avengers*), she begged Goldberg to send her some of the possible scripts that were being considered.

When she read them, she was horrified. 'It just doesn't work,' she flatly told Goldberg. 'Your movie is not what *Charlie's Angels* is all about.'

Rather than getting on his high horse, in April 1999 Goldberg hired Flower Films as co-producers and brought Columbia Pictures on board. And so began the story of the ultimate girl-power flick.

'I saw *Charlie's Angels* as being about three women who are completely in touch with their femininity,' says Drew. 'There's never been enough action movies for women to star in – you don't see a lot of roles for women where they can be strong and capable *and* feminine, all at the same time.'

Drew and Juvonen went back to Goldberg and Columbia with a presentation pitch of magazine clippings, illustrating everything from who they would cast alongside Drew to the colour scheme. 'It may seem unusual,' laughs Juvonen, 'but that's how Drew does the work.'

With Columbia execs on board, Drew commenced preproduction using the skills and knowledge she had picked up during *Never Been Kissed*. Her first port of call was to find another Angel, and she contacted her buddy Cameron Diaz.

'I met Drew when I was modelling – she was working at a coffee shop,' says Cameron. The leggy beauty turned her attentions to acting in the early 1990s and was a sensation in her debut opposite Jim Carrey in *The Mask* (1994). She then took acting lessons and appeared in a number of independent films before memorably starring in *My Best Friend's Wedding*, *There's Something About Mary* and *Being John Malkovich*.

'I was in my car and got a message that Drew wanted to talk to me,' Cameron remembers. 'I called her back, and we talked for almost two hours until the battery on my phone ran out. She said, "It's going to be a chick action movie. We get to be beautiful and tough, and we get to wear badass clothes. In this movie, it's the girls that are going to kick ass." Drew Barrymore is the best saleswoman in the world – if she likes it, you're sold!'

With one down and one to go, the producer drew up a list of possibles to complete the trio and set about finding a director. Drew had known thirty-year-old Joseph McGinty Nichol, aka McG, for several years, and she arranged a meeting.

'I was just praying to hear someone convey all the things that, as a producer, I felt responsible for making happen,' explains Drew. 'McG just said everything I had hoped I would hear a director say.'

There was one slight snag: although McG had made a respectable name for himself as a director, it was not in feature films. After graduating from the University of California, Irvine with a psychology degree, McG became an MTV music-video director for artists such as Smash Mouth and Sugar Ray. The studio was understandably reluctant to entrust a big-budget action movie to a first-timer.

McG presented an impressive three-hour pitch, mapping out the whole film on index cards and acting out several key moments. 'I took my jacket off and I rolled up my sleeves and I started circling the table,' says McG. 'Then I jumped up on a chair and started telling them the minutiae of what I wanted to do with every single scene.' The unorthodox approach worked; the fledgling director was given the go-ahead for his debut.

'Before doing the film, I made a point of watching the entire body of *Charlie's Angels*,' recalls the dedicated director. 'There's the Shelly,

Tanya and Cheryl days, as well as the Farrah, Jackie and Kate days – I saw them all and discovered *Charlie's Angels* is more than just a television show. It's like a piece of the American cloth, global property.'

*

For months, over the summer of 1999, Drew, Cameron and McG tackled lengthy storyboard meetings with a wide variety of writers from Susannah Grant (*Erin Brockovich*) and Akiv Goldsman (*Lost In Space*) to Steve Pink and D. V. DeVincentis (both *Grosse Pointe Blank*). The eventual credits would go to relative newcomers John August, Ryan Rowe and Ed Solomon (*Bill And Ted's Excellent Adventure*).

Working on the script with numerous writers, Drew and Juvonen felt that, as with 1996's *Mission: Impossible*, they would need to recreate the Angels in the present day in order to succeed. 'These will be entirely different Angels,' confirmed Leonard Goldberg. 'We are not remaking the series. We're making a big-screen version of it.'

While they were open to most suggestions, there was one point on which the women remained adamant. They would not fire guns.

'I wanted women who were not afraid to go in and take on life with their own hands and who didn't believe in the cowardliness of flicking a finger and "You're dead",' explains Drew.

The original Angels – Farrah Fawcett, Jaclyn Smith and Kate Jackson – were all offered brief cameos.

'I wanted very badly to pay homage to them and so did Drew,' explains Goldberg. 'There was a scene written for them – a very nice scene in which our three Angels were in an airport and they look over and see Kate, Jaclyn and Farrah going the other way, and sort of acknowledge each other. We had it all staged.'

Smith and Jackson were willing, but Fawcett (who appeared in *See You In The Morning* with Drew) proved the stumbling block; apparently she either wanted a bigger role as a villain, or felt she should take over the voice of Charlie in the ultimate show of sexual equality. No compromise was reached and although Fawcett, Smith and Jackson were absent, John Forsythe reprised his fundamental role from the television series as the mysterious, faceless boss.

In keeping with the modernization, each of the film's three stars was given a brand-new identity: Dylan is the leader, Natalie is the nerd and Alex is the class act. Drew relished the challenge of Dylan and was happy to dismiss most of her CV in the process: 'She's completely badass. I fancied it because I have just played so many nice girls and losers and girls who have never been kissed or barely know how to kiss, or puritans, or these valiant, pure-intentioned, rarely-make-a-mistake characters. I really wanted to play someone who was unashamed and was in touch with her sexuality and in touch with her bravery.'

Cameron was undecided as to which role she wanted as they all appealed in their own unique ways, but eventually chose Natalie. That just left the sassy role of tech-loving Alex to be cast. Drew's initial list spanned Lauryn Hill, Angelina Jolie, Jada Pinkett, Catherine Zeta Jones, Thandie Newton, Michelle Yeoh, Jenny McCarthy, Claire Danes, Liv Tyler, Hilary Swank, Ashley Judd and Penélope Cruz.

'I didn't really watch it, and I didn't find it fun,' said Jolie (*Girl Interrupted*, *Pushing Tin*), who turned the part down. Pinkett (*The Nutty Professor*, *Woo* and married to Will Smith) said, 'I think I'm going to do Spike [Lee]'s next movie [instead],' while the others were variously either uninterested or committed to other films. The hunt for the third Angel took on a media life of its own and claims abounded that Posh Spice, Victoria Beckham, was even approached. Fortunately, that was a fallacy.

In October 1999, with filming scheduled for the following month, Thandie Newton (*Beloved*), signed up to star as Alex. But when freak weather during the filming of *Mission: Impossible 2* delayed the schedule, she was forced to bow out. The producers began to quietly tear out their hair.

Then Drew approached Lucy Liu.

Born in America to Chinese parents, Lucy studied dance, acting and voice and started out as an actress on *Beverly Hills 90210*. Her big breakthrough came in 1998, when she was cast as man-eating Ling Woo on the popular TV series *Ally McBeal*. Lucy's film work included *Payback* with Mel Gibson in 1999; she jumped at the chance to enhance her hardened image in *Charlie's Angels*.

During her audition, Lucy was subjected to the distracting attentions of Drew and Cameron playing with her hair, but she held her own. 'I don't think I've laughed so hard at a reading. I forgot about the job for a minute. It was more about finding friends I was hoping I could get to know better,' says Lucy, adding, 'I was hired as an all-American girl. This is a big step for the Asian community and it's nice to be recognized.'

Drew also secured veteran *Saturday Night Live* comic Bill Murray (*Ghostbusters*, *Groundhog Day*) as the Angels' intermediary boss, Bosley, Sam Rockwell (*Galaxy Quest*) as the kidnapped electronics genius, Tim Curry (*Three Musketeers*) as the prime suspect, Crispin Glover (*Back To The Future*) as the Creepy Thin Man and Matt LeBlanc (*Friends*) as Alex's eye-candy boyfriend.

*

'I spent a lot of 1999 being full of fear,' Drew admitted of Flower Films' biggest year so far. 'I feel like step one was *Never Been Kissed*, we kind of skipped steps two, three, and four, and went to five. I don't think we had any idea of how intense [*Charlie's Angels*] would be . . . On a moviemaking level it was hard – high-stress, big-budget.'

But before the distraught producer even got to the filming stage, she had a few personal issues to deal with. By August, Drew's relationship with Luke Wilson, which had been on the rocks for a while, finally caved in. 'You shouldn't put yourself through hell to keep a relationship going,' she said. 'We were deeply in love [but] Luke follows his own voice and I need someone who can be a little more dependable. We work as friends and we're both cool with how we've ended the romantic part of our relationship.' It was just as well that Drew intended on remaining friends with her ex, as he had already landed a small role in *Charlie's Angels* as Pete, Natalie's boyfriend.

To recharge her batteries, the actress jetted off to the lush Hawaiian island of Kauai on her own, soaking up the tranquil surroundings in solitude. As with her first experience of living alone, holidaying without companions gave Drew some much-needed time to discover inner peace.

'My whole life I have hoped that I would find someone who would make me feel like they weren't going to leave,' she mused. 'I've finally found someone who does that for me, and it's so exciting because it's *me*. It's the weirdest revelation I've ever had. I will always be there for myself.'

Drew also thought about how she could improve future relationships. 'I'm trying to be a less complicated girlfriend [next time],' she continued. 'I'm learning how to think first and speak later, to say something eloquently instead of using the acid tongue.'

Although Drew professed to be happy on her own, it was not long before she was again linked to Jeremy Davies, this time with a little more substance behind the rumours. 'I really didn't pay any attention to him as a "guy" at the time,' says Drew of their first meeting in *Guncrazy*. 'But, looking back, I guess we were flirting even then.'

Barely a month after starting to date, Drew was saying blithely, 'Jeremy's the love of my life. I don't care how crazy I sound, but I'm already so in love that I swoon when I see him.' Despite her proclamations, the relationship was short-lived.

*

As if man trouble wasn't enough, the recurring saga that was Drew's mother resurfaced once more. Jaid had begun to give interviews in which she sobbed about being estranged from her daughter. 'I know when she has a child of her own, she will view me differently,' Jaid stated. 'Perhaps then she will understand why I acted as I did. I did everything for Drew. She didn't magically become a star – I did it.'

Shirking any responsibility for the more unsavoury aspects of her daughter's childhood, Jaid was still brazenly cashing in on Drew's fame. One interviewer tellingly described her: 'Jaid is wafer thin, with tumbling, brown curls, and huge, bee-stung lips. Jaid is childish in her words and demeanour. She talks at a million miles an hour . . . All her sentences seem to centre around "me". She frequently bursts into tears and explains by saying: "I'm just too theatrical for my own good." '

In November 1999, Jaid went one step too far and put Drew's childhood memorabilia up for auction on the internet. Fortunately for Drew, the lots, which included baby clothes, the tiny cowboy hat that Drew wore in *E.T.*, Christmas cards from Jack Nicholson and Kathleen Turner, and a scrapbook from a 1984 trip to Paris, were all ridiculously overpriced and failed to attract their minimum bids.

The auction did not go unnoticed by the press and Jaid was widely derided for such an insensitive, selfish and attention-seeking action. While Jaid defended her latest move, saying, 'Drew is such a magical person. I want people to be a part of her life,' Drew wanted nothing more to do with her mother.

*

Back to the 'real world'. While Charlie's Angels refused to use guns, the fight scenes still needed to be fun and exciting, particularly in the wake of such explosive action films as *Mission: Impossible* and *The Matrix*, which meant that the actresses needed to be physically fit enough to perform the powerful stunts.

McG hired Cheung-Yan Yuen, younger brother of *The Matrix*'s head choreographer Wo-Ping and an award-winning stunt choreographer in his own right. He took his job very seriously and proved a ruthless taskmaster.

'We're going to introduce you to your new best friend,' said Yuen. 'You will learn to love him, embrace him, know him by name.'

'Who is it?' the girls asked enthusiastically.

'Pain,' came the unflinching response.

'In the beginning, we trained six to eight hours a day,' explains Drew, who started working out with Cameron; Lucy played catch-up when she joined, but she had previously studied various martial arts. 'We punched this bag hour, after hour, after hour. You sweat. You bond. You learn things that you never thought you could do. By the end of the day, your hands are covered with broken blood vessels.'

'Drew and I spent months and months with a kung fu master to look like we could fight the bad guys, learning how to kick, jump, jab and hit,' adds Cameron. 'There were days when I thought I couldn't move because I was sore from training. It took a lot of blood, sweat and tears, but we always knew it wasn't going to be easy.'

Drew's character, Dylan, was particularly daring, which meant that Drew had to draw on the fearlessness gained through filming *Bad Girls*. 'I loved to play a woman who did not think twice before jumping off a tall building because she knew she would land perfectly. Before the film I went and jumped off all these incredibly high waterfalls in Hawaii and did all these daredevil-type things. By the end of filming I was sky diving and scuba diving with sharks.'

Drew had to conquer her fear of flying before she was able to jump out of the plane. 'I jumped out with this guy on my back and all I kept thinking is, "Is it possible to die by sheer fear? And how long is it humanly possible to hold one's breath?"' That said, Drew maintains she would do it again.

With the tough training under their belt, the trio undertook a bizarre adventure proposed by *Marie Claire* magazine: accepting the challenge to swap their luxurious hotel rooms for a three-day survival trip in the middle of the Utah desert. They promised to keep diaries of their long weekend, but were forbidden to take food, water, matches, torches, sleeping bags, sunglasses, mobile phones, watches, radios or tents.

They were led hiking and climbing over miles of unspoilt land by Mike, Josh and Jill, guides and survival instructors. Cameron remained fairly unfazed by the trip and enjoyed embracing nature. 'I couldn't have felt more free and safe,' she says. 'It was magical.'

Lucy was a little perturbed by some of the things they had to eat, namely a whole fish. 'We ate everything: skin, fins, bones, eyeballs, cheeks,' she elaborates. 'I woke up with the worst taste in my mouth. I had a cold sweat and Cameron said I looked really pale. They gave me a piece of a cottonwood branch to chew on. That helped me clear my mouth and my senses.' The cuisine aside, she was ultimately pleased by the experience. 'We not only survived the trip, but we also worked well as a team,' she continues. 'I am the luckiest person in the world to have eaten a catfish eyeball, drunk sewer water and dangled from a cliff in their company.'

Despite Cameron's and Lucy's zeal, Drew was actually by her own admission pretty miserable for much of the trip. Her first issue was with obeying authority. Drew did not react well to being told to walk for endless miles with little food or water by the guides. On the second day she had an outburst behind a tree. 'I realized that after I cried in the canyons and pretty much had a little nervous breakdown (I thought you had nervous breakdowns at busy intersections – not in the middle of nowhere and surrounded by nature), I started to open up,' she wrote in her diary.

By the time she got back to the safety of civilization, she was grateful for the event. 'I want to thank *Marie Claire* for giving me an assignment like this,' she said, 'and an opportunity to go out into the woods and the wilderness and gain a whole new perspective on every bone in my body.'

*

With all the preparations out of the way, filming for *Charlie's Angels* finally commenced in January 2000. The labour-intensive shoot was not only draining in terms of mental and physical energy levels; there were also extra pressures.

'The studio gave us a big budget, so immediately that garners negative press,' says Nancy Juvonen, while Drew explains the other factors: 'Any time you even try and touch something that is as well loved and worshipped as *Charlie's Angels*, you already have a couple of things working against you' – namely, nostalgia for the original show and stretching an hour-long programme into a feature-length film.

And then there was the so-called *Charlie's Angels* curse. At the end of the television show's five-year run, Farrah Fawcett broke her contract, was sued for $9 million and blacklisted by Hollywood, her marriage broke up and she fell into porn movies and drug-taking. Meanwhile, Kate Jackson suffered breast cancer twice, underwent open-heart surgery, was married and divorced three times and tragically miscarried in 1992 after sixteen years of trying to get pregnant. These are but two examples of the ongoing damaging effects of being linked to the series.

According to the press (who were actually locked out of the studios), the movie version was faring no better. Rumours of all the problems on set were rife, but how many of the stories were true?

The most pressing issue was the script. Drew had never felt it was right from the first time she read the proposals, but apparently much of the original script was scrapped when no location could be found for the climax. This allegedly resulted in some fourteen writers working on a staggering thirty revisions before a compromise was reached. Critically, though, there was still no ending in place when they started filming. This, of all the rumours, was acknowledged as a serious problem.

'We did indeed have some script challenges,' admits director McG, 'and that put us in a tough spot. But we were able to create a story that supports the weight of the film and gives rise to some great character performances.'

The project had already dragged on while the producers struggled to find a third Angel, but now costs soared, pushing the movie way over budget. And money was the next source of contention.

Cameron and Drew were said to have bickered as although Cameron received the larger upfront salary (approximately $12 million), Drew as producer would exceed her own initial payment (approximately $9 million) with a cut of the profits. Lucy was then supposed to have complained bitterly about not only having a smaller salary (approximately $1.3 million), but also a reduced role and less perks. To an unbiased outsider, it would seem to make sense that the bankable star of *There's Something About Mary* received the highest wage, the producer and *Never Been Kissed* star took the next chunk (with a proportion of the profits), followed by a sitcom actress.

Money aside, one source suggested outrageously that Drew Barrymore, the least streamlined of the three actresses, demanded clean-up work in the editing suite to 'smooth out some of the unsightly lumps and bulges'. Not only was Drew in great shape courtesy of her training, but how long would that clean-up process have taken, if it was even feasible?

The dispute that received the most attention was that between Lucy Liu and Bill Murray. Several versions of the feud exist (which usually indicates serious fabrication): Liu was peeved by the amount of improvisation Murray was doing; Murray slammed Liu for having no comic talent, whereupon she shot back with some expletives; Liu had problems with the script and Murray came to its defence; and Liu hit Murray, who then stormed off set for a day.

Clarifying the last allegation, Lucy laughs, 'The rumours started going crazy that I swung at him – this guy is like 6 foot 2. I wasn't going to pull kung fu on him!' Something obviously happened, though, albeit fairly minor, and Nancy Juvonen offers an impartial point of view on the story's other variations. 'It was tense for a while, but by the end of the day they were hugging each other. Bill plays by his own rules – some days he'd show up when he wasn't needed and other days, when he was needed, he'd turn up late.'

When all the bickering was over, Drew says, 'Bill Murray told us it was like [being] backstage at an all girls' musical. It was honestly different from any other make-up trailer. We would order in tons of food and eat like pigs. We played AC/DC records and talked about boys.'

Producer Leonard Goldberg admits there were some tensions, but not squabbles, between the stars. 'The three girls united instantly,' he says. 'I had words with the girls, the director had words with the girls, I had words with him. We all got together and had good fights with the studio. But the truth is, when you have six or seven people who are very bright and very strong-willed together for six months, you are going to have arguments.'

Director McG is of the same opinion. 'We had some heated conversations about which way to take the film, but that's the passion that I would expect out of a group of creative people,' he says. 'I wouldn't want people to be so uninvolved that they weren't subject to some spirited conversations. Fortunately, we all had a really clear idea about what we wanted to do with this picture.'

The final word goes to Cameron, who produces an interesting analogy: 'Making a movie is probably a lot like giving birth. It's painful, you might have complications, but if you're lucky, you can end up with something you're proud of and will love forever. This is a baby I'm proud of.

'Things didn't always go as planned, they never do, that's just part of the whole process.'

*

When not suffering under the constant media glare, filming for *Charlie's Angels* actually progressed reasonably smoothly. The three girls became very close, synchronizing as only women know how, and gave each other nicknames. 'Pussy Lu, Pussy Pu and Pussy Drew sound a bit rude,' admits Drew, 'but we thought of us girls as having a definite male, toilet sense of humour. It's part of being sisters – you make up names for each other. I'm learning this because I don't have sisters, but this was a wonderful clue for me of what it is like.'

As the actress has always been fond of sleepovers, Cameron and Lucy were invited to one such occasion early in the shoot to watch old episodes of the television series. Having ordered a pizza, when the doorbell rang they decided to give the delivery man a thrill: three Hollywood beauties in their nighties! The poor man was so flustered that he left the property without payment and had to return to collect the money – at which point the Angels all signed a pizza box for him.

One of Cameron's most memorable moments on screen is her dancing, something which she says is a tribute to Drew. 'Her behind has a mind of its own,' Cameron explains. 'We would all be sitting there, and then Drew will start shuffling around, and the next thing you know, her booty will be dancing all over the room – much to our pleasure! So, when the script said that Natalie dances in her bedroom, I thought, "Well clearly, this is a moment to strap on some Spiderman Underoos and give Drew a homage!"'

The clothes were an important part of the Angels' style. Each Angel had an individual look, as opposed to the TV series, in which the three detectives dressed similarly. Likewise, the hair and make-up. Joseph G. Aulisi designed at least fifteen different disguises for the girls, while Barbara Lorenz, the original hairdresser from the television show, was recruited for the film. 'I tried to keep the "Essence of Angel" look very clean, very fresh, very modern,' says Kimberly Greene, head of make-up. 'But I also wanted to have a little, teeny sprinkle of the 1970s, so I kept the lips shiny. It's also very modern as well, but I wanted to keep that feeling and make it a little fun.'

And finally, there is a lovely touch that simultaneously worships Drew's past and keeps movie buffs on their toes: when Dylan escapes death by jumping from an overhanging apartment and stumbles naked through a garden in the L.A. suburbs, preserving her modesty with an inflatable ring, she bangs on the patio door of the very same house in which she filmed E.T., aged six, with Steven Spielberg.

26

CASTING COUCH

For Drew, the whole experience of filming *Charlie's Angels* was invigorating: she was producing her second film, it was a big-budget, girl-power action movie and, far more excitingly, she met and cast anarchic Canadian comedian Tom Green in a cameo role.

Almost four years older than Drew, Tom started out doing stand-up at college. He released a rap album and created a hit radio show while at the University of Ottawa and had his own series, *The Tom Green Show*, on local television by 1994. When MTV bought the show and began airing it in America in 1999, Tom was catapulted to stardom. His peculiar brand of comedy pushed the limits of taste and not everyone found it funny, but those that did appreciated gags usually involving animals (live and dead) in perverse acts and thrusting confrontational comedy onto innocent bystanders. Tom advanced to the big screen as the nerdy college student in *Road Trip* (2000).

Drew, who hardly watched television at all, heard about Tom through the grapevine and soon started tuning in just to watch his show. She quickly became a big fan and found the beanpole buffoon quite attractive too.

At the end of 1999, Drew arranged to meet Tom to discuss a small role for him in *Charlie's Angels*.

'I was just a girl with a crush – it wasn't like the casting couch,' she laughed. 'I met him with his manager and my director. It was all very civilized and respectful. I thought, "Wow, if he would only ask me out." But he didn't.'

Instead, Tom did agree to appear in the film as Dylan's boyfriend, Chad, and when Drew saw him again it was purely business. 'I didn't flirt with him at all at first because I wanted to be seen as a real professional,' she said.

Tom enjoyed his small role as the wacky tugboat captain. 'I was able to ad-lib a few times, like when I fell off the tugboat into the water,' he recalled. 'We were filming a scene in which Dylan was running away from the boat, and it was sad. I ran to see her and (purposely) fell off the end of the tugboat into the water.'*

Tom was only on set for two days, but during the short time he hung out with Drew, he felt a connection and so asked her out. Drew, ecstatic, couldn't say yes fast enough.

'He is actually a very traditional, more normal person in real life,' she said, while acknowledging, 'Tom has taught me to take life less seriously, to laugh and to have fun.' Tom is well known for being a prankster, a practice in which Drew readily participated. The day Drew was disguised as a man during filming *Charlie's Angels*, she was due to meet Tom for dinner, and decided to turn up in costume as a joke. Tom had somehow got wind of her tease and so turned up dressed as a woman.

'That caused quite a stir,' laughed Drew. 'Tom was dressed in a nun's habit with red lipstick and we were making up to each other at the bar, with everyone at the restaurant looking on in total disbelief!'

As with all her previous boyfriends, Drew fell immediately in love with her new man. 'When I met Tom, I had a calmness I'd never been capable of before,' she said. 'Tom's the first man I've ever truly felt comfortable with. No matter what I'm doing – when I'm eating, when I'm stating my opinions, when I'm embarrassing myself by admitting the things I don't like about myself – I know he's not judging me.'

Such statements might have been a little insensitive, given that Drew's ex, Luke Wilson, also had a small role in *Charlie's Angels* . . .

*

During 2000, Drew was busier than ever before. Not only was she filming and producing *Charlie's Angels* and starting a new relationship, but she was also looking out for her next project.

First on the list for Flower Films was an adaptation of Robert Nathan's 1958 novel, *So Love Returns*. The touching story is about a young writer who is shattered by the death of his wife. Unable to deal with his emotions, he becomes a recluse, isolating himself from the

*This scene was actually deleted from the final movie.

world and his two children. He is saved by the appearance of a magical woman who rises from the ocean, to be played by Drew.

It was reported that Flower Films signed up with Middle Fork Productions to produce the indie project with a $5 million budget, but as negotiations dragged on, Drew at last conceded, 'It's such a cute little novel, but we can't find a way to make it work.'

On the lookout for more work, Drew was always willing to consider projects helmed by Tamra Davis. Although their last film, *Sorrow Floats*, never got off the drawing board, the pair embarked on bringing to life another Tim Sandlin book, *Skipped Parts*.

The comedy drama is set in the 1960s and follows the sexual evolution of a teenage boy, Sam Callahan (Bug Hall). The fourteen-year-old is the son of Lydia (Jennifer Jason Leigh), a foul-mouthed, irresponsible loose woman. When the pair are ostracized by Lydia's father, they settle in a small town in Wyoming, where they struggle to fit in. Sam makes friends with his classmate Maurey Pierce (Mischa Barton), the only other reader of literature.

Maurey puts forward an unusual proposal: she asks if they can practise sex so that she doesn't seem inexperienced when she 'loses' her virginity. Sam, who has fantasies about a dream girl (Drew Barrymore), is eager to find out what drives his mother and so gets embroiled in a perverted scenario. When Lydia becomes aware of the situation, she encourages the kids (even crudely instructing them with the use of a taco shell), and her only parental advice is to stop their 'game' when Maurey starts menstruating. As fate would have it, Maurey falls pregnant before she even has a period and the teenagers face becoming parents.

As an adult, it is hard to watch the children's premature sexual relationship without feeling distinctly uneasy and, despite fine performances from all, this 'comedy' fails to evoke any compassion.

While the younger actors were newcomers, the film's main attraction was the big names. Jennifer Jason Leigh had proved herself as a versatile character actress since her professional debut aged sixteen, with award-winning roles in *The Hudsucker Proxy*, *Vicious Circle* and *Georgia*, and was good as the over-the-top mother. Drew, the other big name used to sell the movie, was on screen for less than five minutes in a total of four brief scenes, leaving the viewer feeling more than a little cheated.

Renamed *The Wonder Of Sex*, the film was released straight to video in January 2001 after test audiences indicated a theatrical launch would flop. Fortunately, the failure of *The Wonder Of Sex* did not reflect badly on Drew, who was seen to be doing her friend a favour. It seemed as though the public were willing to be lenient towards the woman they had once judged harshly.

*

In March 2000, Tom Green, Drew's boyfriend of just a few months, was diagnosed with testicular cancer. The comedian had been feeling under the weather for a while and put it down to a miscellaneous injury he had suffered while filming a stunt for his television series. But a check-up at the doctors revealed the worst.

Testicular cancer is a curable form of the disease, particularly if caught early, and Tom swiftly underwent surgery to remove his right testicle and, later, his lymph nodes. In a magnanimous bid to educate the male youth, Tom used his celebrity to make a one-hour special for MTV, documenting his ordeal with his signature brand of humour. While noble in theory, the programme is not always pleasant viewing (Tom's severed testicle makes several appearances) and one wonders if nothing is sacred anymore.

Although Tom survived the treatment, it meant that his relationship with Drew became more serious prematurely. 'I'd hardly had a chance to get to know him when he discovered he had cancer,' she said, 'and that stuff really forces you to confront what's important in life. I'm so proud of Tom and the way he's coped. He's so brave! It must be strange for him because he's so used to throwing himself around and now he has to be calm and steady for a while.'

Despite Drew's ongoing commitment to *Charlie's Angels*, she spent every night at the hospital with Tom. 'It was an interesting way to get to know your girlfriend,' he joked.

'There's always been this theory that laughter can cure cancer, so I tried to practise laughter therapy on him,' she later revealed, but it wasn't always easy. 'I would burst into tears on the set because all the feelings and worries would spill out. I tried my best to hold it together but you can only keep that act going for so long.'

Although the couple had not really had the opportunity to talk about their future, they wisely visited a sperm bank before the operation in case Tom later chose to have children, as the treatment can affect fertility. 'Tom will make a tremendous father, although we've got some time to go before making that step,' said Drew, who had always been keen on having a family one day. 'It seems like a natural course for two people in love and hopefully nothing will stand in our way.'

*

In May 2000, to boost flagging spirits on a seemingly never-ending shoot, Drew held an early wrap party for *Charlie's Angels*, although there was still one month of filming to go. Drew kitted out her house with a dance floor, four bars, a games room with air hockey, a room showing reruns of the original television series and a painting room where canvases and brushes were laid out. It is reported that some one thousand people turned up, with the notable omission of Bill Murray, one of the rumoured feuders.

Throughout the fun both on and off the set, it seemed that Jaid Barrymore was a permanent millstone around Drew's neck, dragging her down at regular intervals. The same month, Jaid was arrested in New York for unlawfully putting up concert posters and carrying a loaded handgun, along with her young boyfriend. 'I explained I had legally purchased this gun in Los Angeles ten years ago at a time Drew and I were being accosted by stalkers,' says Jaid, who had neglected to re-register it when she moved. She was charged with criminal mischief, illegal flyposting and criminal possession of a weapon, and was let off lightly with ten days' community service and six months' probation – mostly because ballistics tests showed the gun was so old and dirty it wouldn't fire.

In June Jaid started promoting a book that she was writing called *Confidential*. Unlike Drew's autobiography, *Little Girl Lost*, this was set to be a tawdry tell-all, revealing details of all her flings, including an alleged proposition by Warren Beatty for a threesome with Drew. 'It's her attempt to set the record straight,' said Jaid's agent, Sheree Bykofsky. 'Drew will learn things she's never known.' Once more, Jaid was using her daughter's fame to steal the limelight for herself.

While Drew lamented that her family was the living definition of the word 'dysfunctional', the actress had always been keen to start her own brood and had frequently spoken of marriage and children with her various boyfriends.

One day in 2000, Drew was driving along and happened to glance into a house on the side of the road. The family were sitting at the dinner table, having a meal together; something which Drew had never experienced and had always longed for. So when Tom presented her with a $86,000 diamond engagement ring in July 2000, the pieces of the jigsaw seemed to fit.

'The minute we woke up that day, something inside told me Tom was going to propose,' said Drew. 'I said yes immediately.'

'The wedding will be a blast, romantic and full of jokes. I have the best fiancé that ever lived; he's romantic, a wonderful gentleman, an incredible listener. He's not just the guy you see on the show.' Could Tom Green be the second of Drew's four fiancés to walk her up the aisle?

27

UNAPOLOGETIC, CONFIDENT AND STRONG

In 2000, director Penny Marshall stepped behind the camera for the first time in five years to bring writer Beverly Donofrio's history to life in *Riding In Cars With Boys*.

Recognizable by her distinct overbite and Bronx accent, Marshall started out as a dancer at a young age. Although successful in competitions and troupe appearances, she also went to university and graduated with degrees in maths and psychology. Marshall's older brother Garry, who had made his name as a television writer, offered her her first film role in his first movie as a screenwriter and producer, *How Sweet It Is* (1968). From there on he gave her roles in his television sitcoms, and one such appearance with Cindy Williams in an episode of *Happy Days* led to her own series: *Laverne And Shirley* debuted in 1978 and continued until 1983.

Marshall moved behind the camera for *Jumpin' Jack Flash* in 1986, starring Whoopi Goldberg. Her second attempt, *Big* in 1988, not only made a megastar of Tom Hanks but also established Marshall's career as a director. Throughout the 1990s, her directorial efforts yielded uneven results, but something about Donofrio's autobiography piqued her interest.

From an early age, Beverly Ann Donofrio displayed a sharp intelligence and a keen interest in literature – she dreamed of going to college in New York and becoming a writer. She had a good relationship with her father, a tough-but-good-hearted cop, but often tried his patience – perhaps her initials were portentous. One day the precocious preteen asked for new boobs for her birthday; the policeman found it hard to deal with his little girl growing up.

Aged fifteen, Beverly and her friend Fay were naturally interested in boys, and after being humiliated by her idol at a party, Beverly sought temporary comfort in the arms of Ray. As a result of their late-night fumble, Beverly discovered she was pregnant, and in order to protect her family's reputation the pair quickly got married. A wife and mother by sixteen, Beverly nevertheless remained determined to finish high school and go on to college. Unfortunately, Ray wrestled with responsibility, squandered all their money on his heroin addiction and eventually walked out. Beverly regales not only her struggle to survive, raise her son, Jason, and get her life back, but also Jason's perspective on being raised by a single mother.

Marshall found it easy to relate to Donofrio's life, as she herself was married with a child by the age of eighteen. 'Part of the story is so very similar to my own life,' she admits. 'This movie is about a girl who makes a mistake, but she keeps on striving and won't let go of her dream. She's a survivor.'

In bringing the story to the screen, Marshall was faced with the challenge of finding an actress who could convincingly play Donofrio at various stages of her life, ranging in age from fifteen to thirty-six. Although *Never Been Kissed* had boosted Drew's career in terms of popularity and ability as a producer, she had done little recently to suggest that she could handle such a complex range of emotions. Marshall wanted the actress to audition extensively before she made any decision.

'You create your own job,' says Drew of the films she produces, 'then you don't have to go through that [auditioning] process because it's such a painful, humiliating and awkward thing to do.' But, like Marshall, she was intrigued by *Riding In Cars With Boys*. 'I was willing to go through whatever Penny's process was,' she continues. 'Every director is different and she's really about matching up people's chemistry.'

Drew auditioned for eight hours a day, over several days, acting out much of the movie. After all that effort, Marshall went unnervingly quiet and months of no contact went by. Eventually, when the director invited the actress out for lunch, Drew assumed it was a polite let-down, to say thank you for being so patient.

'When she said yes, I was so happy!' recalls Drew. 'Then I thought, "OK, this is actually going to be the greatest challenge of my life . . ."'

'I almost got scared when she told me I got it, because I really didn't know if I could pull it off. I was glad to audition because I wanted to prove to myself that I could do it, because I was full of fear.'

*

Filming for *Riding In Cars With Boys* commenced in August 2000 and lasted a gruelling eight months. As the plot ended in 1986, Drew banned herself from any contact with television or music beyond that era. Moreover, she chose a relevant song (often by the Beatles) for each scene and listened to that tune repeatedly during her preparations.

Marshall wisely filmed much of the action in chronological order to help Drew with her transformation. 'I just went really far into the youth for fifteen; wide eyes, bangs, a fresh face, dewy skin, no make-up, and flat shoes,' explains the actress. 'By the time I was thirty-six, though, I was six inches taller, my shoulders were back and my legs were like long celery stalks. My cheeks were raised, and my eyes were higher and everything was different. I just wanted to pay attention to every single detail.'

Drew was understandably nervous about the latter sections, as she could still remember being a teenager but had never experienced single motherhood and was ten years younger than Donofrio's final age in the film. Fortunately, her dedication prevailed, as she says, 'I just lost myself so much in this character, and I became her to such a degree, that my confidence overcame my anxieties.'

Drew especially related to the story as both she and Beverly had had to fight to counteract the popular opinion that they were 'bad girls', although for different reasons. But, however emotional the journey, Drew was glad that Marshall's direction did not pander to sentimentality.

'It's not candy-coated and that's the whole reason I wanted to do it,' she says. 'Bev is very unapologetic, very confident, very strong, and she does things we all do, whether we admit it or not, which is to act unlikeable, selfish, and desperately righteous at times. The truth is, she does triumph, she is a heroic character, but it's done in such a reality-based heroism.'

Drew found the shoot hard, but was greatly helped by the presence of Donofrio herself, guiding her through the emotions and answering her questions.

'Playing me required someone who understood the wild, wilful, prematurely screwed-up person that I was,' says Donofrio, who forged a strong bond with the actress. 'Drew and I met for the first time shortly before shooting began, and we stayed up all night talking about the parallels in our lives.

'She was totally consumed by the role. She really went back to being a miserable adolescent.' Such memories brought back painful insights. 'To go back and feel all that self-hate for making those mistakes, for thinking you are a bad person, was really intense,' says Drew.

Another difficult task was trying to evoke sympathy for an unlikeable character. 'She's not a nice person a lot of the time,' explains Drew. 'She resented her child a lot of the time; she ignored him; she screamed at him.'

At first, she empathized with the character of Jason, left alone and forced to grow up prematurely. But, in playing his mother, Drew had to deal with Beverly's alien feelings of bitterness towards her child. In her own words, she was 'overcome with understanding' for her own mother.

It is very interesting, given Jaid and Drew's history, to see the various dynamics played out in the film. The moment Beverly goes into labour is particularly poignant. 'There's a scene in the film when my character's waters break, and it wasn't in the script, but I screamed "Mum!"' says Drew. 'I was calling out to my real mum, who couldn't hear me.'

*

Aside from the emotional roller coaster of *Riding In Cars With Boys*, Drew also had to master a new accent. 'I'm from California and talk like a Valley Girl, and Bev is from the East Coast and has a whole different sound,' she explains.

Along with Donofrio herself, Drew became great friends with Brittany Murphy, who plays her onscreen best friend, Fay. 'I'm like the salt, she's like the pepper,' says Drew. 'We hit it off immediately. And we fed off each other through the shoot.' Murphy first came to fame in *Clueless* in 1995 and went on to provide the voice of Luanne in the hit animated series *King Of The Hill*. 'The first time we met was like fireworks,' she laughs. 'We got along like a house on fire.'

Sara Gilbert completed the trio of friends; it was the second time she had worked with Drew. 'Drew is really light-hearted, really sweet, and really generous,' enthuses Gilbert. 'Who she is as a person is way more important than who she is as a celebrity.'

In his adult incarnation, Beverly's son, Jason, is played by Adam Garcia, who is actually two years Drew's senior. The Australian newcomer started out as a dancer and was critically acclaimed for his native work in *Hot Shoe Shuffle* and, later, West End productions of *Grease*, *Birdy* and *Saturday Night Fever*. His crossover into film in the late 1990s was successful, particularly with his starring role in *Coyote Ugly*.

'Drew is a lovely, lovely lady,' he says. 'It's bizarre working with someone like that because you can get starstruck, but she didn't want to be treated like a star at all. And it was a shame she was playing my mum because we didn't get to do any kissing scenes!'

Riding In Cars With Boys also reunited Drew with James Woods (who played her father in *Cat's Eye*). 'It's interesting to see the kind of challenges that women face and the mistakes they can make because, biologically, they can be burdened with pregnancy, and all its consequences,' says Woods of what attracted him to the film. 'I knew Drew is a wonderful actress, and I knew Penny is so detail-oriented that we'd probably find some really funny, very human things along the way.'

Gilbert adds to Woods's perception of the director's style, 'Penny likes to keep [filming] frenetic. The cameras are going, she's screaming through the takes, and saying, "Move over here." I think that's part of her thing to make it feel exciting and to get you off guard, so you're not self-conscious. It's not relaxed!'

Indeed, the voyage of self-discovery is a fine piece of work. Drew amply gets to grips with the vast range of emotions involved and, despite the bleak circumstances, there are numerous comedic moments, particularly when Beverly tries to throw herself down the stairs to induce a miscarriage and when she practises with Fay how to tell her parents that she is pregnant. The forced wedding is also a humorous affair, as it is so dire; Drew portrays the perfect picture of teenage misery.

Although key moments, such as Beverly giving birth, are frustratingly omitted, the fact that she really wanted a girl and doesn't bond with her son are more pertinent. As Beverly ages, Drew employs different postures and facial expressions to great effect. She also sports changing fashions in both her clothes and hairstyles, something which helps her transformation – unfortunately, the same cannot be said for Brittany Murphy, and consequently her progression as Fay is less successful.

Although Beverly is not a good mother, Drew manages – quite brilliantly – to evoke sympathy for her position. However, when Beverly asks, 'When does this job end?' all feelings of empathy transfer immediately to her son, who understandably blames her for his emotional instability.

Knowing Drew's past, it is admittedly hard to watch the film without relating events to her own upbringing with Jaid, but if anything, that only adds to the poignancy of the piece.

*

Although manically busy in 2000, Drew somehow managed to provide two voiceovers for animation work by Matt Groening.

Other than Tom Green's MTV show, Drew's only television addiction was *The Simpsons*. Like many, she was hooked on the antics of the realistically outrageous family and joked that Lisa was her role model 'because she's the voice of reason in a family of chaos'.

Groening was encouraged to draw by his cartoonist father from an early age and, after graduating, went to Los Angeles to find fame and fortune. His first strip, *Life In Hell*, was born from the illustrated progress reports he sent home. *The Simpsons* started out as animated segments aired during Fox's *The Tracey Ullman Show* in 1987, but by December 1989 the series about a politically incorrect family had its own time slot. Now one of television's longest-running shows, *The Simpsons* has received some eighteen Emmy Awards. Having provided guest spots for numerous stars, Groening was delighted when Drew accepted the job of voicing Sophie in an episode titled *Insane Clown Poppy*.

Drew had often tried to get involved in children's films, and when Groening pitched a second, much larger project to her, she was more than happy to fit it into her tight schedule. The film was an animated adaptation of the children's book *Olive, The Other Reindeer* and was co-produced by Groening and Drew. The story centres on Olive, a dog who is not very dog-like and is very excited about Christmas. Then she hears a radio broadcast that one of Santa's reindeer is injured and cannot fly. A press release from the North Pole says that unless 'all of the other reindeer' can help, Christmas will have to be cancelled. Olive's mischievous pet flea, Fido, misinterprets the phrase as 'Olive The Other Reindeer' and convinces Olive that not only is this her calling, but the reason she's not a very good dog is because she is, in fact, a reindeer.

The off-the-wall narrative then follows Olive's journey to the North Pole, where she offers her services to Santa. En route she bumps into a musical mailman, who is happy that Christmas is cancelled as his postbags will be lighter and so vows to curtail Olive's mission. Fortunately, the heroine is helped by Martini, a street-vendor penguin, and magically saves the day.

Drew voiced the hyperactive canine – bizarrely insisting on having her own pooches in the sound booth with her – while the supporting cast includes Dan Castellaneta (*The Simpsons*), Peter MacNichol (*Ally McBeal*), Tim Meadows (*Saturday Night Live*) and R.E.M.'s Michael Stipe, who provides voice work and a song.

As one might expect from Matt Groening, the animation is unusual to say the least, bordering on downright scary, and there are several corny word plays. Unfortunately, *Olive, The Other Reindeer* is not enjoyable for either children or adults, the worst part being the songs. Not only are they cringe-making anyway, but Drew's voice doesn't really lend itself well to singing (she was wise to insist on a stand-in for *Everyone Says I Love You*). Just when the farce becomes mind-numbing, the sight of Olive flying with envelope wings provides light relief.

All the same, the film was nominated for a 2000 Emmy Award for Outstanding Animated Program.

*

In November 2000, *Charlie's Angels* was released. The troubled production fared little better in its promotional gimmicks: journalists received silver briefcases at the press junkets, and to get to their freebies they had to key in the release date – unfortunately, someone forgot to program the code into the cases in the first place!

Partly due to all the negative publicity, critics were ready to slate the movie before it had even premiered, but early reviews and test screenings indicated that it would be a smash hit. 'Non-stop action and fun, from its over-the-top start to its giddy, glamorous finish,' said Jonathan Ross. 'There's no denying the pizzazz and playful fun of this big-screen adaptation of the notorious TV series – say what you will: this isn't boring,' wrote *Video Movie Guide*, while *Total Film* added, 'Fling all the mud you want at *Charlie's Angels*, it never pretends to be anything other than what it is: unashamed and instantly disposable popcorn entertainment.'

A month later, Drew and Lucy Liu flew across the pond for the British royal premiere, attended by Prince Charles. Drew started the evening trying to be refined for royalty, but soon realized that no one really relaxed around the prince and so when he was flanked by the two Angels at dinner, she let her hair down and chatted normally.

As always, Drew accepted invitations to most appearances to promote her film, but nothing attracted more attention than her numerous hoax weddings.

On 18 November, Tom set up an intricate 'surprise' for Drew – a wedding ceremony to be held on *Saturday Night Live*. The audience thought it was a skit, but when he dragged Drew out of the crowd, they believed it was for real. She went backstage and agreed to get dressed and walk up the aisle with her bridesmaids. At the last minute Drew bottled out, leaving Tom standing at the altar. Later, they passed it off as an elaborate joke that went too far.

Needless to say, the television show had one of the highest ratings of the season and the stunt created much interest in the *Charlie's Angels* star and producer. At the premiere, the couple continued the farce by claiming that they had in fact married, in Cleveland, after *SNL*.

*

While Tom Green involved Drew in many unorthodox pranks, he was also influential in helping to reconcile her with Jaid. The actress had mellowed in her feelings towards her mother as a result of filming *Riding In Cars With Boys*, but it was Tom who suggested making contact after all the years of bitterness.

'I had no idea how to find her,' admits Drew. 'I had a feeling she was in New York, so Tom and I started making some calls. It was so embarrassing in front of Tom not to know how to contact her, but he never judged me, he just helped me. Finally, I found her number and called.' Jaid agreed to meet up.

Drew was excited and nervous, but the pair sensibly took things slowly. At one dinner together Jaid produced a photo album, and Drew was amazed how much like her mother she looked playing Beverly Donofrio. Things began to make sense.

Tom then pushed the reconciliation further when he invited Jaid to spend Christmas with Drew and his family in Ottawa, Canada. 'I kind of freaked out at the thought,' says Drew, 'but it was really fun. Everybody got along really well.

'It was the first Christmas I'd spent with Mom in over ten years. It wouldn't have worked if Tom's family hadn't been so grounded. It gave us a sense of normality we didn't have.'

Thereafter, Drew and Jaid had many cathartic conversations, airing many of their differences, but finally able to start seeing things from both sides. 'I now see my mother every few months,' concludes Drew. 'We don't have to be best friends, we don't have to support each other and we don't have to get financially involved.'

28

WHAT WOULD YOU DO IF YOU KNEW THE FUTURE?

After the massive success of *Never Been Kissed* in 1999 and *Charlie's Angels* in 2000, Drew Barrymore and Nancy Juvonen's confidence in producing was rightly brimming. They searched for a suitable follow-up for their talents, and were rewarded with *Donnie Darko*.

It could not have been more different from their first two projects.

Donnie Darko was the brainchild of writer and director Richard Kelly, who at twenty-five years of age was just one month younger than Drew. Born and raised in Virginia, he had graduated in film from the University of California at Los Angeles in 1997. With just one 'short' behind him, this was both his first screenplay and his first feature, so any producers he managed to snare would have to put their complete faith in his proposal.

'When I came out of film school I was broke, so I started writing,' Kelly recalls. 'I set out to write something ambitious, personal, and nostalgic about the late 1980s. I thought about a jet engine falling onto a house, and no one knowing where it came from – it seemed to represent a death knell for the Reagan era – and I built the story around that.'

Set in the weeks leading up to the 1988 presidential elections, *Donnie Darko* tells the story of its eponymous hero, a strange teenage boy who is on medication for paranoid schizophrenia. Donnie comes from a 'typical' semi-dysfunctional upper-middle-class family and attends a 'typical' American high school in Middlesex, Iowa, where bullies lurk around every corner, drugs are snorted in the corridors and knives are wielded in the toilets.

Donnie is exceptionally bright and not afraid of voicing his own opinions in the face of authority. Reminiscent of Drew's description of her role in *Poison Ivy*, the director describes his protagonist as 'someone that everyone wants to be, someone that everyone wishes they were, someone that everyone knows that they were at one point in their life and certainly a character that they won't forget'.

One night Donnie sleepwalks out of his house and, in his somnambulistic stupor, he encounters Frank: a 6-foot-tall monster rabbit with a satanic, grotesquely grinning mask and bunny ears.*

Frank may or may not be a prankster, an alien, a messenger of God, the devil incarnate, or a simple flight of fancy, but his message is at once crystal-clear and utterly confusing: the world is going to end in twenty-eight days, six hours, forty-two minutes and twelve seconds.

The next morning Donnie awakens by the side of the road. When he returns home, he finds to his amazement that part of a 747 jet engine has fallen out of the sky, through the roof of his family home and come to rest in his bedroom. Had he been asleep in his bed, the accident would have been fatal. Unsurprisingly, he decides to take Frank's warning very seriously.

Over the course of the next month, Frank continues to visit Donnie, sending him on seemingly destructive missions of vandalism. Donnie believes Frank's instructions will help to save the world and so will do anything he requests, no matter how bizarre it may seem. And so he stops taking his medication.

As Donnie's mental state deteriorates (or is that the mental state of everyone around him?), he has to deal with the inhabitants of his town, namely the attitudes of his family, his girlfriend, his analyst-turned-hypnotherapist, his teachers, his classmates and the town's mentor – a mysterious 'inspirational' self-help speaker and author called Jim Cunningham.

In his quest to discover whether his life is ruled by fate or whether he can change the future, Donnie's research leads him into hallucinations, hypnosis, time travel and a fresh understanding of the apparently co-dependent relationship between good and evil. The doom-laden sense of the inevitable as the clock ticks by to the world's

---

*Obvious but unintentional comparisons can be drawn here with the 1950 film *Harvey*, in which drunkard James Stewart's imaginary friend and saviour is a 6-foot-tall, invisible white rabbit, and the 1994 movie *North*, in which Bruce Willis, dressed as the Easter Bunny, serves as Elijah Wood's conscience and advisor.

denouement leads to a memorably mind-boggling twist in this most ambitious, soul-searching chronicle.

*

The hardest part of finding a backer for *Donnie Darko* was that it was impossible to categorize. As fantasy and reality blur and become one in the story, so the finished product would reflect an unlikely fusion of science fiction, nostalgia and teen romance.

Kelly knew no one in the industry and it took fourteen whole months of dedication and rejection before it looked like his project would even get off the ground.

'At first, I would walk into a room and they would just start laughing, "Come back in five years when you actually have some kind of experience!"' he recalls. 'There was a lot of begging and a lot of screaming and yelling. It was meeting after meeting after meeting, and the response was always: "No, you're too young, it's not gonna happen . . ."'

However, his script was good, and anyone who read it loved it. They just weren't prepared to take a chance on such a gargantuan variation from the norm.

As Kelly progressed through hundreds of Hollywood offices, he attracted the attention of Jason Schwartzman, a young actor who liked the idea of playing Donnie. His agent cannily sent the script on to Flower Films.

On reading the screenplay, Drew was transfixed. If she wanted to risk a major departure, here it was, staring her in the face.

'Nancy and Drew read it and immediately loved it,' Kelly continues. 'I had a meeting with them and I asked Drew if she would play the teacher. She asked if they could be involved in making this film and that was it. Everything in my life changed after that meeting.'

'I was just so amazed,' Drew remembers. 'First of all you have so much trust in someone when they write something so extraordinary and then, speaking with him – the fact he's able to articulate all the genius that resides inside of him . . .' She was lost for words, but she and Juvonen were hooked. They agreed to produce his feature independently, using him as the director and Drew's name to help get the movie off the ground. Drew's association ensured the money started coming in and soon *Donnie Darko* was up and running.

'I was so excited, I would try and do anything I could to enable the movie getting made,' she affirms.

*

The first task in assembling *Donnie Darko* was to cast the lead role. Schwartzman had dropped out due to more concrete commitments. The new Donnie needed to be special: a dark, brooding mix with undeniable geekiness but charisma by the bucketload.

As seemed to be the case with so many of Drew's colleagues, Jake Gyllenhaal came from an eminent Hollywood family as the son of writer-producer Naomi Foner and director Stephen Gyllenhaal. A talented child actor who had made his screen debut playing Billy Crystal's son in 1991's *City Slickers*, Gyllenhaal was decidedly offbeat in his attitude, looks and direction. Still attending Columbia University when he was approached by Flower Films, Gyllenhaal was perfect for the enigmatic Donnie.

'He's incredible,' Drew enthuses. 'I always love and appreciate fate but the road we took to finding him and the fact that he *is* this character – and I swear he *is* this character – it's just the most incredible thing in the world! The more time I spend with him the more blown away by him I am.'

The family connection ensured Jake's real-life sister Maggie would play his onscreen sister, Elizabeth Darko, and with their leading man in place, Flower were fortunate to piece together a solid cast including Mary McDonnell (*Mumford*) and Holmes Osborne (*Election*) as Donnie's parents; Katharine Ross (*Home Before Dark*) as his analyst; Jena Malone (*Stepmom*) as his girlfriend, Gretchen; and Patrick Swayze (*Dirty Dancing*) as the creepy Jim Cunningham. Drew Barrymore and *ER*'s Noah Wyle stepped in line to play two of Donnie's more approachable teachers, and filming commenced in Los Angeles.

Jake Gyllenhaal was particularly excited to be working with Drew, and marvelled at how she juggled her dual responsibility to the film as actress and producer.

'It's interesting to get both perspectives,' he reflects. 'To watch her at work – it was funny because I'd turn to her and say, "God, they don't give you another take," and there was a part of her that wanted to say, "We need another take!" and there was this bit, "Shouldn't we move on?"

'There was this balance and she worked the two brilliantly.'

Drew's character, Karen Pomeroy, was the kind of English teacher every school kid wishes for; for example, she tells the new girl who arrives late to class to 'sit next to the boy you think is the cutest' – and so begins the romance between Donnie and Gretchen.

'I really like this character,' says Drew, who, with her long, centre-parted auburn hair, bears a striking resemblance to the actress Julianne Moore in the movie. 'She doesn't smile a lot, which is nice because I have this ridiculous clown face and I constantly look like some zany freak, and it's very nice to be contained!

'The level of maturity that she has in leading these kids into profound thinking and wonderful literature is so where it's at for me and all I want to do in my life, so to play a woman that's really in touch with that is just great.'

In Karen's first scene she is teaching Graham Greene's short story *The Destructors*, a controversial 1954 publication about a gang of London schoolboys deliberately destroying a beautiful eighteenth-century house which has survived the Blitz. The meaning of the story is beyond the comprehension of Donnie's classmates, but he is inspired by Greene's musing that 'destruction, after all, is a form of creation'.

The book is banned after Donnie's Frank-inspired acts of vandalism start occurring at the school. Ultimately Karen is fired, allegedly because of her slightly off-kilter teaching methods – although this is more to do with keeping certain titles on the reading list and making them available to the students even when they are forbidden.

The real tragedy for Drew with this film is that literally half of her appearances ended up on the cutting-room floor due to time constraints. Kelly originally wrote and filmed an entire follow-up storyline in which Karen replaces *The Destructors* with Richard Adams's classic *Watership Down*, the story of a warren of talking rabbits who flee the destruction of their home by a land developer (Frank clearly making his presence felt here). Through this subplot, the viewer would have come to understand the strange relationship between Karen and Donnie and also her ultimate firing.*

*

There was a danger with *Donnie Darko* being immersed in 1980s nostalgia in that its darker elements could have been eclipsed by cheap laughs and 'do you remember that' winks and nudges – dare one mention, a little like *The Wedding Singer*. Karen's shoulder pads and occasional cultural references (*The Smurfs* cartoon, the TV sitcom *Married With Children* and Stephen King's 1986 novel *It*) echoed that, albeit in a warped fashion.

But somehow any easy referencing was transcended and the finished product stood testament to a childhood in the Reagan years – when nothing really mattered and everyone belonged to the 'Me' generation. One line from the film which was ultimately cut, 'Children

---

*Fortunately for a serious fan of the film and of Drew herself, this whole episode is included as one of the extras on the DVD.

have to save themselves because the parents have no clue,' underlined this mood perfectly.

'Donnie's a teenager but he's very intelligent and a lot of the theme has to do with the fact that you have to save yourself and that your parents can't save you,' Juvonen explained. 'What all these outside influences tell you [is that] you need to make your own decisions.'

Donnie Darko turned out to be a terrific film on countless levels – the kind of feature that the viewer continues to analyse for days afterwards. The school setting is almost as frightening as any personal development for Donnie, and his aggressive confrontations of authority are steeped in reason.

Gyllenhaal is an inspired choice as Donnie. He walks trancelike even when awake and wears hoods all the time – although no doubt fashionable during the 1980s, it also gives a secretive feel only really explained by the shock ending. He ably captures the daily embarrassments of a teenage boy who is also either a genius, or is mentally ill – or both.

The film's dreamlike quality is helped by the excellent soundtrack (Echo & The Bunnymen, Tears For Fears, Duran Duran and Joy Division) paying homage to a certain indie feel, and Kelly's fabulous direction is visually reminiscent of Tim Burton, a director inextricably linked to the 1980s. Even the cast bring back memories: Drew and Patrick Swayze especially.

For a 'teen' movie, all the elements were there (new girl in town, the bullies, the annoying gym teacher, the archetypal 'outsider'), yet as Kelly envisaged, 'they existed on a different level to a point where we could poke fun at these plot contrivances. We put the whole package together in a way that is really provocative, that will hopefully speak to young people and will give them a puzzle to try to solve.'

Said Nancy Juvonen, 'I think that we'd be selling ourselves short if we sold it as a teen movie because it's very mature – I think it's going to inspire teenagers and I hope that they are thankful that we're not feeding them the same mediocre assumptions about their lives.'

Meanwhile, Drew was drawn by the depth versus the dark humour of it all. 'It has this beautiful poetic aspect of how these characters are all so deep and interesting and yet Richard's adding this lightness into it where there's such a lack of a patronising "this is the way it is",' she said. 'It opens the door to all these possibilities.'

*

It was a struggle, but an early incarnation of *Donnie Darko* was completed for the Sundance Film Festival in January 2001.

'We had barely finished in time,' says Kelly. 'We had never showed it to an audience before, so after those screenings I went back and tightened it up a bit.' At the festival, it was nominated for the prestigious Grand Jury Prize, but sadly lost out to Henry Bean's *The Believer*, the stirring story of a religious boy turned Nazi skinhead.

Donnie Darko and its creator, Richard Kelly, seemed to spring from nowhere. The film's twist ending wasn't immediately obvious and proved baffling for test audiences. But they liked it. The word-of-mouth praise soon reached fever pitch and after four months of fretting, Kelly and Flower Films signed a distribution deal with Newmarket Films.

Donnie Darko was released in the autumn in the States and soon accumulated a large cult following.* The following spring, Gyllenhaal was declared one half of *Entertainment Weekly*'s 'It Gene Pool', with his sister Maggie being the other half. He was clearly set for a glittering future both in major Hollywood features and on the London stage. Meanwhile, Richard Kelly had already written his next five movies, born of the frustration of finding a home for *Donnie Darko*.

As for Drew, she had succeeded in producing one of the most thought-provoking movies of the decade so far. Not bad for Flower Films' third effort.

*

Just before her twenty-sixth birthday, Drew was given another sharp lesson in appreciating every day as though it might be her last.

At 3.20 a.m. on Sunday 18 February 2001, she and Tom Green were woken by their dog, Flossie, barking wildly and banging at the bedroom door. Minutes later the couple noticed smoke seeping under the door and the fire alarms sounded.

With Flossie and another of Drew's three dogs at their heels (the third showed up unharmed at a neighbour's house), they escaped out of the bedroom's sliding patio doors to the guesthouse. There they dialled 911 and waited for the Los Angeles Fire Department to arrive.

Shortly after their timely exit, the bedroom ceiling collapsed, underlining how closely they had cheated death, and within minutes, the whole house had gone up in flames. There had been no time to save anything, and Drew watched in horror as her personal possessions burnt to a cinder. Eleven fire trucks and fifty-five firefighters attended the blaze, which had swept through the open-plan property with wooden floors, taking almost an hour to extinguish.

*It took over a year to progress to British shores, where it premiered on 25 October 2002.

The cause proved a mystery – ironically, Drew had given up smoking just three weeks earlier – but it finally transpired that it was a simple electrical fault. The damage was estimated at $700,000, but rather than walk away from the mess, Drew was determined to rebuild her home.

Just as Drew had tried to keep upbeat for Tom during his cancer ordeal, so Tom reciprocated. When she tried to go to sleep the following night in their hotel room, she became paranoid with the lights off.

'I started screaming, "Leave the lights on," and panting and hyperventilating,' she recalls. 'I couldn't sleep. The next night, the same thing happened. Tom said, "OK honey, don't make this into a big thing. You don't want to find yourself in ten or fifteen years unable to sleep with the lights off, having these phobias. Let's nip this in the bud."' Drew saw the sense in Tom's thinking and credits him with getting her back on track.

'The fire destroyed everything I owned,' says Drew. 'It was a difficult time for me. I had to believe the fire happened for a reason.' Rather than dwelling on all that she had lost, she chose to think of it as a cleansing experience and that she should start life afresh – with her fiancé, a revived relationship with her mother and a glittering career ahead of her. Fortunately, Drew was able to repair some of the Barrymore family silver with chemical solutions, and many of her books and photos were saved as the library door had been closed. Sadly, it was believed that the turtles she rescued from Chinatown perished in the basement.

Drew was so grateful to Flossie for sounding the initial alarm that she placed the rebuilt property in a trust fund, so that her dog would be housed no matter what happened. When wounds were healed with time, Tom made distasteful jokes about Drew's devotion to the dog, telling reporters that he had run it over. 'You never know what Tom's going to do,' Drew responded. 'You just learn to live with it, although I'm still not sure sometimes when to take him seriously – and we've been together a while.'

*

'I personally truly love comedy the most, and the more I grow up, the more I appreciate it. I actually would really love to do a movie with Tom Green,' said Drew in 2000.

Unfortunately for Drewbies, Tom reciprocated his role in *Charlie's Angels* with a cameo for the actress in his directorial debut, *Freddy Got Fingered*. Co-written by Tom and his friend Derek Harvie, the film is a feature-length vehicle for Tom's peculiar brand of gross-out comedy. But even Tom's fans were shocked as during the course of the film he accuses his father of molesting his brother, sexually pleasures various animals, licks open flesh wounds, delivers a baby using his teeth and swings it round by the umbilical cord, cuts open a dead moose and wears it, and goes scuba-diving in a toilet.

'Oh, there was constant pressure to change the title, to take out the horse scene, the umbilical-cord scene, the elephant scene,' sighs Tom. 'I'd say, "You've got to keep these things, because they're funny and they freak people out, and that's what we want to do." The good news is, all the scenes made it into the final film.'

Tom couldn't have been more mistaken. *Freddy Got Fingered* was an unmitigated box-office disaster when it was released in April 2001 and was panned by all who had the misfortune of seeing it. *Variety* called it 'one of the most brutally awful comedies ever', while super-critic Roger Ebert said, 'It doesn't scrape the bottom of the barrel – it doesn't deserve to be mentioned in the same sentence with barrels.'

Reminiscent of her *Wayne's World 2* appearance, Drew's blink-and-you'll-miss-it cameo was as a receptionist, but at least the former was seen as cult viewing. *Freddy Got Fingered* was nominated for eight Razzie awards, including Worst Director (Tom Green), Worst Actor (Tom Green), Worst Screenplay and Worst Supporting Actress (Drew Barrymore). Although only joke awards, the Razzies echoed the public's views – the film *was* terrible.

Drew valiantly defended her fiancé. 'They were vicious,' she said of the critics. 'I think he wanted a reaction. So positive or negative, he made a film for a certain audience, gender, age group. And he didn't want to compromise that and I really respect him for that. And I love the movie.'

As the couple had proved with *Charlie's Angels*, what better way to attract attention and promote a film than to pretend to get married?

During one interview for the movie, Tom said that he and Drew were married in a private ceremony a couple of weeks earlier. Drew's publicist, Eddie Michaels, had not heard of the news when first quizzed by reporters, but later confirmed, 'It's true, they're married. I don't have any details, but I can tell you it's true.'

Taking the story a step further, Tom then told Jay Leno on *The Tonight Show* that just before he walked out, Drew whispered to him that she was pregnant. Tom later admitted that this too was a hoax. 'Not only didn't that bother me, I loved it,' said Drew. 'I was backstage when he said it, laughing my butt off. As if I would tell Tom that I was expecting a baby just before he went on live television! The fact that people started running with the story made me love it more.

'We also pretended that we'd married months before. It was all a joke to us because we thought it was weird that people even cared.' Of course the media lapped it all up, as millions of viewers and readers around the world *did* care about what happened to Hollywood's darling.

*

After months of practical jokes, rumoured elopements and an aborted television wedding, Drew and Tom were finally married on 7 July 2001.

The ceremony took place under a large white tent at a private house overlooking the Pacific Ocean in Malibu. Eight-year-old Frances Bean (Drew's goddaughter) was a flower girl and led the procession down the grassy aisle to 'Ave Maria', followed by four bridesmaids in white dresses decorated with yellow daisies, and four suited groomsmen.

Drew, dressed in a backless lace-sleeved cream gown with a white orchid in her short blonde hair, was escorted by her mother. At the altar they joined Tom and his younger brother, the best man. John Barrymore II was notably absent from the occasion.

During the nondenominational ceremony, conducted by a female minister, the couple exchanged personal vows from the heart.

'My wedding was the most beautiful ceremony I'd ever attended,' boasts Drew. 'It was insanely cool. It took place next to the ocean and dolphins swam by as we were saying our vows. It was mind-blowing, just everything I could have ever hoped for. It was romantic and sensual and beautiful.'

Among the one hundred guests were Courtney Love, Adam Sandler, Cameron Diaz, Lucy Liu, Beverly Donofrio, David and Courteney Cox Arquette, Nancy Juvonen, Justine Baddeley and Melissa Bochco. The reception afterwards was a unique combination of Indian food served at tables adorned with scattered seashells and bowls of floating gardenias, a speech about drag racing, a DJ and karaoke, while a nearby banner wished 'Happy Anniversary' to a fictitious couple to fool passing paparazzi. Drew's perfect day was completed when her new husband crooned the John Lennon song 'Imagine' just for her.

'They really wanted to keep it private,' said publicist Eddie Michaels. 'It was a special time for them.' The newlyweds succeeded in keeping the press at bay, refusing to sell any photos of the affair.

After a month-long honeymoon in Hawaii, Drew returned to Hollywood to start the promotional rounds for *Riding In Cars With Boys* and *Donnie Darko*, not to mention working on her next project.

29

ANNUS HORRIBILIS

At 8:45 a.m. New York time on 11 September 2001, the world changed. Two hijacked airliners crashed into the twin towers of the World Trade Center, causing the two 110-storey buildings to collapse onto the surrounding Manhattan streets. It was part of a horrifying terrorist attack on the United States, followed later that day by a similar strike on the Pentagon and a crash in Pittsburgh.

America suddenly became a nation in mourning, but the effects were international and long-lasting. 'If there's one thing we've come to learn by the events of 11 September, it's that "I love you" are the three most profound words that we have,' says Drew, echoing global sentiments. While celebrities joined the public in rallying around Ground Zero, one of Drew's first gestures was a sizeable donation to the American Society For The Prevention Of Cruelty To Animals (ASPCA), an organization that set up a command centre to help stranded pets and their owners.

Like many entertainers, Drew found that her career was affected by the violent events and ensuing war on terrorism. The promotion of *Donnie Darko* hit an unexpected, awful standstill. The chilling real-life events were a mite too close to several of the film's themes (the falling of a plane from the sky; the apocalyptic nature of Frank's messages).

For several weeks the producers worried about whether to change the film itself, and eventually pulled a couple of shots – namely the falling jet engine – from the trailer. But as the film was a period piece, to be viewed in the context of the 1980s, any similarities had to be deemed coincidental and unfortunate.

The release of *Riding In Cars With Boys* on 19 October in America was also hindered, as the requisite publicity coincided with the US retaliation bombing of Afghanistan. Drew had made her political feelings clear the previous autumn when she wore a T-shirt saying: 'I Won't Vote For A Son Of A Bush', and now she was openly distraught by the president's move towards war.

The press junket for the latter film was held at the Four Seasons hotel in Los Angeles, and neither the cast and crew nor the journalists were in the mood to talk about entertainment. Drew was consoled by the chief executive of Sony Pictures beforehand, but wept freely throughout her interviews.

'I didn't think that anyone needed to hear anything from me today,' she said. 'I feel so trivial and so confused and so extraordinarily lost. I've never had to do my job in a time of war, and I don't know how to do my job right now – I'm literally learning in front of you, and that is very humiliating and embarrassing.' Apparently, Drew then spent some time watching films made during World War II and the Vietnam War for inspiration, and was encouraged to discover that, back then, the public had yearned for a bit of Hollywood escapism.

Still, nervous of further terrorist attacks, Drew avoided New York for all events except the premiere of *Riding In Cars With Boys* and another episode of *Saturday Night Live*. Despite having been the butt of cruel jokes about her house fire on the show, Drew agreed to host *SNL* again in October. She had been wary of flying but made the trip to Manhattan and overcame her concerns once rehearsals were underway.

The latest terrorist act was mail maliciously contaminated with anthrax. The day before Drew's live show, an employee at NBC News, in the same building as *SNL*, was diagnosed with the fatal bacterial disease, contracted after opening a letter sent to the newsroom. The disturbing announcement brought the studio to a halt and Drew had to be pacified – exaggerated reports had her running screaming out onto the street. When she returned to her hotel that evening, Tom rallied around her, and with New York Mayor Rudolph Giuliani's message of bravery in mind, Drew returned to the studio to host the show on 13 October.

During the show, Drew referred to the anthrax scare and her reasons for returning, congratulated the audience for also being brave and finally thanked her husband for his support; Tom was sitting in the crowd wearing a gas mask as a joke.

The next New York occasion was the launch of *Riding In Cars With Boys*. The cast and director had agreed to travel to the devastated city.

'The Mayor of New York has asked us to come to New York for the premiere, and we will because they need it,' said Penny Marshall. 'They need the business, they need a distraction from what's going on.' However, studio bosses cancelled the premiere altogether in the wake of the anthrax scare.

Despite the fact that Drew had continued with her commitments in the Big Apple, radio personality Howard Stern openly ridiculed her at Paul McCartney's concert for the New York victims. 'I just want to say one thing to all the celebrities who have stayed away from New York, I say shame on you,' proclaimed the shock jock. 'People like Drew Barrymore. Don't be afraid, honey. It ain't scary here. I mean, it can't be any worse than spending the night with Tom Green alone.'

Drew understandably bristled. She defended herself in an interview saying, 'I was still brave in the end, so I don't know what's wrong with that.' She accused Stern of making a living by 'being mean to other people', adding, 'I just don't even go to the mean kids' area in that playground.'

*

Unfortunately, at the end of the day, *Riding In Cars With Boys* received mixed reviews, and the film that was supposed to be Drew's *Erin Brockovich* fell a little short. For her part, Drew was praised for her performance and grown-up platform (which should have incited award nominations), but the complaints focused instead on the depressing storyline, Donofrio being unlikeable as a main character and the corny ending.

Drew sacked her publicist, Eddie Michaels. The film's negative response was the final straw after a spate of humiliating and bad publicity: *Freddy Got Fingered*, the false weddings, the fire, pregnancy rumours, Drew's initial avoidance of New York and the anthrax scare.

Perhaps harking back to her insecurities as a child, it is notable that during this period Drew also got a new pet – an adorable white Persian kitten. She then turned to her ancestors for comfort and began her own pet project: a documentary about the famous Barrymore acting dynasty.*

'When I was younger, I felt, "How can I live up to my family? I'm Hollywood royalty? Me? A kid who eats macaroni and cheese?" It made me nervous,' she admits. 'I never wanted to let them down, have people say, "God, this acting dynasty, what the hell happened to their

*At the time of writing, the documentary has yet to surface.

granddaughter?" But I finally decided, God is not going to come down and punish me if I don't do them justice. I can only try.'

Drew regularly watched their black-and-white movies, viewing it as a form of documentation on the extended family she never knew. 'People frequently tell me anecdotes about my relatives,' she says. 'The good, the bad, and the weird, they all run through me.

'I feel close to them and see the family resemblance. It might sound cosmic and crazy, but I talk to my grandfather every day. He is guiding me towards a better path than he took himself. I feel him around me. I have conversations with him in my head.'

*

Chuck Barris had dreamed of success and a bevy of beautiful women as a youth, but despite scoring a hit with the song 'Palisades Park' and a job with Dick Clark on *American Bandstand*, his hopes eluded him. That is, until the 1960s, when he became the popular host of *The Gong Show*, a new television genre. Over the next decade he also went on to create and produce *The Dating Game*, *The Newlywed Game*, and a handful of other successful game shows. Eventually, bored of the shows and their critics, Barris left America for the South of France, where he wrote his autobiography.

In his memoir, *Confessions Of A Dangerous Mind*, Barris also claimed controversially to have been a secret agent for the CIA. Caught up in the deadly world of spy games, the assassin soon found his own life threatened by the KGB.

Fascinated with the fantastical story and interested in filming a biopic, numerous directors, studios and producers came and went throughout the 1990s. '*Confessions* had been in the works for quite some time, but a number of obstacles prevented it from going in front of the cameras,' says Barris. 'Mike Myers pulled out at the last minute [as the lead], financial people, the director pulled out, and the deal kept going down – I thought it would never happen.'

In the new millennium, Barris discovered he had cancer purely by chance, when a friend insisted he had a CAT scan. Having found the tumour so early, an operation was all that was needed for Barris to cheat death once more.

Chuck Barris's *Confessions Of A Dangerous Mind* was adapted into a screenplay by none other than Charlie Kaufman (*Being John Malkovich*). It was a bizarre meeting of minds: a surreal screenwriter adapting a delusional memoirist.

Hollywood heart-throb George Clooney had been involved with the project for almost as many years as it had been going. The nephew of famed singer Rosemary Clooney, he had made his television debut aged five on his father's talk show, *The Nick Clooney Show*. In his early twenties, George Clooney re-emerged in numerous failed television pilots and several series before the medical drama *ER* made him a household name in the 1990s.

Clooney made a successful transition to film at the end of the decade with *Three Kings* and *O Brother, Where Art Thou?*, hitting the big time with a remake of *Ocean's Eleven* in 2001. He had already turned his hand to producing, and when *Confessions Of A Dangerous Mind* needed a director to spur it into action, he stepped up for his debut.

'I didn't feel confident that I could tell the story,' admits Clooney, 'but I knew I could work with actors. I also thought if I was *ever* going to direct anything, why not direct the best script around?

'I figured if I had a good script and good actors, then I couldn't *completely* fail. I'm a fan of films from the mid-1960s to the mid-1970s, and I wanted to bring to *Confessions* what I think was most important with those films: a point of view.'

Had he fallen for Barris's fanciful tale? 'It was important for me not to ask him the question when I met him,' continues Clooney. 'I wanted to be able to tell the story, true or not. I wanted to be able to say I think it's a really fascinating story – if it's not true – that someone as successful as Chuck Barris felt the need to write that story. So I felt it was important not to know the answer, but I have opinions on it.'

Elaborating on his theory, Clooney explains that *Confessions* is about a man who wakes up and suddenly realizes that he isn't the man he thought he was. Furthermore, he is blamed entirely for the destruction of television and begins to believe the hype himself.

*

Like George Clooney, Drew had been interested in *Confessions* for years, and as usual, it was Nancy Juvonen who had filtered out the script.

'Nancy is so smart; she foresees so many things,' says Drew. 'About six or seven years ago, she'd read these Charlie Kaufman scripts, *Being John Malkovich* and *Human Nature*, and said, "He's amazing and I want you to read him." I read them and then read Charlie's *Confessions Of A Dangerous Mind*.'

Drew became obsessed with playing Barris's love interest, Penny; a partly fictional character, she was actually an amalgamation of various women Barris knew. 'I think she's a combination, but I know there is one woman he was particularly thinking of,' says Drew.

Up against stiff competition from Gwyneth Paltrow and Renée

Zellweger, Drew won the role, not least because of her long-term commitment to the project. When asked if she believed in Barris's spy career, she too was careful to avoid a straight answer. 'I know he has an amazing imagination and I'm impressed with the way he articulated it into a novel. I also love when people tweak the history as we know it.'

All Clooney needed was a leading man, a suitably quirky actor to play Barris. Sean Penn, Ben Stiller, Johnny Depp and John Cusack were all interested in the part, but Clooney was waiting for someone special. When he met Sam Rockwell on the set of *Welcome To Collinwood*, the director mentally cast him for this role.

As the son of artists, Rockwell had enjoyed a bohemian upbringing, travelling between San Francisco and New York. His mother introduced him to the world of theatre and he made his stage debut at the age of ten. In his twenties he became known as a powerfully idiosyncratic actor in numerous independent films, capitalizing on his appeal of versatility and offbeat sexiness.

Although he had broken into mainstream movies as the villain in *Charlie's Angels*, Rockwell was still a relative unknown, which went in his favour. 'I didn't want someone too famous to play the role,' recalls Clooney. 'In my opinion, you cannot have famous people playing famous people – it doesn't work. Sam was the guy for the part, ready to break and hadn't yet.'

Due to the unknown quantity of Clooney as a director and Rockwell as a lead, Miramax insisted on a screen test, and so they shot a few scenes from *The Gong Show* in full costume with dollies, tracks and real directing. After seven years of negotiations, in November 2001 *Confessions Of A Dangerous Mind* finally got the green light. Clooney roped in his *Ocean's Eleven* buddies Brad Pitt and Matt Damon for blink-and-you'll-miss-them cameos, and managed to get Dick Clark, Jim Lange, *Gong Show* regular Jaye P. Morgan, and Gene Patton (a.k.a. Gene Gene the Dancing Machine) to appear as themselves, with the shoot set for the following year.

*

While waiting for filming on *Confessions Of A Dangerous Mind* to start, Drew found her home life had hit a rocky patch. The actress tellingly revealed to *Rosie* magazine: 'I want our marriage to have some time, because this business can be hard on relationships. It's really tough to make it work.'

On 11 December 2001 Tom and Drew quietly separated. A week later, Green, renowned for his unpredictable behaviour, filed for divorce, citing that old chestnut, irreconcilable differences.

'I thought we'd ease into a public separation, but apparently Tom wanted to do something dramatic. And he did!' said a shocked Drew at the time. 'We talked about issuing a press release in a few weeks, after we've sorted some of our personal business out, but it looks like he changed his mind.

'It would have been nice if Tom had checked with me – or even told me – but I guess he has his own agenda now. It's very sad to see everything end this way because I really loved the guy – and he loved me, too.'

With the divorce of Hollywood's other golden couple, Tom Cruise and Nicole Kidman, finalized the previous month, the press were well versed in speculating on the reasons for celebrity splits.

Numerous stories emerged from 'friends' and 'sources' detailing how their separate careers drove them apart. When Tom's film *Freddy Got Fingered* proved disastrous, Drew allegedly shrugged it off, suggesting that he could have a bigger role in *Charlie's Angels 2* to make up for it. Tom was said to be furious that she didn't take his career seriously. Equally, the relative failure of *Riding In Cars With Boys* was rumoured to have caused a rift. The more outrageous reports claimed that Tom was insanely jealous of Drew's female flirtations, fearing that she would return to her lesbian past, while apparently Drew couldn't sleep at night due to Tom's 'elephant-like' snoring.

As with all break-ups, the real cause was a far more mundane combination of several factors. Due to the intense nature of their relationship during its early stages (Tom's cancer; wedding and pregnancy hoaxes; Drew's reconciliation with Jaid; the house fire; the events of 11 September), Tom and Drew hadn't really spent any time as a 'normal' couple. 'When it came down to just living a regular life, things seemed strange and something was lost between us,' says Drew. 'I realized that we didn't have the same ideas about our life together that we had before we got married.'

Furthermore, Drew had always worked hard, but with her extra responsibilities as producer and her total commitment to *Riding In Cars With Boys* and *Donnie Darko*, she really hadn't had any time for Tom.

Then there was their social life. 'When I come home after a day at work, I'm beat – I'm exhausted and I want a foot massage and a hot cup of tea,' says Drew. 'I thought Tom wanted simple stuff like that, too. It seemed like, after we got married, all he wanted to do was have dinner out and go to boring Hollywood parties.' Drew's weariness with such events was well known, but apparently she didn't find out about Tom's lust for nightlife until after the wedding.

Finally, Drew recalls the day she glanced into a house while driving and craved the ideal life of the family she saw sitting down to dinner. 'I never stopped to ask, "Was that family happy?" ' she now explains. 'We always look at things from the outside. If someone had been driving past when I eventually got to sit down to dinner with [Tom], they'd have thought the situation looked good. But it wasn't. Then I realized I'd fucked up. But maybe I had to get inside the window to learn that.'

When they first parted, Tom issued the statement: 'Drew is a wonderful woman, I love her very much. I wish our marriage could have worked out, I wish her much happiness.' Sadly, Drew laments that he never took the time to tell her that face to face – his press release seemed like a publicity stunt – and because she then went on to film *Confessions Of A Dangerous Mind*, they never really got a chance to talk after the split and so lost touch completely.

All the same, the divorce, finalized in October 2002, was possibly the most amicable affair in Hollywood history. They waived the right to examine each other's accounts and, while Drew kept the Los Angeles house, Tom retained their Studio City home, giving his ex an 'equalizing' payment of $307,603.

*

Two thousand and one proved to be Drew's *annus horribilis*, yet she did everything she could to remain positive.

'I try not to get upset or depressed about things because after all that's happened to me I just believe that the only way to stay sane is to maintain your calm and look at life as a beautiful journey,' she says poetically.

After such a traumatic year, Drew could be forgiven for giving in to her weaknesses, but she was able to deal with the difficult moments alone without resorting to the escape route of drugs. 'If you've gone through addictions and suffered emotionally there's always a slight fear factor at work,' she admits. 'I feel stronger and happier than ever.

'You gradually realize that you've gained a certain emotional maturity and nothing is going to be so bad that it's going to shake you or bring you down from that state of security.'

Drew sought company and spent Christmas with Nancy Juvonen and her extended family in Wolfeboro, New Hampshire. 'She's doing just fabulously,' beamed Juvonen's stepmother, Karen. 'She just relaxed and had a wonderful family holiday, and that's exactly what she wanted to do.' Afterwards, the actress escaped to Hawaii for the New Year. Then, at the beginning of January 2002, she flew to Montreal to immerse herself in filming *Confessions Of A Dangerous Mind*.

*

In *Confessions*, Drew's character, Penny, first meets Chuck Barris (her roommate's boyfriend) when he raids her refrigerator in the nude. A forward girl, Penny confides that in her quest for multi-ethnic lovers, she has yet to have sex with a Jew. She captivates him, he amuses her and they fall in love. She soon becomes a constant in his chaotic life, sticking by him through the manic highs and rock-bottom lows of his career. As Chuck periodically returns to Penny throughout his life, she illustrates the era for the viewer as she embraces and personifies each decade.

'I start as a beatnik, then I become a hippie, then a woman of the 1980s,' says Drew. Although the actress naturally related to the last phase, she loved sporting fifties hoop skirts and a faux-suede jacket embellished with flowers from the 1970s.*

After she has endured years as his long-suffering girlfriend, Chuck finally makes an honest woman of Penny. That is not to say he is faithful during their relationship – his wandering eye proved a challenge for Drew in tackling the character. 'When I read this script, I became almost animalistically possessive, because I knew that I could make her more than a doormat or someone who was terminally needy,' she explains. 'I wanted her to be a life-grounding force, a reminder of what was real out there.'

Drew's main concern had always been that Penny should not be portrayed as being bitter or gloomy – the point was that she was an independent girl who enjoyed Barris's company. However, the actress was not quite sure how to handle the scene where Penny discovers Barris in bed with another woman.

'She's so unlike myself – if I caught my guy with another girl in the room, I'd flip out. Instead I thought, wouldn't it be interesting if her reaction was untypical and calm and quiet?' says Drew. 'When we were filming that scene I tried it a couple of times, keeping it very low. George is such a good director, he said, "Don't even shake and cry, just monotone and soft." That's the take in the movie and it's by far the best one.'

Although now separated from Tom, Drew obviously recognized certain qualities of her ex in Barris. 'Chuck was funny and playful, an "ideas" man – and that's very sexy to women,' she continues. 'OK, he was weird, too, but that's part of the bargain. She just loves him. The heart chooses what the heart wants and sometimes we can't rationalize it.'

As her mind frequently wandered to her own fragile state, so she leaned heavily on George Clooney. 'I wasn't in great shape emotionally

*Drew was so taken with the seventies jacket that Clooney bought the garment for her.

but I was lucky I had George to talk to during filming,' she acknowledges. 'He would give me a wink once in a while to check out how I was doing – that meant as much to me as anything else.'

'When we were filming *Confessions*, she had a lot going on,' says the director. 'She had every excuse for bad behaviour, but there was none of that. She lit up the room. You just wanted to give her a hug. She's delicate in that sense, and I don't know anyone who knows her that doesn't want to protect her.'

Personal issues aside, Drew praises Clooney's professional ability. 'He's one of the best directors I've ever worked for,' she says – not bad for Clooney to be classed alongside Steven Spielberg, Woody Allen and Joel Schumacher for his first attempt. 'He makes your acting better. He really watches you like a hawk, and then comes in and tweaks and adjusts things that you're doing, and just makes them better.'

Drew turned to Clooney for help with the scene where Chuck finally tells Penny about his secret identity – they are driving away from their wedding and when she hears the news, there is a stunned pause before she breaks into hysterical laughter. 'After a few takes, I just couldn't laugh naturally anymore,' admits Drew, 'so I asked Clooney to put a walkie-talkie in the car and say something that would make me laugh.'

Rockwell delivered his line. Then there was a pause.

'Corn,' said Clooney. Drew looked suitably puzzled.

'Corn in my doody this morning,' he concluded, with split-second timing.

'I let the cacophony come out full throttle!' recalls Drew.

*

'Penny and Chuck are so perfect for each other and yet he takes her for granted,' explains Sam Rockwell. 'In a way it's a typical kind of relationship between a man and woman that goes awry. You just hope he will get it together.'

That Drew and Rockwell had already worked together, and so recently, undoubtedly helped their scenes. 'Had we not known each other, I'm sure it would have been a little different,' says Drew. 'We were so close at that point because not only did we spend six months on *Charlie's Angels* together, but we became good friends and have been very social since then. So, there was an amazing shorthand.'

This bond relieved the awkwardness of the film's nude scenes. 'I haven't had a love scene like that in a while,' she continues. 'I just got into it and did it, then afterwards I was shy and embarrassed. But [Sam and George] are so wonderful, and I feel very protected.'

'She's a breath of fresh air,' reciprocated Rockwell. 'She lights up the room. She's a real movie star. And she brings it out of you.'

Needless to say, leaked rumours from the set suggested that the pair became an item, but both parties denied they were anything more than 'just good friends'.

The atmosphere on set was fun, but Clooney, renowned in the industry for his practical jokes, was too busy concentrating on both directing and acting (as Chuck's CIA boss) to fool around. Instead, he fell victim to one of Drew's pranks.

'She called, crying and screaming and said that the cops had her at the border and that she'd been arrested,' he growls. 'We sent over some producers to fix it but of course she was lying – but that's gonna backfire on her!' Clooney threatens to get his own back when she least expects it.

As the cast and crew averaged ten-hour days, George Clooney completed his masterpiece under budget and ahead of schedule. '[George has] a really amazing way of articulating what his vision is and what he wants,' concludes Drew. 'He's incredibly objective.' She was particularly surprised by his ability to be confident, especially for a first-time director, without a hint of arrogance.

*

When not filming, Drew kept busy with a renewed interest in charity work. 'As long as I lay my head down on the pillow at night, and I can say I was a decent person today, that's when I feel beautiful,' says the compassionate actress.

Twenty-two female celebrities designed their own heart-shaped necklaces for auction at Sotheby's in February 2002 by the Women With Heart Program™. The individual pieces were created by top platinum jewellery designers and the money raised was donated to a charity of the celebrity's choice. Drew's gently curved simplistic design had a particularly romantic feel and her recipient was Green Chimneys, an organization that houses around one hundred children with a history of homelessness or a family background of alcohol and drug abuse. Green Chimneys helps by encouraging a nurturing relationship between the children and animals, to help them relearn trust and love. This cause was particularly pertinent to Drew, who frequently sought comfort with her pets as a child.

Her next creative charitable outlet was to design a one-of-a-kind Mercedes-Benz pedal car for the Paediatric Aids Foundation, a cause that Drew had supported since 1996. The various celebrity models were also being auctioned off, this time on the eBay website – as expected, Drew's car was sparkling green and featured a field of daisies.

In March 2002 *E.T. The Extra Terrestrial* was re-released on DVD to mark its twentieth anniversary. Steven Spielberg commented that it was like 'a good bottle of vintage Bordeaux, it just gets better with age'. He's right: the film doesn't appear to have dated – or is that just camera trickery?

As Spielberg is a notorious perfectionist, he wanted to correct a few niggles before reissuing the film, for instance where E.T.'s mouth didn't form quite the right shape, or when the arm movement wasn't exactly how he had envisioned. With the aid of new technology, Spielberg was able to literally iron out these kinks so that the modern viewer would be none the wiser.

Interestingly, since Spielberg had had children himself he had become aware of the inappropriate presence of guns in children's films, and although there is only one brief scene with two armed policemen in *E.T.*, he took the opportunity to replace the shooters with walkie-talkies.

The footage included as an extra on the DVD explaining these changes and the techniques used is quite fascinating. Other bonus material includes various outtakes which show just how advanced Drew was for her age.

*

Being young, free and single, as Drew turned twenty-seven in February 2002 the tabloids linked her with an endless stream of suitors. She was said to be enjoying the support of singer Robbie Williams at AA meetings, although she was known to have given up attending the group years earlier. Next on the list was billionaire Brandon Davis, grandson of oil baron and movie mogul Marvin Davis, followed by Alec Puro, the drummer for rock group Deadsy.

When journalists couldn't find any suitable male candidates, they remembered that Drew had swung both ways and reports flooded the media that Drew was seen in passionate clinches with several unnamed women in nightclubs. As the papers really scraped the bottom of the barrel, rumours then flew around that she was reunited with Luke Wilson, weeks after he split from Gwyneth Paltrow.

Drew denied most of the above relationships, although, tellingly, she never commented on the late-night lesbian sessions . . .

But then there was mention of Fabrizio Moretti, the drummer for rock band the Strokes. The press had hit the jackpot, and Drew later confirmed that the two were an item.

Fabrizio, born 2 June 1980, was five years younger than Drew and was raised in Rio de Janeiro, Brazil. The son of a cruise-ship musician, the energetic drummer showed an early interest in music, but before choosing it as a career he wanted to become an art teacher. Fabrizio is a gifted artist, both in sculpting and painting, and his work has been auctioned for charity.

The Strokes were formed by five friends in 1998 and have been credited as single-handedly fuelling the rock revival with their debut, *Is This It?* in September 2001. The band spent most of 2002 on tour before returning to the studio to work on their follow-up album.

Backstage at one of the Strokes' concerts in April 2002, Fabrizio and Drew first crossed paths. Conforming to Drew's penchant for tall men, Fab (as he is known) is 6 foot, dark and handsome.

'Fabrizio is a total gift,' said Drew. 'A beautiful person. I love watching him play his music. And he's so relaxed. It means I can have this love in my life and still have room to focus on work and friends.'

Indeed, Drew gave little time to her budding romance, as she was already heavily involved in the inevitable *Charlie's Angels* sequel.

30

JIGGLE TV

The second movie adaptation of the television series was entitled *Charlie's Angels: Full Throttle* and started filming over the summer of 2002.

The first headache was dealing with a rapidly escalating budget. While Cameron Diaz and Lucy Liu were willing to return, their fees had jumped by several million dollars due to the phenomenal success of the first feature: Cameron was set to follow Julia Roberts's landmark of being the first woman to command $20 million for a role, and Lucy Liu was also looking to join the big league.

Drew took a salary of around $14 million, but having bought the movie rights before joining forces with the studio, she looked set to earn a substantial additional sum. With Pete (Luke Wilson) and Jason (Matt LeBlanc) returning as Natalie's and Alex's love interests respectively, and many guest appearances by other big names on top of regular production costs, the finances soon reached dizzying heights.

'We're looking at it as this is our second case, our sophomore year,' said Drew. 'We were freshmen, now we're sophomores, so it's a little bit more adult. We've grown, we know things now and I think that's reflected in the tone but it's still really true to what it is.'

The movie revealed a little more about the personal lives of the three Angels, with Dylan's ex, Seamus (Justin Theroux), seeking revenge. While Dylan's past unravels, Alex has to deal with her father

(John Cleese) misunderstanding her vocation. On the investigation side of the plot, a pair of rings, coded with special information to access the FBI's Witness Protection Program database, have been stolen. When several supposedly protected informants are murdered, the Angels are brought in to find the culprit. The villain turns out to be Madison Lee, an ex-Angel who decided that crime was more financially rewarding than crime-fighting.

Such a powerful adversary required an actress with clout and the lady Drew wanted was the inimitable Demi Moore. Making a name for herself in the 1980s in the Brat Pack, Moore hit A-list status in 1990's *Ghost* opposite Patrick Swayze. With controversial career choices during the 1990s (*Indecent Proposal*, *The Scarlet Letter* and *Striptease*), a high-profile marriage to Hollywood heart-throb Bruce Willis and frequent flashings of surgically enhanced flesh, the actress was rarely out of the papers.

After the 1997 flop *G.I. Jane* and her divorce from Willis the following year, Moore stayed out of the limelight and focused on being a full-time mother to her children, Rumer, Scout and Tallulah. She was willing to grace the big screen again in *Charlie's Angels: Full Throttle*, but, living up to her former industry nickname of 'Gimme Moore', she demanded an extortionate paycheck; Drew is believed to have reduced her own wage in order to increase the offer.

Refuelling the previous rumours that Lucy Liu and Bill Murray fell out during the making of *Charlie's Angels*, the comedian refused to return, no matter how appealing the financial incentive. For the new Bosley, the producers turned to another comic who had appeared in a number of films in the early 1990s and had recently been seen on the big screen in *Ocean's Eleven*: Bernie Mac. He was delighted to take on the role.

'We're brothers from another mother,' Mac tried to explain of the complicated background story. 'You see, Bill [Murray's character] and [my character] are related, but our father just messed around. His Bosley was also adopted as a kid . . . don't ask. The other thing I can tell you is that our father eventually brought him home and introduced us as brothers.'

Whatever Bosley's origins were, his character is the same as the original: a bumbling fool who, when caught up in a world of danger and sex, finds he is in over his head. 'We wanted to send a message that said, "Look you don't need to be a lily white, Anglo girl to live in this Charlie's Angel world,"' adds returning director McG. 'Cameron Diaz is half Cuban, Lucy Liu is of Asian descent, Bernie Mac is African American – we're saying, feel good about your own skin, shake what your momma gave you, get in the back of this convertible and let's make it happen.'

While negotiations with the original Angels for cameos failed the first time round, Jaclyn Smith came on board for the sequel. 'They put together such an emotional scene where Kelly Garrett (Smith) imparts her Yoda-like wisdom to Dylan,' explains McG. 'It was one of those moments where you couldn't believe it was really happening.' Various other past Angels are also honoured in a photo gallery, although Farrah Fawcett and Kate Jackson are conspicuous in their absence as the actresses refused permission to use their pictures without remuneration.

Crispin Glover returns, reprising his excellent performance as the Creepy Thin Man, while other cameos include the singer Pink (who provides the title track), Demi Moore's ex-husband, Bruce Willis, and for those with keen eyes, Sam Rockwell. 'I did a walk-on,' recalls Rockwell. 'I happened to be visiting the set, but I don't think people will be able to spot it.'

The three stars were again required to train intensively for two months with Cheung-Yan Yuen as they reprised their physical roles. This time, they were joined by Demi Moore, who, although fast approaching her fortieth birthday, performed the strenuous stunts herself.

The action in the sequel was even more daring and a few of the moves left very real injuries. Drew snapped her coccyx when she forgot to wear protective pads and hit a chair wrongly, Lucy's bandanna burst into flames during a welding scene, Drew's backside also caught fire and her harness broke during a driving sequence. After the last accident, Drew said, 'That was too much excitement. Filming these movies you get pumped with adrenalin – you really feel immortal. But hanging on to the hood of a car that's fishtailing at 50mph isn't funny. Finally, I slid off the car crying, "I'm not meant to die!" I was peeing in my pants.'

Cars feature heavily in this second instalment, but at the end of the day, *Charlie's Angels* is all about style and the women don even more guises than for the first movie, if that's possible. 'There are so many different costumes,' elaborates Drew. 'One day we're in motocross gear, the next day we're coming out of a Greek statue. Then we're in evening gowns, and next we're dressed like roller derby girls.' Costume designer Joseph Aulisi laughs at the mixture of references used (from *BMX Bandits* to current fashion): 'I just try to have a lot of humour in the clothes.'

*

While the premise of *Charlie's Angels* is female empowerment, the television series was at first slammed by critics – labelled 'Jiggle TV' as the preposterous plot lines required the stars to constantly appear in skimpy outfits. In the first movie version, the sexual appeal of Drew, Cameron and Lucy was played up, but most of the time it remained respectable. But in the second girl-power flick, the cheap thrills that aim purely to titillate are even more outrageous.

Firstly, there's the scene in which the girls become erotic dancers to obtain information inside a club – as research, the actresses attended the real-life risqué Pussycat Dolls show led by Carmen Electra and Christina Applegate. Then there's the point at which the Angels jump out of the sculpture naked. 'That was an exercise in trust,' asserts McG. 'It takes a lot of trust in the director to agree to be naked on set and on the screen. I explained to them that it would be a very powerful scene and since we would be playing with shadow and light, there was really nothing to worry about. So when they jump out of the sculpture, the Angels really are completely naked.'

And finally, there's the curious moment when Madison nuzzles Natalie's face. 'Madison is a very animalistic woman,' explains Cameron. 'We have a fight scene, and Madison and I hit and kick each other. She has me trapped and doesn't know what to do next. She's trying to consume me and get everything on me. That's what urges her to lick me. It's a primal urge.'

Nancy Juvonen was less understanding about its importance. 'The licking of Cameron's face is a question for McG because to me it's not inherent in the story. It's not an important character thing that needed to happen.' In fact, it caused a bit of an uproar on set. 'We argued about that,' says Leonard Goldberg. 'McG thought it was very important to the character, but if I had a little daughter, I wouldn't want her to see that.' Interestingly, the final cut is less provocative than the extensive footage shot – perhaps Juvonen and Goldberg won the argument.

Capitalizing on Cameron's Spiderman-clad bottom-wiggle in the first film, she performs another sexy dance to 'Hammer Time'. 'Cameron can move. She can pop go the weasel until the weasel go pop,' drools Bernie Mac. 'That girl can make your imagination just go to the left a little.'

Drew, who is very free with her body and has been known to strip completely while changing on the roadside, only encouraged McG.

'They've all seen me naked, I've seen them naked,' says the director, citing the time they attended the Super Bowl Of Motocross in particular. 'We got a big limo van, put on old Mötley Crüe records, and Drew and I stripped down. It's sort of fabulous the way we all trust one another, most particularly Drew. Drew is very into the body, very natural. It's a splendid thing.'

And of course the actresses played up their closeness during promotion – constantly touching and stroking one another – ensuring that every red-blooded male would go to see the film at least once. 'Lucy has the most gorgeous ass I've ever seen on any woman – hands-down,' raves Drew. 'She has what I call *frutas grandes*, because it's like a delicious peach and, if I were a guy, Lucy's ass is the ass I would want. But I'm lucky because I'm her girl pal so I get to squeeze it every day.'

Such exploitation on screen and behaviour off the set, plus the fact that the Angels sit around waiting for Charlie to click his fingers, could seem to undermine their position as independent women. Fortunately, this is counterbalanced by the Angels' strength and control – not to mention numerous flashes of finely toned male flesh.

*

The hype surrounding the second film was no less than the first, and once again rumours were rife that rivalry had broken out into arguments. This time it was suggested that Moore was the cause of the problems, insisting that she had her own beauty stylists and the same perks as the veteran Angels. Whether or not there were troubles on set, Moore upstaged the girls at the premiere, proving the point that she didn't conform to teamwork.

While filming dragged on throughout the latter half of 2002, Drew had more important issues to worry about than any supposed petty squabbles. In August 2002 Drew received some worrying death threats from a knife-wielding man named James Hufstetler, who apparently had murderous designs on Drew and people of the Jewish faith. Drew wisely stepped up security after the incident at the Beverly Hills Hotel on Sunset Boulevard. Drew frequently used this venue for meetings but fortunately wasn't there at the time.

It was during this period that Drew reneged on her vegetarian lifestyle, as she was bored of shopping in the same stores. 'I don't eat a tonne of meat,' she says, 'and I don't wear a tonne of leather. But I don't put strict limitations on myself. I didn't wear certain designers because I didn't want any animals to suffer for beauty, so I was literally dressed in clothes by one chain store at one point. But I got tired and wanted to play again. Dressing is like an art form – it's so much fun.'

In September she was reported to have broken up with Fabrizio Moretti due to their clashing schedules and was seen stepping out with guitarist Joel Shearer. By November, she was firmly back with Fabrizio.

'I'm very happy with him,' she commented, although she elaborated on her reticence. 'People have heard plenty about my personal life, and I'm going to spare them. I realized that I was a real adult in my workplace, but that when it came to my personal life I was still quite young. So I thought, well if things in your life don't work, try everything the opposite, you know? If talking about everything in your personal life is exposing you in a way where maybe you feel raw and vulnerable, don't talk.'

Drew was happier speaking about her career, in particular *Confessions Of A Dangerous Mind*, which was released in December 2002 in America and the following spring in England.* Along with George Clooney and Sam Rockwell, Drew attended all related events, plugging the film at every given opportunity.

The reviews were generally good from all points of view: Clooney was praised for his directorial debut; Rockwell was considered an inspired piece of casting and he and Drew proved their worth as actors; Roberts was noted as making an interesting femme fatale; and Kaufman's script was as unconventional as Barris's memoir.

If there is a criticism to be made about *Confessions*, it is the take-it-or-leave-it nature with which Barris's claim of being a CIA agent is handled. The film portrays it as absolute truth and any viewer not paying attention could be left wondering where the intrigue was. Once the premise is established that Barris is a television game-show host by day and assassin by night, the film becomes a little slow in its cyclical pattern, finally picking up for the climax.

'I just think a lot of great people came together on this – whether it's real or an idea – and told a very interesting story that I think a lot of people can weirdly relate to,' summarizes Drew. 'Everyone fantasizes about the dual life, I think. But all in all, I just think it's an amazing story.'

Unfortunately, by the time the film was released, Ron Howard had beaten the team to it with another unreliable autobiography of a schizophrenic character, *A Beautiful Mind*, the previous year. Still, *Confessions* was more accessible, as Barris was a well-known television personality.

*

Director Joel Schumacher once commented, 'No one falls in love like Drew Barrymore. Not Elizabeth Barrett Browning, not Heathcliff or

---

*At the time of going to print, there were reports that Miramax didn't feel the film received enough attention on its first release and, in an unusual move, were going to re-release it with a new promotional campaign in August 2003.

Cathy, not Romeo and Juliet.' He was not wrong, but for once she seemed to be under a little more control.

By the year's end, Drew's relationship with Fabrizio Moretti had become quite serious and the couple made space in their hectic schedules to spend their first Christmas together. Drew's presents for her nearest and dearest in 2002 were huge dictionaries. 'I do a theme every year,' she explains. 'One year it was record players, this year it's dictionaries. They're all vintage. I love old things.' One assumes Fabrizio was as impressed with his second-hand lexicon as Drew was with the exquisite Elsa Peretti necklace he bought her . . .

Reports abounded in January that the drummer had proposed to the actress over the festive season and that Drew had accepted. It seemed that Drew's impetuous past had preceded her and she carefully corrected the press.

'We're not engaged,' she responded. 'We're so happy and calm that we want to let things naturally unfold. I don't need to rush into anything now. Our love is fundamental, kind, supportive and communicative. There's nothing gossipy or scandalous about it. It's just a beautiful thing in my life.'

Furthermore, she explained why she wouldn't get married so hastily a third time, to Fabrizio or anyone else for that matter. 'I'm very grown-up in my approach to moviemaking, but as a woman, I'm still quite young,' she said. 'I'm certainly not ready for marriage again until I get to know myself better. I am not rushing into anything anymore. I have made some spectacular mistakes and the trouble is, I have made them in public. So I am not going to say or do anything silly.'

Fortunately for their relationship, Fabrizio was as busy with the Strokes as Drew was with her career. As soon as the over-running *Charlie's Angels: Full Throttle* shoot ended, she was on a different film set both acting and co-producing, in meetings with Adam Sandler for another collaboration, and planning further ventures for Flower Films.

*

Duplex, a dark comedy with Drew cast opposite Ben Stiller, was the first project that held her attention.

The son of comic actors, Stiller was making home movies by the age of ten. His big-screen debut was in Steven Spielberg's epic *Empire Of The Sun* in 1987, but he found fame on television as a cast member of *Saturday Night Live*, which led to his own MTV series, *The Ben Stiller Show*. In 1994 he turned his hand to directing with *Reality Bites*, and *The Cable Guy*, a box-office flop starring Jim Carrey.

Stiller made a stunning recovery in 1998, appearing in the cringe-making *There's Something About Mary* with Cameron Diaz, followed by *Meet The Parents* and *Keeping The Faith* in 2000, and *The Royal Tenenbaums* and *Zoolander* the year after.*

Duplex was a co-production between Flower Films and Stiller's company, Red Hour Films, and the pairing was made by Meryl Poster of Miramax, who had been trying to match Drew and Stiller in a comedy for ages. The screenwriter was Larry Doyle, who had worked on *The Simpsons* but never before on a feature film. Greg Mottola (*The Daytrippers*) was originally signed as the director, but was swiftly replaced by Danny DeVito (an accomplished director as well as actor, whose credits included *Hoffa*, *Throw Momma From The Train*, *The War Of The Roses* and *Matilda*). If handled properly, *Duplex* had the potential to be a successful quirky comedy along the lines of *Home Fries*, and an ideal showcase for Drew.

Due to directorial changes, the filming schedule for *Duplex* was delayed from November 2002 to February 2003 before it finally got underway, wrapping in just three months. The story is set in New York and is based on the cutthroat industry that is the property market.

Drew and Stiller play Nancy and Alex, a young affluent couple desperate to get ahead. Currently living in a small studio apartment on the Lower East Side, they find their dream home, a converted duplex in the perfect neighbourhood, but the asking price is a little more than they can afford. 'I take that chance because I believe in us,' says Drew of her character. Unfortunately, their new home comes with an extra feature: an elderly rent-controlled upstairs tenant, Mrs Connelly (Eileen Essell), who proves to be less easy-going than they anticipated.

'The world just closes in on them, and everything is about her and what takes place inside this duplex,' continues Drew. 'They're living in a contained world. They can't see outside. They start to lose their perspective.' As Nancy and Alex's life crumbles, they start plotting various ways to remove Mrs Connelly . . . enter James Remar (*Sex And The City*, *Boys On The Side*) as the undercover hitman posing as a pornography producer.

The atmosphere on set was light-hearted, with all cast members getting on well and frequently ad-libbing.

'I enjoy working with Drew, I find her to be a true professional,' says Stiller. 'She's very giving as an actress, she's very easy on the eyes, and she's funny too!' Drew reciprocated, saying, 'He makes me laugh so hard that I unfortunately might have ruined a few of his best takes! I've

*In May 2000 Stiller married Christine Taylor – Drew's Madonna-wannabe friend in *The Wedding Singer*.

had to modify my character to add that she thinks her husband is really funny. He does these amazing improvs and he just goes off. I don't know where he comes up with this stuff!'

One day on the way to work, Stiller tripped and bumped his head, an injury which was incorporated into the movie. 'We're shooting a scene where I've gotten burned, because we sneak into the lady's apartment upstairs and I accidentally get blown up by her oven,' he explained of the cover-up.

Entertainment aside, Drew felt unusually constrained by her character. 'She's very uptight, very yuppie-ish, and she dresses very conservatively,' she complained. 'I wanted sex and rock 'n' roll in my life so desperately, I couldn't take her turtlenecks anymore. I wanted to kill her! She's just very tickety-boo – that's what Nancy [Juvonen]'s mom used to say. It means organized and logical.

'I'm not like that. I don't have an outfit that matches, I don't have a thing that's in place anywhere. I'm trying as I get older to get a better system, but it's just a disaster.'

With a stellar comedic supporting cast including Harvey Fierstein (*Mrs Doubtfire*), Swoosie Kurtz (*Liar, Liar*), Maya Rudolph (*Saturday Night Live*), Wallace Shawn (*Toy Story* and *Toy Story 2*) and Justin Theroux (*Charlie's Angels: Full Throttle*), *Duplex* looked set to be a smash on its release in the autumn of 2003.

*

In March 2003 Drew attended the Global Vision for Peace party in Los Angeles at the home of co-founder Xorin Balbes. Reconfirming her commitment to philanthropy, Drew read out a statement from the Dalai Lama, the spiritual leader of Tibetan Buddhism and Nobel Peace Prize winner, in protest against the war on Iraq. 'Violence leads to more violence. It's not the solution,' said Drew, feeling honoured and humbled to read the message.

Hollywood's response to the war had been to downplay the Oscars, but instead the powerful medium was used to promote the message of peace. Drew was frequently seen making the two-fingered peace sign, and it even inadvertently appeared on the poster promoting *Charlie's Angels: Full Throttle*.

But Drew was not hanging around, and she immediately launched herself into another new project, a reunion with Adam Sandler (*The Wedding Singer*). Having attended the premiere of *Anger Management*, Sandler's latest film with Jack Nicholson, Drew was ready to start filming *Fifty First Kisses*.

Written by George Wing, with revisions by Adam Sandler and Tim

Herlihy, this romantic comedy is very much along the same lines as *The Wedding Singer*: it is a vehicle for Sandler to showcase his loveable goofball character, again. While this may have worked well the first time, that does not mean it needs to be repeated, particularly with the same co-star. That said, it looks likely to be a funny, feel-good flick and a box-office hit on its proposed release date of Valentine's Day 2004.

Sandler plays Henry Roth, a veterinarian at a Hawaiian aquarium who enjoys short-term affairs with visitors to the island, but otherwise leads a regular life revolving mainly around work. He meets Lucy (Barrymore) in a breakfast bar and strikes up a rapport, becoming enchanted by her. When she takes offence at his direct approach the following day, Henry is confused, but the proprietor of the café explains that Lucy was in a car accident and consequently suffers from short-term memory loss (*à la Memento*). On paper, the rest of the plot sounds sadly predictable – Henry has to make Lucy fall in love with him all over again every single day (*à la Groundhog Day*).

Filming in the early part of 2003, *Fifty First Kisses* was shot on location in Hawaii and on set in Los Angeles, with Rob Schneider (*Saturday Night Live*, *Deuce Bigalow: Male Gigolo*) and Sean Astin (*Lord Of The Rings* trilogy) playing Sandler's best friend and brother respectively. Co-produced by Happy Madison (Sandler's company) and Flower Films, the romantic comedy was directed by Peter Segal (*Anger Management*).

*

When Drew was not acting, she was busy promoting her upcoming film, *Charlie's Angels: Full Throttle*. Capitalizing on the appeal of the three Angels, the studios created pre-release hyperbole with all manner of merchandising: a cartoon, a console game, and a special-edition DVD of the first movie with added extras. The massive marketing campaign marked an unusual move by three big companies – Sony Ericsson, Ferrari and Cingular Wireless – who joined forces in a joint promotional drive, also backed by campaigns from Best Buy, Billabong and Ray-Ban.

Drew, Cameron and Lucy attended the Los Angeles premiere on 18 June 2003, all dressed in white outfits to show their unity (this was where Demi Moore upstaged them by arriving later with an odd entourage consisting of her toyboy boyfriend, three children and ex-husband). The three stars then flew across the pond to attend the British launch in Leicester Square, delighting fans with an impromptu walkabout.

The film received a rapturous reception, aptly summed up by *heat* magazine's Charles Gant: 'It's an endless parade of surface pleasure.

The logic that connects each scene may not be terribly compelling, but who cares when the girls escape from a beautifully choreographed explosion by landing feet first on flying planks and then sliding down a metal rail?' Unfortunately, after a year of action follow-ups (*X-Men 2*, *The Matrix Reloaded*, *2 Fast 2 Furious*), sequels were beginning to wear a little thin – perhaps *Charlie's Angels* won't push its luck with a trilogy.

EPILOGUE

THE AVOCADO GIRL

Truly

Drew's comeback has been slow and steady, but since the mid-1990s she has really proven herself as a first-rate actress, professional producer and down-to-earth celebrity.

Coping with fame in 2003 is a lot easier than the first time around, some twenty years earlier. 'I'm fortunate because I've been doing it my whole life,' she explains. 'I can't imagine what it must be like in midlife to suddenly have to cope with it.' She manages to go out and live a relatively normal life by donning a cap, shades and, intriguingly, a slightly altered facial expression. 'I sort of change the shape of my face,' she says, 'I don't even know that I do it anymore.'

It is undoubtedly Drew's friends who are her grounding force: Justine Baddeley, Melissa Bochco and Nancy Juvonen in particular, and her more recently acquired celebrity pals, Edward Norton, Courtney Love and Adam Sandler.

'Your friends are your release – they're who you have the most fun with. And yet when the going gets tough those people turn around and suddenly they're not just making you laugh, they're being a rock and giving you their advice,' she says wisely. 'Their influence is incredible. Best friends are what you need most.'

Drew started smoking again in 2003, and although she drinks in moderation, she has never showed any signs of giving in to her alcohol addiction. 'I drink beer because I love the little tingle it gives on your shoulders,' she says, 'and I love wine with meals.' Since losing weight while training for *Charlie's Angels*, Drew has kept slim by taking up yoga and eating a high-protein diet, having renounced her vegetarianism.

The former wild child is a self-confessed lover of a 'traditional', 'normal' lifestyle. When she gets some time to herself, Drew still loves reading; her favourite writers include e. e. cummings, Carl Jung, Truman Capote, Henry Miller, Anaïs Nin, Dorothy Allison, Sir Thomas More and Charles Bukowski. 'I'm always reading [about] six books at a time,' says the woman who is a regular at Book Soup on Sunset Boulevard.

Another hobby, a passion which she shares with Lucy Liu, is photography. 'I love taking pictures of the beach – I'd like to be a *National Geographic* photographer,' says Drew. 'It's shooting people that's hard, getting that spontaneity.' The actress develops her own pictures and often frames them as gifts for her friends.

For someone who says, 'I wouldn't get out of bed in the morning if I didn't believe in love,' Drew rarely gives herself a chance to cement a relationship with her thirst for work, but perhaps by taking things slowly with Fabrizio Moretti, their union might become something more permanent. Hopefully she can break her long cycle of doomed two-year romances.

And as for children? Approaching her thirties has had the reverse effect on Drew's maternal instincts. 'I have the opposite clock,' she explains. 'When I was younger, I wanted babies. Now, I'm not ready at all. I just want to be very realistic and make my choice. Do it at the time when I'm the smartest, the least selfish, the most patient.'

It seems that Drew really has performed a complete and genuine about-face from her youth.

Madly

'I never have believed in regret, and hopefully I never will,' says Drew philosophically of her troubled past. 'It has opened my eyes and kept me strong, and it's allowed me to be a humble, appreciative and grateful person.'

Since her abrupt wake-up call in her mid-teens, the actress has learned to live life one day at a time. 'The best thing you can do is turn your pain into your strength and try to be a positive force and make the most of this life you've been given,' she continues. 'And cherish every day, every breath, and try to breathe that back into the world, in making a family or being artistic. Just make the most of your life, because the only person who will stop you is you.'

These are philosophical words from a woman not yet thirty, but then again, Drew packed a lot of life's richest experiences into her first fifteen years. Her early meltdown hasn't dampened her spirit, and while she now leads a calmer, more normal life, she has acquired an insatiable drive to prove herself within her profession. It seems she cannot turn down a challenge, be it as an actress or producer. She has been known to try writing screenplays herself, and how long will it be before she steps behind the camera as a director?

Having spent most of her twenties concentrating on building up Flower Films, in 2003 Drew was inundated with new projects. As soon as Drew finished promotion for one film, so the next was released and her hamster wheel of filming-and-promoting continued.

She has been toying with the screenplay for *A Confederacy Of Dunces* for some time; indeed, the novel of the same name has been causing a stir ever since it was first published in 1980.* The story, set in New Orleans during the 1960s and revolving around an obese, rude and repulsive misanthropist who treats his mother despicably, tends to provoke extreme reactions of either love or hate.

A film adaptation has been in the pipeline for over twenty years and for a while Steven Soderbergh has been attached as co-producer, along with Drew and Juvonen. Scott Kramer will collaborate with Soderbergh on the script, and in 2002 David Gordon Green reportedly came on board as the director. However, production had not commenced at the time of writing and still seemed a long way off.

Another film which Drew has been connected to for many years is a remake of *Barbarella*. The 1968 original, starring Jane Fonda as a sexy forty-first century space-babe, was based on the French comic strip of the same name, and has since become known as a classic slice of camp sci-fi. Flower Films wants John August (*Charlie's Angels*) to write the screenplay and so production has been on hold until his schedule is clear, but with studios cashing in on the success of the revamped *Charlie's Angels*, this flick may well see the light of day in the next few years.

However, as with *Angels*, it will not be a remake – more of an update. 'The new film will be about society and utopia. It will still have some flower-child ideas,' explains Nancy Juvonen. The story is said to be about a woman (Barrymore) who uncovers the secret behind her tiny planet's good fortune and finds herself leading a revolution. 'This will be a new Barbarella,' adds Drew. 'I'm not going to play the Jane Fonda character.'

Again raiding the Hollywood back catalogue rather than finding

*The late author, John Kennedy Toole, was posthumously awarded the Pulitzer Prize the following year.

new material, Drew has also spoken of a sequel to *The Wizard Of Oz*, called *Surrender Dorothy*. Working with producer Robert Kosberg and Warner Brothers, Drew began developing the venture in 1999, but as yet nothing has materialized. Although she would be stepping into Judy Garland's ruby-red slippers as Dorothy Gale, Drew was keen to point out, 'I'm *not* going back to Emerald City and Judy Garland of 1939.' Instead, the plot is believed to be set in modern-day New York City, where the Wicked Witch isn't dead and is out to seek revenge.

Three other, less well-publicized projects in the pipeline are *Entering Esphesus*, based on the 1971 book by Daphne Athas about the lives of three school-aged sisters; *Kinky Boots*, a Disney feature starring John Cusack about a family of shoemakers who make erotic footwear to save their business; and *The Science Of Sleep*, a fantasy supposedly to be directed by Michel Gondry, co-starring Patricia Arquette and Rhys Ifans.

It will be interesting to see the personnel list for future features as, just as Fox gave Flower Films its big break, Drew in turn deserves to be recognized for showing faith in relative unknowns – Michael Vartan and Raja Gosnell (*Never Been Kissed*), McG and Lucy Liu (*Charlie's Angels*), Richard Kelly (*Donnie Darko*), and Sam Rockwell (*Confessions Of A Dangerous Mind*) would surely agree.

'Drew has a more sincere instinct for giving than anyone of our generation I've met in this business,' says Edward Norton, pointing out, 'You kind of remember: she's a *Barrymore*.'

Deeply

With two comedies due out in the next year – with almost interchangeable co-stars, Ben Stiller and Adam Sandler – and two proposed remakes of classics on the back of *Charlie's Angels*, it seems that Drew is stuck in a rut.

With a few exceptions, she appears to have a cyclical approach to her work: she breaks into a genre, establishes herself in that field, then moves on. As a child she started with fantasy horrors, then moved on to family dramas; as a teenager she juggled road movies and lethal Lolita roles; in her twenties she tried a few dark comedies, followed by feel-good romantic comedies and remakes. But this is where she seems to have hit a dead end.

When she has successfully broken the mould, Drew has produced some of her finest performances: *Mad Love*, *Riding In Cars With Boys* and *Confessions Of A Dangerous Mind*. Unfortunately, with her gruelling experiences as Casey Roberts and Beverly Donofrio in mind, she clearly prefers lighter material, as she says: 'Making a movie, you have to play a character for so long – you live and breathe her. It affects your mind, and I want to be in a happy place these days.'

Drew has ably held up the Barrymore name in terms of her acting ability, so it's a shame that she is rarely willing to tackle something a little more daring – something that could result in the elusive Oscar. Looking at recent winners – Nicole Kidman (*The Hours*), Halle Berry (*Monster's Ball*), Julia Roberts (*Erin Brockovich*) – somehow Drew's cutie-pie characters don't cut the mustard.

On the other hand, after all her years of worrying about the public's perception of her, Drew is past doing things for the approval of others. So long as she is happy – and she clearly is – little else is of concern to her. If she is recognized as an actress of the highest calibre with the accolade of an Oscar, that would be wonderful, but providing she enjoys her work and she continues to entertain audiences, that's enough for her.

As she said years earlier, the profession is so unpredictable that she could lose it all within a year. Little seems to bother her now. 'Some people just won't let go of me and *E.T.*, but that's cool,' she says. 'It's where my history is. I'll always be a Barrymore, I'll always be in *E.T.*, I'll always be the back-and-forth wild child.'

So much has been said and written about Drew Barrymore, every aspect of her private life subjected to intense public scrutiny from birth, that it is a testament to her strength and courage that she has survived. But she has done more than that: she has positively thrived and, although she occasionally talks as if she's on a different plane, she has remained remarkably down-to-earth. As George Clooney, friend, director and co-star on one of her more interesting ventures, aptly sums up: 'Drew is about as innocent a human being as I've ever met. Incredibly sweet. An open book.'

FILMOGRAPHY

Films are listed in reverse order of production; the date is of release.

Fifty First Kisses	2004
Duplex	2003
Charlie's Angels: Full Throttle	2003
Confessions Of A Dangerous Mind	2002
Freddy Got Fingered	2001
Donnie Darko	2001
Olive, The Other Reindeer	2000
The Simpsons	2000
Riding In Cars With Boys	2001
The Wonder Of Sex (a.k.a. *Skipped Parts*)	2000
Charlie's Angels	2000
Titan A.E.	2000
Never Been Kissed	1999
Ever After	1998
Home Fries	1998
The Wedding Singer	1998
Best Men	1998
Scream	1996
Everyone Says I Love You	1996
Wishful Thinking	1997
Batman Forever	1995
Mad Love	1995
Inside The Goldmine	1994
Boys On The Side	1995
Bad Girls	1994
Wayne's World 2	1993
Beyond Control: The Amy Fisher Story	1993
2000 Malibu Road	1992
Doppelganger: The Evil Within	1993
Guncrazy	1992

Sketch Artist	1992
Poison Ivy	1992
Waxwork II: Lost In Time	1991
Motorama	1991
No Place To Hide	1992
Getting Straight	1989
Far From Home	1989
See You In The Morning	1989
A Conspiracy Of Love	1987
Babes In Toyland	1986
Strange Tales: Ray Bradbury Theatre	1986
Star Fairies	1986
Amazing Stories	1985
The Adventures Of Con Sawyer And Hucklemary Finn	1985
Cat's Eye	1985
Firestarter	1984
Irreconcilable Differences	1984
E.T. The Extra-Terrestrial	1982
Bogie	1980
Altered States	1980
Suddenly Love	1978

BIBLIOGRAPHY

Barrymore, D. and Gold, T., *Little Girl Lost*, Simon & Schuster, 1990.

Brite, P., *Courtney Love: The Real Story*, Orion, 1997.

Donofrio, B., *Riding In Cars With Boys*, Virago, 2001.

Freer, I., *The Complete Spielberg*, Virgin, 2001.

Furman, L. and E., *Happily Ever After*, Ballantine Publishing Group, 2000.

Halliwell's Film And Video Guide, HarperCollins, 1999.

Halliwell's Who's Who In The Movies, HarperCollins, 1999.

Hamlyn History Of The Twentieth Century, Reed International Books, 1995.

Kemp, M., *True: The Autobiography Of Martin Kemp*, Orion, 2000.

King, S., *On Writing*, Hodder & Stoughton, 2000.

Peters, M., *The House Of Barrymore*, Simon & Schuster, 1990.

Rossi, M., *Courtney Love: The Queen Of Noise*, Pocket Books, 1996.

INDEX